THE SYSTEM OF PUBLIC SACRIFICE
IN FOURTH-CENTURY ATHENS

AMERICAN PHILOLOGICAL ASSOCIATION
American Classical Studies

Series Editor

David L. Blank

Number 34

The System of Public Sacrifice
in Fourth-Century Athens

by
Vincent J. Rosivach

Vincent J. Rosivach

The System of Public Sacrifice in Fourth-Century Athens

Scholars Press
Atlanta, Georgia

The System of Public Sacrifice in Fourth-Century Athens

by
Vincent J. Rosivach

© 1994
The American Philological Association

Library of Congress Cataloging in Publication Data
Rosivach, Vincent J.
 The system of public sacrifice in fourth-century Athens / Vincent J. Rosivach.
  p. cm. — (American classical studies ; no. 34)
 Includes bibliographical references.
 ISBN 1-55540-942-3 (cloth : alk. paper).— ISBN 1-55540-943-1 (pbk. : alk. paper) .
 1. Sacrifice—Greece—Athens. 2. Public worship. 3. Athens (Greece)—Religion. I. Title. II. Series.
BL793.A76R67   1994
292.3'4'09385—dc20   93-47180
                                              CIP

Printed in the United States of America
on acid-free paper

ACKNOWLEDGEMENTS

Major portions of this study were written during my tenure as a Faculty Resource Network Scholar in Residence at New York University and during a sabbatical leave awarded by Fairfield University's Faculty Research Committee; I thank both institutions, and particularly David Danahar, my former dean, for the generous support shown me. Special thanks are also due to Michael Jameson for his encouragement, thoughtful comments and helpful suggestions, and for his tolerance of my sometimes differing views.

CONTENTS

ABBREVIATIONS	ix
INTRODUCTION	1
1. THE FREQUENCY OF SACRIFICE	9
2. SUPPLYING THE VICTIMS	68
3. ACQUIRING THE VICTIMS	107
CONCLUSION	143
SUPPLEMENTARY NOTES	148
BIBLIOGRAPHY	165

ABBREVIATIONS

Titles of periodicals are generally abbreviated following the system in *L'année philologique*. Note also the following:

IG 1^2 = *Inscriptiones graecae*, vol. 1, editio minor, ed. F. Hiller de Gaertringen (Berolini 1924).

IG 1^3 = *Inscriptiones graecae*, vol. 1, ed. 3, fasc. 1, ed. D. Lewis (Berolini et Novi Eboraci 1981).

IG 2^2 = *Inscriptiones graecae*, vols. 2-3, editio minor, ed. I. Kirchner (Berolini, pars prima 1913; pars altera, fasc. prior 1927; pars altera, fasc. altera 1916).

IG 7 = *Inscriptiones graecae*, vol. 7 = *Corpus inscriptionum graecarum Graeciae septentrionalis*, vol. 1, ed. G. Dittenberger (Berolini 1882).

LSCG = F. Sokolowski, *Lois sacrées des cités grecques* (Paris 1969); references are to item numbers, not pages, unless otherwise indicated.

LSJ = H. G. Liddell and R. Scott, *A Greek-English Lexicon*, 9th ed., revised by H. S. Jones (Oxford 1940).

LSS = F. Sokolowski, *Lois sacrées des cités grecques: Supplément*, (Paris 1962); references are to item numbers, not pages, unless otherwise indicated.

PA = J. Kirchner, *Prosopographia Attica* (Berolini 1901-1903).

RE = Pauly-Wissowa, *Real-Encyclopēdie der classischen Altertumswissenschaft* (Stuttgart 1893-).

SEG = *Supplementum Epigraphicum Graecum* (1923-).

SIG^3 = W. Dittenberger, *Sylloge Inscriptionum Graecarum*, 3rd ed. by F. Hiller von Gaertringen (Leipzig 1915-1924).

Fragments of Attic comedy are cited according to the edition of R. Kassel and C. Austin, *Poetae Comici Graeci*, vols. 3.2, 4, 5 and 7 (Berolini et Novi Eboraci 1983-89), except for the fragments of Alexis, Ameipsias and Antiphanes, which are cited according to the edition of J. M. Edmonds, *The Fragments of Attic Comedy*, vol. 2 (Leiden 1959), and the fragments of Menander, which are cited according to the edition of A. Koerte, *Menandri quae supersunt*, vol. 2, 2nd ed. by A. Thierfelder (Lipsiae 1938).

For convenience I have given the inaccurate title "Calendar of Nikomakhos" to the calendar of the *polis*' "ancestral sacrifices" which was included in the late fifth-century recodification of "the laws of Solon." The surviving fragments of this calendar, from the two stages of the recodification (in 410 and following, and in 403 and following), were originally inscribed respectively on either side of the same marble slabs, and are cited here as follows:

Inventory no.	*earlier stage*	*later stage*
EM 6721+8001	$IG\ 1^3$ 241	$IG\ 2^2$ 1357a
EM 286		$IG\ 2^2$ 1357b
Ag. Inv. I 727		*Hesp.* 1935, p. 21
<not given>		*Hesp.* 1941, p. 34
Ag. Inv. I 4310		*Hesp.* 1941, p. 35
<now lost>	$IG\ 1^3$ 238	$IG\ 2^2$ 845
Ag. Inv. I 251	$IG\ 1^3$ 239	*Hesp.* 1934, no. 34
Ag. Inv. I 687+ 1026a+1026b	$IG\ 1^3$ 240	*Hesp.* 1941, p. 36
Ag. Inv. I 945+ 591+590	"	

Hesp. 1934 = Meritt (1934); *Hesp.* 1935 = Oliver (1935); *Hesp.* 1941 = Dow (1941). In general see Dow (1961); for the inappropriateness of the title "Law Code of Nikomakhos" see Clinton (1982).

INTRODUCTION

As for sacrifices and sacrificial victims and festivals and sacred lands, the *dêmos*, knowing that it is not possible for each one of the poor to sacrifice and feast and banquet and live in a great and beautiful city, has found a way for these things to be. And so the *polis* sacrifices many victims at public expense, but it is the members of the *dêmos* who feast and share the victims among themselves ([Xen.] *Ath. Pol.* 2.9).

And the *dêmos* as a whole spends more for its common banquets and distributions of meat than it does for the administration of the *polis* (Theopomp. 115 F 213).

Broadly speaking, religion may be viewed as the interplay of creed and cult, of what people believe and of what they do as a consequence of their beliefs, and conversely of what they do and of the meaning they assign to their cultic acts. Our ancient sources for Greek religion tell us a good deal about cult but very little about creed, in no small measure because the Greeks in general considered what one believed to be of much less importance than what one did. Yet the massive presence of religion in literature, in art, in architecture, and in civic and domestic life makes it clear that the Greeks took religion very seriously, and that their cult practices were not a matter of simple routine or hollow show. The one-sided nature of our sources has led many scholars to examine the details of cult practices in an effort to reconstruct the religious beliefs behind the acts, and much of what has been written on Greek religious practices is written from this point of view. The present study of Athenian public sacrifices also considers cult practices, but not to get at their causes or meanings. Rather, it moves in the opposite direction, as it were, focusing instead on some of what one might call the non-religious consequences of these religious acts. Without in any way denying the religious importance of public sacrifices for the participants, we have chosen to ask a series of questions which deal with socio-economic dimensions of these religious acts under three general topics: the frequency of sacrifice (Chapter 1), the supply of victims (Chapter 2) and their acquisition (Chapter 3).

The sacrifices (*thusiai*) which we shall study here were public ones, both in the sense that they were sponsored by the *polis* or by one of its sub-units, and in that they were attended by Athenians in their capacity of citizens.[1] The pattern of public sacrifice in Athens was a complex one since Athenians were citizens not only of the *polis* but also of a variety of smaller units (demes, tribes, phratries, etc.), all of which were in many ways miniature versions of the *polis*, replicating the practices of the *polis*, including the sponsoring of public sacrifices for their members.[2] Of necessity then our study of public sacrifice will require us to consider not only the sacrifices of the *polis* but those of these sub-units as well.

The diet of the typical fourth-century Athenian relied heavily on grain (*sitos*), either wheat or barley.[3] This *sitos* was supplemented primarily with vegetables and fruits, and also with fish, poultry products, cheese, various sausages and other processed foods when available. Fourth-century Athenians rarely ate fresh meat (*krea*, understood for our purposes as prime cuts of beef, mutton, goat meat, and pork) except at religious sacrifices, when the meat of the sacrificed

---

[1] And indeed that as communal activities they reinforced the sense of social cohesion within the citizen body, as Plato recognized (*Lgg.* 738D-E, cf. 771B-772A).

[2] On the sub-units as miniature versions of the *polis* see most recently Osborne (1990); on the centrality of religion to the life of the *polis* and vice versa see Sourvino-Inwood (1990).

[3] On the importance of grain in the Athenians' diet see especially Foxhall and Forbes (1982). For the place of barley in the Athenians' diet see also Gallo (1983).

animals was grilled and/or boiled[4] on the spot and distributed to those in attendance.[5] While some public sacrifices were attended by only a relatively few citizens, at many others meat was distributed to the citizen population at large, either that of the *polis* as a whole or that of the sub-unit (deme, tribe, etc.) sponsoring the sacrifice. Since in Athens most animals slain in public sacrifices were also bought with what might generally be called public funds, the complex accumulation of sacrifices carried out by the variety of political units (*polis*, tribes, demes, etc), and particularly those sacrifices involving a widescale distribution of meat, may be viewed in their totality as a significant system of resource redistribution whereby the Athenian community transformed income from a specific set of sources into nourishment for the citizen population at large, a point already recognized by the so-called "Old Oligarch" in the passage quoted above at the start of this Introduction ([Xen.] *Ath. Pol.* 2.9).

While the "Old Oligarch" is almost certainly wrong when he says that the redistributive aspect of the sacrificial system was in origin an outgrowth of the democracy's pursuit of the interests of the poor,[6]

---

[4]For both types of cooking cf. e.g. the parody of a sacrificial *kreanomia* at Eur. *Kyk.* 241-46.

[5]Cf. Durand's definition of *thusia* as "sacrifice sanglant grec alimentaire" (1979, 126). Many times our sources do not even mention the religious dimension of sacrifice but speak only of dining on the sacrificed animal (so e.g. [Xen.] *Ath. Pol.* 2.9; Plato, *Lgg.* 782C; Aristot. *Pol.* 1321^{a}35-37; Isaios 9.21; *IG* 2^2 1204.12-15; *IG* 2^2 1214.11-17; note that at Menander, *Sikyon.* 183-91 the speaker is interested only in getting his share of the animal, and he does not even mention—much less attend—the actual sacrifice; note also that at the beginning of Plato's *Republic* Kephalos is out in the courtyard sacrificing [328C] while the guests are already inside). Conversely, failure to share the meat of a sacrificed victim with others was a sign of shamelessness (Theophr. *Char.* 9.2). For the link between *thusia* and *hestiasis* cf. e.g. θύσαντα τὰ ἱερὰ ἑστιᾶσαι ἐκεῖνον, Antiphon 1.16; θύσας ἐπιδειπνεῖς, Aristoph. *Eq.* 1140; εἰς τὰς θυσίας τοίνυν, ἐν αἷσπερ οἱ ἄλλοι Ἀθηναῖοι.

[6]The origins of the system are doubtless much older than democracy and probably lie in Greece's more primitive past when "big men" reinforced their preeminent position in communities by distributing largess to their dependents.

the existence of democracy in Athens inevitably affected the system of public sacrifice, probably in respect to funding and perhaps also in other ways which are less obvious. Because Athenian democracy was unique, both in its ideological commitment and in the resources it could command, the conclusions which this study draws and the evidence used to reach those conclusions must of necessity be limited to Athens itself. Our focus will be on the fourth century because most of our documentation (and certainly our most important documentation) comes from this period. Such evidence as we have from the fifth century suggests, but is inadequate to prove, that Athenian sacrificial practice then was not significantly different from what it was in the fourth century. In this study, fifth-century evidence will be used only when it supports or complements what we already know from our fourth-century sources. Evidence dealing with Athenian public sacrifice after the fourth century is not used however, because the loss of democracy as surely affected the system of public sacrifices in the third century and later as the existence of democracy did in the fifth and fourth.

Most of the evidence used in this study comes from inscriptions, and it is important to keep in mind the particular nature of such evidence. Each inscription is specific in that it tells us what some governmental unit (deme, tribe, etc.) did or intended to do at one particular moment in history. In a study of religious practice, however, this limitation of an inscription's data to a single and specific moment is less of a problem than it might first appear, particularly in the case of lengthier inscriptions such as the sacrificial calendars which we will examine in detail in Chapters 1 and 2. Athenian religious practice was intrinsically conservative, and thanks to this conservatism we can be reasonably certain that the general picture which emerges from e.g. a deme's sacrificial calendar remained by and large the same over an extended period, even as we also recognize that changes in detail were probably inevitable in time and may even have been the occasion for reinscribing the calendar. Indeed, when we can identify the reason why a particular inscription was erected (e.g. to define financial responsibilities for sacrifices), it is usually a reasonable assumption that while one or more of the details associated with the purpose of the inscription may reflect a change, at least the details not so associated reflect previous practice which probably continued unchanged.

Inscriptions are also specific in that each tells us what one, and only one, particular governmental unit (deme, tribe, etc.) did. This kind of specificity could be an advantage if we had a relatively complete series of documents which would allow us to identify norms and trace variations from these norms over time and place. Unfortunately, very few inscriptions survive dealing with the many aspects of Athenian religion which will concern us here, and certainly not enough to enable us to identify what is norm and what is variation. All we can do instead is to examine the inscriptions we have and look for patterns which may indicate a possible range of activity. Thus, for example, while no individual deme inscription can tell us how often any other deme sacrificed, several deme calendars taken in combination can suggest approximate upper and lower limits of frequency within which the sacrificial activities of other demes would likely have fallen.

Because our sources are too few and too particular to enable us to make precise projections of general Athenian practice scholars have either avoided the quantitative issues completely or they have been content with vague generalities ("the Athenians sacrificed with great frequency") to express their views. In order to move beyond such generalities this study expresses many of its conclusions with the formula "in the range of" followed by a number. In such cases we are to imagine the range of possibility as a scale running from half as large as the number given to twice as large; within this range we are more confident that the actual number which corresponds to reality lies closer to the mid-point of the scale than at either extreme, but as we narrow the range by moving from the extremes toward the midpoint we become progressively less confident that the number corresponding to reality is still within our narrowing range. Thus, for example, when we say that an average fourth-century Athenian had the opportunity of annually attending in the range of as many as forty-five sacrifices at which meat was distributed, what we mean is that, on the basis of the evidence discussed, we can be somewhat confident that the number was neither less than forty nor more than fifty, that we can be substantially more confident that the number was neither less than thirty nor more than seventy-five, and that we can be all but certain that the number of sacrifices was neither less than twenty-two nor more than ninety (i.e. neither less than half nor more than twice as large). Ranges of this sort are certainly less satisfying than precise numbers, but they can still be useful in giving us a general sense of what happened, at least by helping us exclude what did not.

In what follows we will also have the occasion from time to time to estimate the size of the population of different demes. For this purpose I have used the Kleisthenic quotas of *bouleutai* from the several demes as determined by Traill,[7] divided by five hundred (the membership of the *boulē* until its reorganization in 307/6), times 27,500 (the mid-point of the 25,000-30,000 range for adult male citizens during the fourth century argued by Hansen[8]). Of these factors, the use of the bouleutic quotas calls for further comment. It is generally agreed that Kleisthenes allocated seats in the *boulē* to the several demes in proportion to the size of their adult male populations at the time of his reforms, and that these bouleutic quotas were not changed, except in special circumstances,[9] until 307/6. In 307/6 the

---

[7] All of the figures on bouleutic quotas used in this study are drawn from Traill (1975) 59 and 67-70, and Tables I-XII.

[8] Hansen (1986) 68-69.

[9] E.g. a smaller deme could not provide its quota of demesmen (Traill 1975, 58). I am not persuaded by M. H. Hansen's argument (1983) that the seats in the *boulē* were reallocated in 403/2 according to the then current population; if Hansen is correct, however, his view would only strengthen the claim being made here that the bouleutic quotas found in fourth-century documents can be used to determine the relative populations of the several demes.

INTRODUCTION 7

size of the *boulē* was increased from five hundred to six hundred by increasing the bouleutic quotas for forty-nine of the one hundred thirty-nine demes. In twenty-four of these forty-nine cases the quota was increased by one,[10] an increase which was merely part of the adjustments required by the 20% increase in the membership of the *boulē* from five hundred to six hundred, and not the consequence of a relative increase in population; the increase of two or three *bouleutai* in five other demes with Kleisthenic quotas of nine or more is probably also to be explained in a similar fashion.[11] The increased quotas in the remaining nineteen demes, however, can only be explained by an increase in the population of these demes relative to that of the remaining one hundred and twenty. In other words, the changes in the quotas of these nineteen demes is clear evidence that the reorganization of 307/6 took into account the relative populations of the several demes, and that on the basis of the new bouleutic quotas only nineteen demes can be shown to have increased significantly in population relative to the other demes.[12] The Kleisthenic quotas thus appear to

---

[10] Such increases may simply mean that a particular threshold was crossed, entitling the deme to a second seat, and cannot be taken as evidence that the deme's population had increased significantly (in other words, an increase from one seat to two does not necessarily mean that a deme doubled its population).

[11] Kephale increased from nine to twelve, Euonymon from ten to twelve, Alopeke perhaps from ten to twelve, Eleusis from eleven to thirteen and Akharnai from twelve to fifteen.

[12] In his discussion of the reorganization of 307/6 Traill (1975, 58-61) accepts relative shifts in the populations of the demes as part of the rationale for the changes in the bouleutic quotas, but argues on two grounds that this cannot be only explanation, first that no deme *lost* representation as a result of the reorganization of 307/6, and second that the resulting quotas are not always consistent with the individual demes' share of the total of individuals whose demes are known (as calculated by Gomme [1933, 55-65] on the basis of Kirchner's *Prosopographia Attica*). As to the first of these arguments, I would suggest that political considerations alone could have precluded the possibility of reducing any deme's bouleutic quota (note, however, that any deme whose quota remained constant had a proportionately smaller representation when the *boulē* increased in size from five hundred to six hundred members).

provide a reasonably secure basis for estimating the relative population of the remaining one hundred and twenty demes during the fourth century. When we have occasion to deal with demes whose bouleutic quotas were increased by more than one in the reorganization of 307/6, we will note both the Kleisthenic and the later quotas.

As to the second argument, Gomme's figures can tell us something about the relative populations of people who are likely to appear in the epigraphic record, but are inadequate evidence for the relative total populations of the demes. The number of demesmen known to us is in part a function of wealth (wealthier individuals were more likely to be commemorated on stone), of geography (some demes, especially those in remote areas, are less well excavated than others closer to the city or other important centers), and of the accidents of chance survival. Poorer demes and those off the beaten track would thus provide fewer individuals likely to be remembered in the epigraphical record, making that record a less than reliable witness to the relative populations of these remoter and poorer demes.

1. THE FREQUENCY OF SACRIFICE

While our principal concern in the present chapter will be with public sacrifices, we may note prefatorily that personal piety also inspired private sacrifices by individuals, especially among the wealthy who could afford them.[1] Even such private sacrifices, however, frequently had a public dimension when others were invited to share the sacrificial meal.[2] Thus, for example, when in Menander's *Dyskolos* Sostratos' mother decides to sacrifice a sheep to Pan, her purpose is wholly personal, to convert an ill-omened dream about her son into a favorable one, but she still invites a large number of people to join her in the sacrifice and in the meal which will follow.[3] Similarly at Isaios 1.31 Kleonymos sacrifices to Dionysos as an act of private devotion, but he also invites καὶ τοὺς οἰκείους ἅπαντας . . . καὶ τῶν ἄλλων πολιτῶν πολλούς. Perhaps more interestingly, in Xenophon's *Oikonomikos* Sokrates reminds the wealthy Kritoboulos that a man in his position must lavishly entertain foreigners and provide meals and otherwise help his fellow citizens if he is to maintain

---

[1] On private sacrifices see Stengel (1920) 105-6. Private individuals could officiate at their own private sacrifices, particularly when these were conducted at home, or they could have priests officiate for them at some public site (thus θύων . . . πολλάκις μὲν οἴκοι, πολλάκις δὲ ἐπὶ τῶν κοινῶν τῆς πόλεως βωμῶν, Xen. *Mem.* 1.1.2); for the former cf. e.g. Isaios 8.16 where it is said of Kiron αὐτὸς δι' ἑαυτοῦ πάντ' ἐποίει, in his sacrifice to Zeus Ktêsios; for the latter cf. e.g. Dem. 59.166.

[2] Naturally not all private sacrifices had such a public dimension. At Isaios 8.16, for example, Kiron limited attendance at his private sacrifices to Zeus Ktêsios his family, and excluded slaves and outsiders (ὀθνείους). Still, the fact that Isaios' speaker feels it necessary to specify that slaves and outsiders did not participate in these sacrifices of Kiron suggests that such participation of slaves and/or outsiders was far more typical than not.

[3] Men. *Dysk.* 393-418. The slave Getas enters carrying a heavy load of rugs upon which the banqueters will recline while eating (cf. 402-5, with Handley [1965] 202 on 404 f.).

his reputation and have their political support, but first and foremost he must sacrifice πολλά τε καὶ μεγάλα if both gods and men are not to find him intolerable (Xen. *Oik.* 2.4-5). Kritoboulos' sacrifices are private, and in no sense does he perform them as an agent of the state, but they nonetheless have a public—and indeed political—dimension both in the way their magnificence enhances Kritoboulos' reputation and in the way the food they provide for his fellow citizens puts those citizens under an obligation to help Kritoboulos politically at some point in the future.[4]

At a minimum private sacrifices can join others to the sacrificer through the common meal which the sacrifice occasions, and inviting an acquaintance to a sacrifice is surely the best way of getting oneself invited in return to his sacrifice and to the meal it will provide (Xen. *Mem.* 2.3.11). And in at least some instances, as the case of Kritoboulos shows, private sacrifices can become part of the broader pattern of *philotimia*, i.e. the ostentatious expenditure for the public good provided by the wealthy in anticipation of public recognition and gratitude, which was typical of the socio-political behavior of much of Athens' upper class.[5]

---

[4]For this obligation upon the elite to benefit their neighbors through the modalities of sacrifice cf. Isaios 3.80, where a wealthy man is expected to feast (ἑστιᾶν) the women of his deme on behalf of his wife at the time of the Thesmophoria, and to do whatever else it is fitting to λῃτουργεῖν ἐν τῷ δήμῳ. By contrast Theophrast. *Char.* 10.11 describes the "cheapskate" who feasts his fellow demesmen but slices and serves only small pieces of meat; the *hestiasis* in Isaios 3.80 would appear to be a deme liturgy (unless λῃτουργεῖν is used metaphorically), but that in Theophrast. *Char.* 10.11 is almost certainly a private sacrifice (it is difficult to imagine how a liturgist would be involved in slicing up and serving the meat at a public sacrifice). Theophrastos' vignette thus suggests that the wealthy were also under a social obligation to provide food *via* private sacrifices for other members of their deme.

[5]On *philotimia* see Whitehead (1983) 55-74; and, more generally, Veyne (1976). See also Davies (1981) 91-92.

THE FREQUENCY OF SACRIFICE

Unlike private sacrifices, which were performed by individuals for their own personal ends, public sacrifices were performed by agents of a larger community for the benefit of that community. For convenience we may distinguish here between public sacrifices performed under the general supervision and direction of the central government (i.e. the *boulē* and *ekklēsia*) on behalf of the whole *polis*-community and those performed by smaller units within the *polis*. These smaller units would include most prominently the demes[6] to which all citizens belonged, as well as the trittyes and tribes into which the demes were grouped; they would also include the *genē* and phratries which were still "public" in the sense that we are using the word here, even though, unlike the deme/trittys/tribe organization, the *genos*/phratry organization was not coextensive with the entire citizen body of the *polis*. We have evidence from inscriptions for sacrifices on the level of the *polis*, the demes, the trittyes, the *genē* and the phratries,[7] though of course, given the limits of our sources, not for every deme, trittys, etc.; and although it is impossible to prove, it is nonetheless a reasonable assumption that every subdivision of the *polis*-community offered some sacrifices for the benefit of its members. Benefit here should be understood both in the sense that the gods' favor was sought for its members and in the sense that some or all of its members could share in the meal prepared from the sacrificial animal(s). In fact, participation in these public sacrifices was a function of citizenship in the *polis*, deme, etc.,[8] such that all citizens *qua* citizens normally had

---

[6]Cf. the lexicographers' distinction between δημοτελῆ and δημοτικά sacrifices (Hesykh. s.v. δημοτελῆ ἱερά: καὶ δημοτελῆ μέν, εἰς ἃ θύματα διδῷ ἡ πόλις, δημοτικὰ δέ, εἰς ἃ οἱ δῆμοι, similarly Bekker, *Anec.* 1.240.28-30; Harpokrat. s.v. δημοτελῆ καὶ δημοτικὰ ἱερά; note also δημόσιον ἢ δημοτικόν in the law quoted in [Dem.] 43.71).

[7]In general see below, note 14. For sacrifice on the level of the phratry note *IG* 2^2 1237, which details perquisites for priests conducting sacrifices for the phratry of the Demotionidai.

[8]This right to share the meat of sacrifice by virtue of one's citizenship in the unit offering the sacrifice is clearly implied, for example, in deme decrees granting non-demesmen a share of the meat equal to that of demesmen, in

a right to the benefits of the public sacrifices of the *polis*, as well as those of the deme, trittys, etc. into which they were either born or adopted.[9] And conversely, when one's citizen's rights were lost or impaired, one could no longer attend these public sacrifices.[10]

Besides these private and public sacrifices, sacrifices were also offered to individual deities by voluntary associations of worshipers (*orgeônes*, *thiasôtai*) for the benefit of their members. Such cult associations were organized along the same lines as the demes et al. and may be grouped with the latter for our purposes. It should be noted, however, that we have much less evidence for such voluntary cult associations, but it is unclear whether this is because by their nature such associations were less likely to erect inscriptions or be mentioned by our literary sources, or simply because there were relatively fewer such associations.

Inasmuch as the Athenians sacrificed on a variety of political levels, from that of the individual deme up to that of the *polis* as a whole, in principle we could determine the frequency with which they publicly sacrificed by taking the sum of all the sacrifices which occurred on all these levels throughout the year. Given the nature of our sources, however, it is impossible to calculate such a specific combined sum. As it is, we have very little evidence about the frequency of sacrifice, and almost all of what we do have concerns sacri-

---

recognition of services rendered by the honorand to the deme (e.g. *IG* 2^2 1187.16-23; *IG* 2^2 1204.12-17).

[9]On rare occasions victims provided by a public unit may be reserved for the members of a smaller group (so e.g. the goat and the sheep handed over to the Pythaistai in the Erkhia Calendar [*SEG* 21.541], Γ.35-37 and E.35-37; on the number of Pythaistai see also below, notes 30 and 31); significantly, however, even on these occasions the smaller group receiving the victim always appears to be composed exclusively of citizens of the unit sponsoring the sacrifice.

[10]So e.g. Antiphon 6.4 describing the fate of one convicted of murder: εἴργεσθαι πόλεως, ἱερῶν, ἀγώνων, θυσιῶν, ἅπερ μέγιστα καὶ παλαιότατα τοῖς ἀνθρώποις; cf. Dem. 57.47.

fices by either the demes or the *polis* as a whole, with almost nothing about sacrifices by trittyes, tribes, phratries and *genê*. Further, most of our evidence about the demes and the other subunits is epigraphic, with all the limits that evidence of this sort has.[11] Fortunately, however, while the total number of surviving inscriptions dealing with sacrifices in the demes and other units is quite small, several of these inscriptions are extraordinarily detailed, presenting calendars of sacrifices with dates, victims, anticipated expenditures[12] and other concerns, and it is the wealth of detail in these inscribed calendars which makes the present study possible. In what follows we will first examine three deme calendars, from Erkhia (*SEG* 21.541), from Thorikos (*SEG* 33.147), and from Marathon (*IG* 2^2 1358).[13] Next, as illustrations of sacrificial practices on a level between the deme and the *polis* we will consider the sacrifices on the Calendar of the Marathonian Tetrapolis (a regional cult association of four demes) which is also found in *IG* 2^2 1358, the same inscription containing the Marathon Deme Calendar, as well as the sacrifices in a document of the Salaminioi *genos* (*SEG* 21.527).[14] Finally we will examine the so-

---

[11] On these limits see above, Introduction, pp. 4-5.

[12] The financial purpose of *SEG* 21.527 (the inscription containing the Salaminioi Calendar), is stated quite clearly (lines 82-84): . . . ἐγγράψαι τὰς θυσίας ἁπάσας καὶ τὰς τιμὰς τῶν ἱερέων . . . ὅπως ἂν οἱ ἄρχοντες . . . εἰδῶσι ὅ τι δεῖ ἀργύριον συνβάλλεσθαι εἰς τὰ[ς] θυσίας. As noted below (p. 15), the intention behind the arrangement of the Erkhia Calendar appears to have been to produce five columns of almost equal expenditures.

[13] Previous study of these calendars has focused for the most part on their religious content (so, most comprehensively, Mikalson [1977]). By contrast, their economic content has been by and large ignored except for the data they provide for prices of sacrificial animals (so e.g. van Straten [1987] 166).

[14] Other extant calendars (all incomplete) include *IG* 1^3 250 (= *LSS* 18, detailing sacrifices to Eleusinian gods, from the deme Paiania), *IG* 1^3 244 (= *LSCG* 10, from the deme Skambonidai), *IG* 1^3 255 (= *LSCG* 11, on which see below), *IG* 1^3 246 (= *LSCG* 16, probably from an unidentified deme [so e.g. *LSCG ad loc.*; see further below, note 94], although Lewis in *IG* 1^3 *ad loc.*, following Prott [1896] no. 2, believes that it could be from a tribe, phratry or *genos*), *IG* 2^2 1363 (= *LSCG* 7, from the deme Eleusis), *SEG* 21.542

called *Dermatikon* Accounts (*IG* 2² 1496), a record of the sale of victims' hides by the *polis*, for the evidence which it provides concerning the major sacrifices which were conducted for the *polis*-community as a whole.

The Erkhia Calendar (*SEG* 21.541, *LSCG* 18).[15]

This calendar from the second quarter of the fourth century details a series of sacrifices conducted by the moderately large inland deme of Erkhia.[16] Each item on the calendar lists the month and day of the sacrifice, the deity to whom the sacrifice was offered, the place

---

(= *LSS* 132, from the deme Teithras), "The Calendar of Nikomakhos," (the recodification of the *polis*' "ancestral" sacrifices completed some time after 403), and *IG* 1³ 234 (= *LSCG* 1, possibly an earlier version of the calendar of "ancestral" sacrifices). All of these calendars are too fragmentary to be of much use for our purposes here (but see below, notes 72 and 94). There is also a calendar from outside our period (*IG* 2² 1367 = *LSCG* 52, possibly from the first century A.D.). Note also *IG* 2² 1356 (= *LSCG* 28, probably from an unknown deme) detailing perquisites for priests from various sacrifices. *IG* 1³ 255 (= *LSCG* 11) is usually identified as a the calendar of an unknown trittys on the basis on the word τριττύι on line 9, but the dative is a bit odd; Jameson *ad loc.* calls attention to the datives Γλεόντων φυλῆι Λευκοταινίων τριττυι in the "Calendar of Nikomakhos" (*Hesp.* 1935, p. 21, no. 2, lines 35-37) where the dative appears to indicate that the animal in question (an *ois leipognômôn*) is allocated to the trittys for its sacrifice; if the dative is used in the same way at *IG* 1³ 255.9, *IG* 1³ could not be a trittys-calendar, and is likely to be a *polis*-document of some sort.

[15]The text followed here is that printed in *SEG* 21.541 based on Daux' original publication (1963), and incorporating his subsequent corrections (1964, 676-77).

[16]For the calendar's date see Daux (1963) 615; for Erkhia's location see Vanderpool (1965). Erkhia provided six or seven of the five hundred members of the Kleisthenic *boulê* (vs. a median representation of two and an average representation of 3.6); its representation increased to eleven of the six hundred *bouleutai* after the reorganization of 307/6 (all figures are drawn from the tables in Traill (1975)); on the usefulness of the number of members a deme provided to the *boulê* as an index of the deme's population see above, Introduction, pp. 6-8.

where it occurred, the anticipated cost of the victim, and occasionally additional specifications, some of which appear to pertain to the distribution of the meat. The Calendar is arranged in five columns on the stele, the purpose of which arrangement appears to be financial, to divide the expenses of sacrifice into five almost equal totals;[17] within each column the sacrifices are arranged in chronological order, and Daux has shown that the text as we have it is in fact a re-edition into five columns of a single, now lost, chronologically ordered list.[18] The calendar has survived intact except for the loss of a few lines at its bottom containing information on the month of Skirophorion and the summary totals for three of the five columns.

Since the principal concern of the present chapter is with the distribution of meat from sacrifices, in the following analysis of the Erkhia Calendar, as in the analyses of the other calendars below, I will ignore victims which were totally destroyed (*holokaustoi*) in the act of sacrifice. I will also ignore sacrifices of piglets (*khoiroi*) which often served as purificatory victims and were thus unlikely to be eaten at least on these occasions,[19] and which in any event would not supply much meat for a general distribution. The Erkhia and other calendars usually allow us to identify male and female victims,[20] but since both male and female victims would provide approximately the

---

[17]On this point see especially Dow (1965, 194-95), although I do not agree with Dow on the purpose of this division (on which see further below, Chapter 3, note 92).

[18]Daux (1963) 615-17; the key to recognizing the unitary nature of our calendar's prototype was the observation made to Daux by R. F. Healey, S.J. that the sacrifice to Semele at A. 44-48 is ἐπὶ τοῦ αὐτοῦ βωμοῦ as the sacrifice to Dionysus at Δ.35-40 (Daux [1963] 617, n. 1). F. Sokolowski's view (*LSCG*, p. 42) that the five columns represent five different years in a quinquennial cycle of sacrifices appears to be only a bad guess.

[19]Jameson (1965) 163; Jameson adds "Pigs, though not always offered in holocaust, were small and cheap victims and served as a convenient means of achieving the effect of total destruction."

[20]Male victims were typically offered to male deities, female victims to female deities; male victims also usually cost more than female ones (on the higher prices for male victims see below, pp. 101-6).

same amount of meat I will not distinguish here between the two; for similar reasons pregnant victims will not be specially noted. Public sacrifices to different deities, both in Erkhia and elsewhere, were often grouped together on a single day, and can thus be understood as elements in a single sacrificial event. The information on both date and place of sacrifice on the Erkhia Calendar allows us to identify which individual sacrifices were parts of a single sacrificial event with greater certainty here than on any of the other deme calendars. The following list of sacrificial events on the Erkhia Calendar is arranged by month to permit comparisons with the other calendars to be studied below.

Sacrificial Events on the Erkhia Calendar

Hekatombaion (June/July):

(1) 2 goats,[21] both οὐ φορά[22]

Metageitnion (July/Aug.):

(1) 4 sheep, 2 of which οὐ φορά, ἐν ἄστει[23]
(2) 1 sheep, οὐ φορά
(3) 1 lamb,[24] οὐ φορά

---

[21]Even though the sacrifices occur in different places in Erkhia (ἐς Σωτιδῶν, Γ.8-9; ἐπὶ τ[ὸ] Ἄκρο, Δ.8-9), the two places need not have been very far apart. Since both sacrifices are to Artemis, it is probably best to take them as parts of a single ritual act begun in one location and completed in another. Cf. the three sacrifices in three different places ἐν ἄστει on the same date at A.1-5, B.1-5 and Δ.13-17.

[22]See below, pp. 18-19, on the meaning of this expression.

[23]See above, note 21.

[24]The lamb is to be all-black (παμμέλαιναν, A.9-10). Black sacrificial victims may elsewhere indicate sacrifices to chthonic deities in which the victims were totally destroyed, but since victims to be sacrificed in this manner are clearly designated by the notation *holokaustos* elsewhere on the Erkhia

THE FREQUENCY OF SACRIFICE

Boedromion (Aug./Sept.):
    (1) 5 sheep

Pyanopsion (Sept./Oct.):
    (1) 1 sheep, οὐ φορά

Maimakterion (Oct./Nov.):
    (no sacrifices)

Poseideon (Nov./Dec.):
    (1) 1 sheep, οὐ φορά

Gamelion (Dec./Jan.):
    (1) 2 sheep (1 of which to be handed over to Pythaistai)
    (2) 4 goats (1 of which to be handed over to Pythaistai)
    (3) 1 lamb
    (4) 3 sheep

Anthesterion (Jan./Feb.):
    (1) 1 sheep, ἐν ἄστει
    (2) 1 kid

Elaphebolion (Feb./March):
    (1) 2 goats (both to be handed over to women), οὐ φορά

Calendar (B.19-20; Γ.22-23; E.22-23) one would infer from the absence of such a label for this victim that it was not totally destroyed in sacrifice. Indeed, whatever the precise meaning of the rubric οὐ φορά, there is no doubt that it refers to meat which is distributed after sacrifice (the same rubric is applied to the animals whose meat is to be distributed to women [γυναιξὶ παραδόσιμος, A.48-50; similarly Δ.37-38]), and its presence here must mean that meat from this all-black victim was also to be distributed to those in attendance.

Mounikhion (March/April):
    (1) 1 sheep
    (2) 1 sheep, οὐ φορά
    (3) 1 sheep, οὐ φορά

Thargelion (April/May):
    (1) 2 goats (1 of which to be handed over to Pythaistai), 3 sheep[25]
    (2) 1 lamb, οὐ φορά
    (3) 1 sheep, οὐ φορά

Skirophorion (May/June):
    (1) 4 sheep, 1 of which οὐ φορά[26]

According to this calendar then, the deme of Erkhia sacrificed victims, and presumably distributed their meat, on a minimum[27] of twenty-one different days during the year. Even if relatively few people would be fed by a single lamb (three occasions) or a single kid (one occasion), on the remaining seventeen occasions at least one sheep or goat was sacrificed, and on nine of these seventeen occasions, two or more animals were sacrificed. Further, on six of the eight occasions when a single sheep was sacrificed the rubric οὐ φορά is appended to the item in the calendar. If, as is generally assumed,

---

[25] Although the five victims were sacrificed in three different places (ἐμ Π[υ]θίο [i.e. -ου] A.54-55; ἐμ Πάγωι; B.58-59 and Γ.57-58; ἐν ἀγορᾶι, E.50-51; and simply 'Ερχιᾶσιν with no further specification, Δ.50), their sacrifices all appear to be part of a single sacrificial event. Cf. above, note 21.

[26] In addition to this event on Skirophorion 3 there was a second sacrificial event on Skirophorion 16, but the item has been lost from the stone except for its date. Under the monthly label for Skirophorion in column E there was also at least one more victim which has also now been lost from the stone; the victim(s) there may have also been sacrificed as part of either the event on the 3rd or that on the 16th.

[27] See previous note.

this rubric means that the meat was to be consumed on the spot and not carried away, then on these six occasions the prescription, whose original intent was probably cultic, had the added effect of making the meat of the single animal go further by limiting the amount of meat which any one person could have.[28] The single sheep sacrificed to Zeus Melikhios ἐν ἄστει in Anthesterion may be a special instance, with relatively few demesmen making the trip to town for this late winter event, in which case the absence of the οὐ φορά rubric is understandable. In contrast, multiple victims were sacrificed ἐν ἄστει in Metageitnion in late summer, a more congenial season for travelling, and hence a time when a larger number of demesmen living in Erkhia were likely to come to the city than in the rawer weather of Anthesterion.[29] As for the victims to be handed over to (the?) Pythaistai, I would only note that we have no way of knowing how many Erkhians

---

[28] Dow (1965, 210) sees this desire to insure an adequate supply of meat for all participants, rather than anything religious, as the primary purpose of the οὐ φορά prescription, but he is probably mistaking a beneficial side-effect of the prescription for its original intent. In *IG* 7 235 (= *SIG*³ 1004), lines 31-32, a fourth-century inscription from Oropos dealing with the duties of the priest of Amphiaraos, the removal of meat from *private* sacrifices from the *temenos* of Amphiaraos is prohibited; again the origin of the prescription may well be cultic, but it also benefited the priest, who would receive the uncomsumed meat (note that private sacrifices might be shared with friends, etc., but there could be no question of a general distribution of meat to the public at large; absent the prohibition, the sacrificer would simply take any leftover meat home for himself).

[29] Metageitnion was also an excellent time for country demesmen to visit the city since it was a time of low agricultural activity between the spring harvest and the fall vintage and plowing. There is no reason to take these multiple victims sacrificed ἐν ἄστει as evidence that a substantial number of demesmen had moved from Erkhia and taken up permanent residence in the city.

were Pythaistai, though the number is unlikely to be very small,[30] and it might even in fact be quite large.[31]

There are two reasons for believing that the Erkhia Calendar which we have been considering (sc. that inscribed in *SEG* 21.541) probably does not contain all of the sacrifices which the Erkhians would have celebrated during any given year. First, the calendar itself bears the title Δημαρχία ἡ μέζων, implying that there was also a Δημαρχία ἡ μείων. Dow, it is true, has argued the view originally suggested to him by R. F. Healey that the expression Δημαρχία ἡ μέζων means something like "the increased (scope of) authority of the Deme," imagining that the deme government had increased its authority in religious matters by assuming the expenses which had previously been met by wealthy hereditary priests.[32] This notion, however, that well into the fourth century hereditary priests paid for the expenses of the deme's cult rests on what I believe is a faulty view of how deme sacrifices were financed, as will be seen below in Chapter 3. Besides, whatever the exact meaning of Δημαρχία, it must have something to do with the person or office of the demarkh, as Jameson has pointed out,[33] and cannot refer abstractly to the authority of the deme as Dow would have it.

---

[30]It is unlikely that the Pythaistai would be assigned an entire victim if they were very few in number.

[31]Their name indicates that the Pythaistai were some kind of a religious fellowship. Membership in such fellowships was not necessarily very exclusive; cf. e.g. the large number of Athenians who were initiates in the Eleusinian Mysteries.

[32]Dow (1965) 194-95.

[33]Jameson (1965) 155, note 1, approved by Woodhead, *SEG* 22.131. I cannot accept Bicknell's suggestion (1976, 603) that the δημαρχία ἡ μείων contained sacrifices performed by Erkhia as part of its membership in a three-village union of Kytherros, Erkhia and Konthyle, since it is hard to see what meaning either δημαρχία ἡ μέζων or δημαρχία ἡ μείων would have in this case; note also that at least in the case of the Marathonian Tetrapolis (*IG* 2² 1358 = *LSCG* 20) the demes' sacrifices appear on the calendar of the Tetrapolis and not vice versa.

It is also noteworthy that the Erkhia Calendar contains only annual sacrifices, and there is no indication of any biennial and quadrennial sacrifices such as we find on some other similar documents. It is of course always possible that the Erkhians performed only annual sacrifices, but it is perhaps more likely that the biennial and/or quadrennial events were inscribed elsewhere and have now been lost; indeed, to judge from the multi-year cycles in the Marathonian calendars discussed below, there probably were also fewer sacrificial events on the biennial/quadrennial calendar than on the annual calendar, in which case the biennial/quadrennial calendar could well be the Δημαρχία ἡ μείων, the shorter calendar of sacrifices for which the demarkh was also responsible.[34] Alternatively, the Δημαρχία ἡ μείων may be a shorter calendar detailing sacrifices to Eleusinian gods, who are absent from the Δημαρχία ἡ μέζων, sacrifices which would similarly be the responsibility of the demarkh.[35] In any event, since the title Δημαρχία ἡ μέζων implies a Δημαρχία ἡ μείων, whatever that may be, it is clear that the Erkhian Calendar as we now have it lists perhaps most, but certainly not all, of the sacrifices and sacrificial events which took place in the deme of Erkhia in any given year.

Finally, one may observe that the sacrifices on the Erkhian Calendar are not spaced out evenly throughout the year, but the major events with the largest number of victims cluster in two periods, the first between the months of Thargelion (April/May) and Boedromion (August/September) and the second in the month of Gamelion (December/January).

---

[34]Following up on an unpublished paper by R. Parker, Whitehead (1986, 63-64) proposes a variant of this idea, viz. that the δημαρχία ἡ μέζων and the δημαρχία ἡ μείων were two years in a biennial cycle, the former with more sacrifices (annual and biennial) in it, the latter with fewer.

[35]Cf. the separate calendar for sacrifices to Eleusinian gods in IG I³ 250 (= *LSS* 18) from the deme Paiania (I thank Michael Jameson for calling the absence of Eleusinian cults to my attention).

The Thorikos Calendar (*SEG* 33.147, not in *LSCG*).[36]

This calendar, from the smallish coastal deme of Thorikos,[37] was probably inscribed in the 430s, and would thus be perhaps as much as eighty years earlier than the calendar from Erkhia.[38] The calendar is arranged chronologically by month. Under each month's rubric, individual items list the name of the god to whom the sacrifice was made, the kind of victim to be sacrificed (but not its price), and occasionally other information. The inscription is mutilated on its upper left, so that most of the information concerning the month of Thargelion has been lost; on the right side the ends of lines have been lost beginning near the end of Boedromion (21) and continuing to the end of the inscription (65), though this loss is less serious than the loss of Thargelion, and most of the lost text can be easily restored.

Dates within the month are provided for some items (either by the number of the day within the month, or by the name of a major feast), but other items are undated except for the month's rubric. This imprecise dating, compared with that on the Erkhia Calendar, makes it somewhat more difficult to identify multiple sacrifices which were part of single sacrificial events on the Thorikos Calendar. In order to determine the *minimum* number of separate days upon which the demesmen of Thorikos offered sacrifice, in the following table I have

---

[36]The text followed here is essentially that of Daux (1983) 152-54. Earlier editions of this inscription were published by Vanderpool (1975, 37) and by Dunst (1977, 243-45). Both Vanderpool and Dunst depended on what we now know were faulty and incomplete transcriptions, while Daux' is the first edition based on a direct observation of the stone. For commentaries see Dunst (1977) 249-64; Daux (1983) 161-71; and Parker (1987) 145-47.

[37]For the date see Daux (1983) 152. As an index of Thorikos' population, it provided five members for the *boulē* (compared with a median of two and an average of 3.6 per deme); its representation increased to six of six hundred after the reorganization of the *boulē* in 307/6 (all figures are taken from the tables in Traill [1975]; see also above, Introduction, pp. 6-8).

[38]For the date see Lewis (1985) 108, n. 3; Jameson (1988, 115, n. 7) dates the inscription to the 430's or 420's. Daux (1983, 152) had dated the calendar to the first half of the fourth century, perhaps between 385 and 370.

combined each month's sacrifices into single events except when the calendar specifically tells us that sacrifices fell on different days, that they were celebrated in places distant from each other, or that two different sacrifices were both in honor of the same deity. Again, I have not included the sacrifices of piglets (*khoiroi*) or the sacred tables (*trapezai*) since these apparently did not entail a major distribution of meat.[39] Also, no distinction has been made between male and female victims, nor between those labeled κριτόν, πρατόν or ὠνητόν, and those with no such labels.[40]

Minimum of Sacrificial Events on the Thorikos Calendar

Hekatombaion (June/July):

(1) 1 goat[41] and 1 *teleos*[42]

---

[39] On piglets see above, p. 15 with note 19.

[40] Κριτόν/-ήν: 13-14, 17, 18, 19-20, 20, 47-48, 53, 54; πρατόν: 9, 11-12, 26, 35; ὠνητόν, line 15. The significance of these labels is quite uncertain, but given their identical forms as passive verbal adjectives it at least seems reasonable to assume that they all refer to the same aspect of the sacrificial process (thus it is unlikely e.g. that κριτόν and ὠνητόν refer to the acquisition of victims while πρατόν refers to the sale of their meat; *pace* Parker [1987, 145, commentary on l. 11], I do not see how the Greek οἶν πρατόν, "a sold sheep," can be made to mean that the meat of the as-yet-to-be-sacrificed animal is to be sold after the sacrifice]). In any event κριτόν cannot describe requisitioned victims (as distinguished from purchased ones) since the label κριτός/-ή is used in the so-called "Calendar of Nikomakhos" to describe victims for whom a purchase price is also budgeted (*Hesperia* 4 [1935] 21, no. 2, lines 22, 70). Indeed, it is possible that the three adjectives refer to some other quality of the victims, and have nothing to do with how they are acquired.

[41] Because of the loss of most of the calendar for Hekatombaion, it is impossible to say with certainty what preceded its first surviving entry (Δελ]φίνιον αἶγ[α]) at the end of line 6. Most of lines 7-9 are also lost. The first part of line 7 may have contained the date of the next sacrifice which was offered to Hekate, whose name appears at the end of line 7, and there seems to be space for the victim to be sacrificed to her in the lost beginning of line

Metageitnion (July/Aug.):

(1) 2 *teleoi*
(2) *horkômosion*[43]

---

8. The illegible end of line 8 and/or the beginning of line 9 would contain the name of the god to whom the teleos (the next item in this table) was sacrificed at the end of line 9.

[42] The adjective *tele(i)os* describes a fully mature animal (see further below, Supplementary Note A), and we find the adjective applied to sheep, goats and oxen, and even to a sacrificial swine (cf. Eustathius' discussion of age terms for animals [1625.33 ff.] based on Aristophanes of Byzantion's περὶ ὀνομασίας ἡλικιῶν; for the swine, *IG* 2² 1356.12-13 with note 138 below). Occasionally *tele(i)os* is used substantively, without a noun indicating the kind of animal intended; this is true of all of the uses of *teleon* in the Thorikos Calendar. According to Dunst (1977, 262) a victim described as *teleos* may be any kind of animal of the right age, but such casualness about victims seems to run contrary to the care which the Athenians typically took (and which the demesmen of Thorikos took elsewhere on this Calendar) to sacrifice specific kinds of victims to specific gods. But the Thorikos Calendar also lists sacrifices for which a sheep or a goat is specified, and it is difficult to see why, if the victims described as *teleoi* were also meant to be understood either as sheep (the animals most commmonly sacrificed) or as sheep or goats depending on the deity, the Calendar specifically mentions a sheep or goat for some sacrifices but uses *teleos* for others. It would seem that the only explanation for the appearance of all three categories (sheep, goats and *teleoi*) in the Thorikos Calendar is that in those sacrifices for which the victim is specified as *teleos* the choice of the victim is neutral, and that an animal described as *teleos* can be either a sheep or a goat (though probably not an ox, which would be in a different class in both size and cost). Note also that both times that λειπογνώμων, another age term, is used in the Thorikos Calendar, it is adjectival, modifying the expressed noun αἶγα (34, 43).

[43] "Une victime pour la prestation du serment," (Daux (1983) 154); the word is used elsewhere in this sense in the plural, but is apparently so used in the singular only here. Dunst (1977, 252) mistakenly identifies the *horkômosion* as the place where the *euthunai* are to take place (cf. Plut. *Thes.* 27). The provision for *horkômosia* both here and below in Skirophorion is an interesting example of the interpenetration of the religious and the civil in deme life, since both *horkômosia* were for the *euthunai* of the deme's officials. I have not found any evidence to show what were typical or appropriate victims for a deme's *horkômosia* (in oaths, the choice of victims appar-

THE FREQUENCY OF SACRIFICE 25

Boedromion (Aug./Sept.):

    (1) *Prêrosia*[44]
    (2) 1 sheep[45]
    (3) 2 sheep
    (4) 1 lamb, ἐπὶ Σούνιον, and 1 goat
    (5) 2 *teleoi*
    (6) 1 *teleos*, ἐφ' ἁλῆι

Pyanopsion (Sept./Oct.):

    (1) 1 *teleos*
    (2) 2 *teleoi*

Maimakterion (Oct./Nov.):

    (1) 1 ox

Poseideon (Nov./Dec.):

    (1) *Dionusia*[46]

---

ently depended on the seriousness of the occasion and the resources of the participants, so e.g. a boar, a ram and a bull for a murder trial before the Areiopagos [Dem. 23.68]). There is also some uncertainty as to whether victims used in oaths could also be eaten; Burkert (1985, 252) discusses the matter briefly and appears to incline toward the view that they were eaten. For my own part, I would think that the Athenians were too sensible to waste good meat in this way, and I would therefore assume that anything bigger than a *holokaustos khoiros* was in fact eaten.

[44] According to Daux (1983, 164) the accusative plurals Πρηρόσια (13) and Διονύσια (31) are not dating devices (which should be in the dative; cf. 27, 32) but rather references to holidays the details of whose rites were presumably published elsewhere.

[45] This offering to Zeus Polieus is accompanied by a series of ritual prescriptions (13-16) which clearly distinguish it from the sacrifices to Kephalos (and Prokris) and Thorikos (and the Heroines of Thorikos) which follow (17-19).

[46] See above, note 44.

Gamelion (Dec./Jan.):

    (1) 1 victim[47]

Anthesterion (Jan./Feb.):5-27

    (1) 1 goat and 1 sheep

Elaphebolion (Feb./March):

    (1) 4 *teleoi*,[48] 1 sheep and 1 lamb[49]

Mounikhion (March/April):

    (1) 1 *teleos* and a *trit[toa*[50]
    (2) 3 goats, 2 sheep[51]
    (3) [1 goat[52]], ἐπὶ Μυκηνον (*sic*)

---

[47] An offering to Hera on the occasion of the *Hieros Gamos*; the description of the victim has been lost with the end of line 32.

[48] With the reading "Ἡρακλείδα[ις τέλεον] proposed by Parker (1984).

[49] It is noteworthy that a pregnant ewe is sacrificed to Demeter but only an *arna* to Zeus (38-39). By contrast, earlier in the calendar Demeter and Zeus Herkeios were given equal victims (*teleoi*, 21-22 in Boedromion). In both places, the sacrifice to Demeter is listed first, before the sacrifice to Zeus. This is a good illustration of how the priorities of religion in the demes do not always correspond to those of the *polis* or of mythology.

[50] The *trittoa* was a sacrifice of three different animals, e.g. a boar, a goat and a ram (*LSJ* s.v. τριττύς II citing schol. Aristoph. *Plout.* 820). Eustathios (1676.34 ff.) cites as examples of *trittoai* a ram, a bull and a swine; two sheep and a cow; a cow, a goat and a sheep; and a swine, a goat and a ram. Note also the τρίττοαν βόαρχον ("beginning with an ox") at *IG* 1³ 5.5.

[51] I.e. one sheep sacrificed to Demeter (43-44) and one sacrificed to Zeus Herkeios; the sheep to Zeus Herkeios appears as an addendum both on the left side of the stone (-ι Ἑρκείωι: οἶν) and on the right ([Διὶ Ἑ]ρκείωι: οἶν), one of which I assume is a doublet of the other. Items (1) and (2) for Mounikhion must be separate events since they both have sacrifices to Artemis and Apollo (40-41, 42-43).

[52] The entry for the victim has been lost from the end of line 45; Daux restores [τράγον], which would be an appropriate victim for this sacrifice to Dionysos.

Thargelion (April/May):
  (1) 1 lamb and 6 sheep

Skirophorion (May/June):
  (1) *horkômosion*[53]
  (2) 2 sheep
  (3) 1 ox, 2 sheep[54]

According to their calendar then, as we have analyzed it here, the demesmen of Thorikos sacrificed one or more animals on a minimum of twenty-one separate occasions, to which the Prêrosia and the (Rural) Dionysia[55] should probably also be added, for a minimum total of at least twenty-three different days upon which the demesmen of Thorikos offered sacrifice, and the actual number of days may have even been higher. The two sacrifices combined above as a single event in Anthesterion, for example, may well have been in fact two separate events since they were offered to Dionysos and Zeus Meilikhios, and it is unlikely that sacrifice would be offered to these two quite different gods on the same day as part of the same sacrificial event. It is also conceivable that in Elaphebolion only the four *teleoi*

---

[53] The *horkômosion* (52) must be a separate category of victims (and not merely a caption for the victims that are next listed) since the deities to whom the oaths are sworn (Zeus, Apollo, Demeter [60-61]) are different from those to whom the next-listed victims are offered (Athena and Aglauros [53-54]). In effect the calendar ends at οἶν (57); the oath is then added as an appendix referring back to *horkômosion* on line 52, and perhaps also on line 12. Note also that at line 12 *horkômosion* is the last item in the month of Mounikhion, and no victims are listed between it and the heading for the new month Boedromion, just as, by our interpretation, no victims are listed for the *horkômosion* on line 52.

[54] Items (2) and (3) should be separate events since each contains a sacrifice to Athena (53, 54). Cf. above, note 50, on items (1) and (2) in Mounikhion.

[55] See above, note 44.

were sacrificed on the same day to the Herakleidai, Alkmene, the Anakes and Helen, while the sheep and the lamb were sacrificed on a different day to Demeter and Zeus. Similarly in Mounikhion (item 2) the three goats may have been offered on one day to Leto, Artemis and Apollo, and the two sheep may have been sacrificed on a different day to Demeter and Zeus Herkeios. Finally, in Thargelion the lamb offered to Zeus was probably sacrificed on a different day[56] from the sheep sacrificed one each to Hyperpedios, Nisos, Thras[. . .], Sosineos and Rhogios. Thus instead of on a minimum of twenty-one or twenty-three days, the demesmen of Thorikos may perhaps have carried out sacrifices on as many as twenty-four or twenty-six different days.

With the exception of the lamb and perhaps the goat (here χίμαρος rather than αἴξ) sacrificed ἐπὶ Σούνιον (i.e. away from Thorikos) in Boedromion, the single lamb sacrificed to Zeus in Thargelion, and also possibly of the animals used for the two *horkômosia*, all of the sacrifices on the Thorikos Calendar involve large animals (sheep, goats and oxen),[57] and on at least thirteen different days (not counting the Prêrosia and the Dionysia), either an ox or more than one sheep or goat was sacrificed. There is no indication that any of the victims listed above were totally destroyed (*holokaustos*) in the sacrifice, and so we must assume that meat was distributed to the demesmen present on every one of these occasions.

Although there were sacrifices in Thorikos in every month (if we include the Rural Dionysia in Poseideon), the largest number of sacri-

---

[56] Note that this item contains the rubric ἐπαυτομένας also found among the prescriptions which set apart the sacrifice to Zeus Polieus in Boedromion (see above, note 45). Parker (1984, 145) would read ἐπ' Αὐτομενας (sic), "To Automenai" (presumably a place name), but Daux (1983, 172-73) gives good reasons against such an interpretation. On the other hand, I am not convinced by Daux' explanation (1983, 171-73) that ἐπαυτομένας refers to women crying out in honor of Zeus, but I have nothing better to offer.

[57] The goats labeled λειπογνώμονα (34, 43) are older animals (on the adjective λειπογνώμων, see further below, Supplementary Note A).

fices took place in the month of Boedromion (August/September) and in the months Elaphebolion (February/March) through Skirophorion (May/June). The pattern is quite different from that which we saw earlier on the Erkhia Calendar.

Finally, whatever title the calendar may once have had[58] was probably inscribed at the start of its first line which has now been lost. However, given the large number of sacrifices on the calendar, even in the absence of a title it is almost certain that we are dealing with a calendar of annual sacrifices, not of biennial or quadrennial ones. Moreover, unlike the Erkhia Calendar, nothing in the Thorikos Calendar suggests that there had once also been a complementary calendar of biennial and/or quadrennial sacrifices, though the possibility cannot be excluded.

The Marathon Deme Calendar (*IG* 2^2 1358, *LSCG* 20).[59]

This calendar from 400-350 is part of an inscription which originally contained a list of sacrifices performed jointly by the Marathonian Tetrapolis and individually by the four demes of the Tetrapolis (the large deme of Marathon and the smaller demes of Trikorynthos, Oinoe and Probalinthos).[60] The surviving text contains a reasonably complete listing of the sacrifices performed by the deme of Marathon and a fragmentary though still useful list of the joint sacrifices of the Tetrapolis.[61] For the moment our focus will be on the sacrifices

---

[58]E.g. τάδε θύεται Θορικίοις suggested by Vanderpool (1975, 41).

[59]The text followed here is that of *IG* 2^2 1358.

[60]Marathon provided ten members for the *boulê*, Trikorynthos three, Oinoe four and Probalinthos five, compared with a median of two and an average of 3.6 per deme; the representation of these demes in the *boulê* was unchanged in 307/6 (all figures are drawn from the tables in Traill (1975); see also above, Introduction, pp. 6-8).

[61]The surviving text is arranged in two columns. For the identification of the sacrifices in the left column as those celebrated jointly by the Tetrapolis and those in the right column as those celebrated by the deme of Marathon see Prott (1896) no. 46. The two columns are not inscribed *stoikhêdôn*; it is

performed separately by the deme of Marathon; we will return below to the joint sacrifices of the Tetrapolis.[62]

The calendar for the deme of Marathon appears in the rightmost of the two surviving columns of the inscription; most of the line ends have been lost, the damage being most severe in the first nine lines of the column. The first line is totally lost except for two letters, but the genitive plural Μα]ραθωνίων in line 2 shows that the list of sacrifices for the deme of Marathon probably began with the first line of this column. The sacrifices are arranged chronologically within three successive groups, annual sacrifices (1-33), a first cycle of biennial sacrifices (34-39, with the rubric τάδε τὸ ἕτερον ἔτος, προτέρα δραμοσύνη, 34), and a second cycle of biennial sacrifices which alternated with the first (39-53, with the rubric τάδε τὸ ἕτερον ἔτος θύεται μετὰ Εὔβουλον ἄρχ[ο]ντα Τετραπολεῦσι. ὑστέρα δραμοσύνη, 39-40). The calendar for the deme of Marathon ends at line 53, and the following line starts that for the deme of Trikorynthos, of which only two lines and a fragment of a third survive.

Separate months are labeled within each cycle on the deme calendar.[63] Under each month individual items contain the name of the god to which the sacrifice is offered, the victim(s) to be sacrificed and their anticipated cost, and occasionally an indication of the date or the

---

probably significant that the space allowed for the first column (containing the Tetrapolis' sacrifices) is substantially narrower than that allowed for the second column (containing the Marathon deme sacrifices), but the nature of the significance is unclear. The last three extant lines of the right column begin the calendar of sacrifices in the deme of Trikorynthos. The stone is broken at the bottom, so the length of columns is uncertain, but it seems clear that, whatever their length, there must have been at least one more column (and perhaps two) to continue the listing of the sacrifices performed by Trikorynthos and the other two demes.

[62] For the joint sacrifices see below, pp. 36-40.

[63] The months are also arranged into three-month periods, each with its own label (πρώτης τριμήνο, δευτέρας τριμήνο, etc.). The reason for this arrangement is unclear, but it does not appear to be important for our concerns here.

place where the sacrifice was performed. Most items also provide for a fee to be paid to the priest(s) (*hierôsuna*) increasing with the number of victims sacrificed, and the appearance of this fee in the calendar may be understood to mark the end of a group of one or more sacrifices performed together as parts of a single event. As in the calendars studied earlier, I will again ignore the sacrifice of piglets (*khoiroi*) and sacred tables (*trapezai*) since these do not appear to have involved a significant distribution of meat.

Sacrificial Events on the Marathon Deme Calendar

Hekatombaion (June/July):
    (1a) 1 ox and 3 sheep (yr. 1 only)[64]
    (2a) 1 sheep (yr. 1 only)
    (1b) 1 sheep (yr. 2 only)
  (no annual sacrifices[65])

Metageitnion (July/Aug.):
    (1b) 1 ox and 1 sheep (yr. 2 only)
    (2b) 1 sheep (yr.2 only)
    (3b) 1 sheep (yr. 2 only)
  (no annual sacrifices[66])
  (no sacrifices in yr. 1)

---

[64]"Yr. 1" and "yr. 2" refer to the alternating years of the two cycles of biennial sacrifices.

[65]I.e. no *major* sacrifices, unless there was something in the now lost second half of line 2. A *khoiros* and a *trapeza* appear on the stone on line 4 for either Hekatombaion or Metageitnion (the month-label has been lost) as offerings to the Hero, who is mentioned on line 3, and presumably to the Heroine, who is usually paired with him.

[66]See previous note.

Boedromion (Aug./Sept.):

    (1) 1 ox and 1 sheep[67] (every year)

Pyanopsion (Sept./Oct.):
    (no sacrifices)

Maimakterion (Oct./Nov.):
    (no sacrifices)

Poseideon (Nov./Dec.):

    (1) 1 ox and 2 sheep[68] (every year)
    (2) 1 ox (every year)
    (3) σπυλια[69] (*sic*) (every year)

Gamelion (Dec./Jan.):

    (1) 1 sheep (every year)
    (2) 1 sheep ἐπὶ τῶι μαντείωι (every year)

---

[67] Restoring the end of line 6 Κουροτρόφω[ι χοῖρος ⊢ ⊢ ⊢, [ἱερώσυνα - - -]; cf. line 31.

[68] The victim for the Heroine has been lost from the stone (8) but the *hierôsuna* of 7 dr. would fit the sacrifice of one ox and two sheep (cf. 20-21); since one ox and one sheep are already listed to be sacrificed (probably to the Hero, but the name is lost from the end of line 7), it seems likely that the victim to the Heroine would be a second sheep. The 150 dr. budgeted for the ox in line 8 is extraordinarily high (90 dr. are budgeted for each of the other oxen in the inscription [6, 20, 21,35, 55; and restored in 9, 43]); the figure of 150 could be nothing more than an engraver's error (so Pritchett [1956] 256) but with the end of line 7 lost and the price followed by erasures on line 8, perhaps one should restore the text at the end of line 7 and the start of line 8 δύο] | βοῦς ΗΠ^Δ[ΔΔΔ] (i.e. 180 dr.).

[69] The word σπυλια is a *hapax legomenon* (*LSJ* s.v.), but whatever its meaning, the accompanying figure of 40 dr. is quite high and must represent a considerable amount of potential meat (by comparison, three male sheep would cost only 36 dr.).

THE FREQUENCY OF SACRIFICE

        (3) 2 sheep[70] (every year)
        (4) 2 sheep[71] (every year)

Anthesterion (Jan./Feb.):
        (1b) 1 swine (yr. 2 only)
        (2b) 1 swine (yr. 2 only)
    (no annual sacrifices)
    (no sacrifices in yr. 1)

Elaphebolion (Feb./March):
        (1) 1 goat ἐπὶ τῶι μαντείωι (every year)

Mounikhion (March/April):
        (1) 1 ox and 2 sheep (every year)
        (2) 1 ox and 2 sheep (every year)
        (3) 4 sheep (every year)

Thargelion (April/May):
        (1) 2 sheep (every year)

Skirophorion (May/June):
        (1) 1 sheep (every year)
        (2) 1 sheep (every year)
        (3) 1 sheep (every year)
        (4b) 1 sheep (yr. 2 only)

---

[70] The victim for Zeus Hypatos is missing from the stone at the end of line 13, but a sheep for Zeus + the sheep for Iolaus + a *khoiros*, both still on the stone (14), would be right for the *hierôsuna* of 2 dr. 1.5 ob. (15). This event should be separate from the sacrifice to Gê ἐπὶ τῶι μαντείωι, for which no *hierôsuna* is provided.

[71] The victim for the Hero Phêraios has been lost from the stone at the end of line 15, but a sheep would be appropriate in view of the sheep offered to the Heroine (16) and the *hierôsuna* of 3 dr. for both.

The deme of Marathon thus sacrificed major victims on eighteen different occasions, including annual and biennial sacrifices, in the first year of the biennial cycle, and on twenty-three different occasions in the second year of the cycle. All of the victims were large animals, and no lambs or kids were slain. There is no indication that any of these animals was totally destroyed (*holokaustos*) in sacrifice, and so we should assume that meat was distributed to the demesmen in attendance on every one of these occasions.

The large number of oxen (six each year) and the absence of goats suggest that Marathon was a more prosperous deme than Erkhia or Thorikos, prepared to distribute more and better meat to its demesmen.

Once again the major sacrifices are not distributed evenly throughout the year but cluster instead in two periods, in the months of Poseideon (November/December) and Gamelion (December/January) and in the months from Mounikhion (March/April) to Hekatombaion (June/July).

To summarize briefly our progress thus far, by using various criteria we have been able to group the sacrifices on the three calendars we have been studying into sacrificial events, i.e. days upon which one or more victims were sacrificed to one or more gods. Excluding those sacrifices at which the victims were totally destroyed or were too small to provide much meat, we have established that the deme of Erkhia offered sacrifices at which a significant amount of meat would be available for distribution to the demesmen on at least seventeen different days annually, and probably more if, as seems likely, the deme also had a cycle of biennial sacrifices, the record of which has now been lost. We have similarly established that the deme of Thorikos offered sacrifices at which a significant amount of meat would be available for distribution on at least seventeen and perhaps as many as twenty-four different days each year. Finally we have established that the deme of Marathon offered similar sacrifices on eighteen or twenty-three different days, depending on the year in its

THE FREQUENCY OF SACRIFICE 35

cycle of biennial feasts. As we have seen, the seasonal patterns of sacrifice differ substantially from deme to deme, probably reflecting the particular religious sensitivities and history of each deme. Choice of sacrificial victims also varies from deme to deme, with Marathon, for example, offering no goats and fewer sheep than the other demes, but at least six oxen compared with two or three from Thorikos and none from Erkhia. Variations in victim-types are again probably a function of the different religious sensibilities of the demes, and perhaps also of their financial resources and their size. Despite the different seasonal patterns, however, and despite the variety in types of victims from deme to deme, it is nonetheless remarkable that the annual total number of sacrificial events is roughly the same in all three demes, a coincidence which suggests that at least the frequency of sacrifices in these three demes may be reasonably representative of the broader patterns of deme practice in general.[72] If the sacrificial practices of Erkhia, Thorikos and Marathon are indeed in any way typical of those of the other demes, we may conclude that in the fourth century B.C. the ordinary Athenian could attend, if he so chose, sacrifices sponsored by his deme at which meat would be distributed on roughly twenty different days each year.

As noted earlier, the Athenians offered public sacrifice on a variety of political levels between that of the deme and that of the *polis*.

---

[72]That the practice of these three demes was typical of broader deme practice is also the impression one gets from the fragmentary remains of other deme calendars (cf. above, note 14). *IG* 1³ 250 (from the deme Paiania) contains at least seven sacrifices in the extant portions of its first column, whose top and bottom are missing, and at least four sacrifices in the extant portions of its second column, whose top is also missing, *IG* 1³ 244 (from the deme Skambonidai) shows traces of entries for at least six sacrifices in its extant portion. In *IG* 1³ 246 (from an unknown deme) only the portion for Thargelion survives, where two sacrifices (a *teleos* and a sheep) are listed. In *SEG* 21.542 (from the deme Teithras) the portion for Boedromion survives, showing two sacrificial events (each with its own *hiereôsuna* [sic]) with a sheep sacrificed at each event.

We have two calendars complete enough to be of use to us from political units on these intermediate levels, the Calendar of the Marathonian Tetrapolis (a cult association in northeast Attica combining the deme of Marathon with the smaller demes of Trikorynthos, Oinoe and Probalinthos[73]) and a calendar which is part of a larger document belonging to the *genos* of the Salaminioi. Both calendars will serve as examples of the sacrificial practices of political units larger than demes but smaller than the *polis*.

The Calendar of the Marathonian Tetrapolis (*IG* 2^2 1358, *LSCG* 20).

This calendar from 400-350 appears to have once taken up all of the significantly narrower left-hand column of the same inscription which also contains the Marathon deme calendar in its wider right-hand column.[74] The first three lines of the left-hand column have been lost, along with whatever caption they may have contained; approximately the first half of each surviving line has also been lost, as has the bottom of the column. Despite the column's fragmentary condition, some notation, usually the kind of victim and/or its anticipated cost, has survived for almost all the sacrifices[75]; the difficulty then is not so much in determining how many animals were sacrificed

---

[73]We also know of several other similar associations of demes, the Trikomoi (Eupyridai, Kropidai and Pelekes), the Tettrakomoi (Peiraieus, Phaleron, Thymaitadai and Xypete), the League of Athena Pallenis (probably Akharnai, Gargettos, Paiania and Pallene) and perhaps the Epakreis (Plotheia and other demes, unless the Epakreis are the trittys to which Plotheia belonged). On the Epakreis see Parker (1987) 140; for the other associations see Whitehead (1986a) 184-85 and note 46 for sources and bibliography.

[74]The text followed again is that in *IG* 2^2 1358. For additional details on the inscription see above, p. 29 with note 61.

[75]Information on one or two sacrifices has disappeared with the loss of lines 1-3; other sacrifices were probably lost with lines 38 and 46; and there was perhaps some further loss at the end of the extant text. The names of almost all the deities to whom these sacrifices were offered have also been lost.

but rather in allocating these victims chronologically, and particularly into annual and multi-year cycles.

Within the Tetrapolis Calendar the year is divided into three-month periods, an arrangement we saw earlier in the deme Calendar from Marathon. On the Tetrapolis Calendar the extant or restorable rubrics appear in the following order: [τετάρτης τ]ριμῆνο (4), τετάρτης [τριμῆνο] (20-21), δευτέρας τρι]μῆνο (27), [τετάρτης τρι]μῆνο (29), τετάρτης [τριμῆνο] (32-33), [δευτέρας τριμ]ῆνο (40), [τρίτης τριμή]νο (42), [τετάρτης τριμῆνο] (44);[76] the rubric - - - δραμ]οσ[ύ]νη also appears on line 39. Now unless the items listed in the Tetrapolis Calendar follow no order at all—which is highly unlikely—, then we must have here at least five separate sacrificial cycles, to account for the five appearances of the fourth (i.e. the year-end) three-month period, which is what the rubric δραμοσύνη (39) would also suggest. The presence of only one sacrifice per three-month period in lines 40-43 seems to indicate that the sacrifices in this particular cycle were relatively infrequent; if this was in fact the case, then the now lost beginnings of lines 46-53 could easily have included three-month rubrics for one or more sacrificial cycles in addition to the five already required by the extant text. Finally, after the completion of the first cycle (1-12) the text reads: τάδε τοῦ τῶν ἐν | [- - - - ἐ]νιαυτοῦ ἕκαστον | - - - - -α ἑξῆς ὡς γέγραπται (13-15) which appears to introduce a second cycle of annual sacrifices mandated by some special enactment of the Tetrapolis,[77] in contrast to the first cycle which presumably contained "traditional" annual sacrifices whose origin went

---

[76]The correctness of the restorations is assured in all cases either by the letters extant on the stone or by the name of the month which follows.

[77]Cf. ὡς γέγραπται (15). Four sites are mentioned, each presumably with its own sacrifice: the incomplete]τον τὸν ἐν τοῖς (16), π]αρὰ τὸ Ἐλευσίνιον (17), ἐν Κυνοσούραι (18), and παρὰ] τὸ Ἡρακλεῖον (19). Kynosoura is a promontory on the Marathonian coast facing Euboia (Hesykh. s.v.). The Herakleion is probably a local shrine to Herakles, and the Eleusinion is also likely to be a local site in some way associated with the Eleusinian cult, and not the great Eleusinion in the *astu*. See also below, note 78.

back beyond memory. Using these clues, and bearing in mind how much of the Tetrapolis Calendar has been lost, I tentatively propose the following summary:

Contents of the Marathonian Tetrapolis Calendar

First Cycle ([lines 1-10] "traditional" annual sacrifices):
- (1) one or perhaps two sacrifices sometime before Mounikhion
- (2) Mounikhion (March/April)   1 sheep
- (3) Thargelion (April/May)   1 sheep
- (4) Skirophorion (May/June)   1 sheep

Second Cycle ([lines 11-23] newer annual sacrifices):
- (1) sometime before Mounikhion   4 victims[78]
- (2) Mounikhion (March/April)   1 sheep

Third Cycle ([lines 24-31] first biennial cycle?):
- (1) Hekatombaion (June/July)   1 goat
- (2) Pyanopsion (Sept./Oct.)   1 sheep
- (3) Mounikhion (March/April)   1 goat and 1 tel]eios[79]

Fourth Cycle ([lines 32-36] second biennial cycle?):
- (1) Mounikhion (March/April)   1 goat and 2 sheep

---

[78] Since there would not have been enough additional space on the stone for separate dates for each of the four sacrifices, it is a reasonable assumption that all four sacrifices occurred on the same day as part of the same sacrificial event (cf. e.g. the multiple sacrifices ἐν ἄστει in Metageitnion, presumably all on the same day, on the Erkhia Calendar). If the sacrifices are all part of the same event, this would support the argument that the four sites of these sacrifices were all local, especially that the Eleusinion mentioned on line 17 was not *the* Eleusinion in the *astu*. Information on the kinds of victims offered in these sacrifices has been lost from the stone.

[79] On *teleios* see above, note 42.

Fifth Cycle ([lines 37-45] first quadrennial cycle?):

    (1) Pyanopsion (Sept./Oct.)   1 ox
    (2) Gamelion (Dec./Jan.)   1 swine
    (3) Mounikhion (March/April)   1 goat

Other Victims ([lines 46-55] perhaps other years in the quadrennial cycle):

    (1) months uncertain: 5 sheep and 2 goats

The first thing one notices here is that there are fewer sacrificial events on the Tetrapolis Calendar than there had been on those of the demes studied earlier; and if I am correct in my belief that at least some of these sacrifices occurred only once in the course of biennial and quadrennial cycles, then the number of sacrifices sponsored by the Tetrapolis in any given year will have been even lower.

It is also noteworthy that the Tetrapolis seems to have sacrificed fewer animals at each event than the deme of Marathon did, with the exception of the first group of sacrifices in the Second Cycle which seems to have brought together a substantial number of the Tetrapolis' citizens. I would conclude from this—exception being made for the first group of sacrifices in the Second Cycle—that relatively fewer Marathonians, for example, attended the Tetrapolis' sacrifices than attended those of their own deme, but this is rather what one would expect. All the same, all of the victims were apparently adult, and in absolute terms a fully grown sheep or a goat, and *a fortiori* an ox, could still feed a substantial number of people.

The Tetrapolis calendar also shows a distinct cluster of sacrifices in the month of Mounikhion (March/April) which was also the month with the largest number of sacrificial victims in the Marathonian deme calendar. In Mounikhion at least then, the Tetrapolis calendar reenforces the emphasis of the deme calendar rather than e.g. providing sacrifices when the deme did not. It would appear from this that whatever considerations produced the clustering of sacrifices in Mounikhion on the two calendars did so independently, and the scheduling of sacrifices in the deme calendar was not intended, in this case at least, to fill a void left by the Tetrapolis.[80]

Finally, everything indicates that the citizens of the Tetrapolis could attend its sacrifices in addition to (and not instead of) those of their home deme. Thus, for example, beyond the eighteen to twenty-three sacrificial events each year sponsored by their home deme, the Tetrapolis provided perhaps seven to ten additional opportunities for the demesmen of Marathon (and of the other demes of the Tetrapolis) to participate in sacrifices annually.

The Salaminioi Calendar (SEG 21.527, LSS 19).[81]

In 363/2 the two branches of the *genos* of the Salaminioi erected a stele bearing the agreement which they had reached dividing the properties owned by the *genos* between its two branches while assuring the continuation of their joint cults. Appended to the text of the agreement is a calendar of the joint sacrifices to be funded from the rents which both branches would now collect separately, each on its own share of the farm land which the *genos* had previously owned jointly at the shrine to Herakles which it maintained at Sounion. The text of the calendar has survived virtually intact. Items are listed chronologically by month beginning with Mounikhion.[82] Each item contains the name of the deity to whom the sacrifice is offered, the

---

[80] Because the Tetrapolis Calendar is so fragmentary it is impossible to tell if there were or were not similar clusters elsewhere in the year. Counting annual, biennial and quadrennial events, there were two sacrifices in Pyanopsion and one each in Hekatombaion, Gamelion, Thargelion and Skirophorion, but there were also 12 or 13 other events which cannot be assigned to a specific month, of which at least 5 or 6 must have been before Mounikhion.

[81] The text followed here is Ferguson's (1938, 3-5). The sacrificial calendar is contained in lines 85-94 of the inscription.

[82] The Salaminioi thus follow a sacred calendar which is different from that of the *polis* and its demes. This may be an indication of the antiquity of the Salaminioi, if they adopted their calendar before the *polis* calendar was standardized to begin with Hekatombaion.

THE FREQUENCY OF SACRIFICE

victim to be offered and its anticipated cost. Sacrifices which occur on a single day are marked by a cumulative entry for firewood and miscellaneous expenses following the last sacrifice in the group.[83] Dates within the month are occasionally specified. As in our treatment of the previous calendars, in the following table sacrifices of piglets (*khoiroi*) are ignored since they would not have supplied a significant amount of meat for distribution.

Sacrificial Events on the Salaminioi Calendar

Hekatombaion (June/July):
    (1) 1 swine at the Panathenaia

Metageitnion (July/Aug.):
    (1) 1 swine

Boedromion (Aug./Sept.):
    (1) 1 swine

Pyanopsion (Sept./Oct.):
    (1) 1 swine
    (2) 1 swine at the Apatouria

Maimakterion (Oct./Nov.):
    (1) 2 sheep

---

[83] Thus in Mounikhion the combined total for firewood and miscellaneous expenses (87-88) separates the first event from the second with its own sum for firewood, etc. (88). Similarly in Pyanopsion, the only other month in which two events occur, each sacrifice is followed by its own firewood fee (92-93). In contrast, in Maimakterion there are two sacrifices (to related gods, Athena Skirias and Skiros) but only one fee for firewood to cover both sacrifices (93), indicating that both sacrifices were part of a single sacrificial event.

Poseideon (Nov./Dec.):
    (no sacrifices)

Gamelion (Dec./Jan.):
    (no sacrifices)

Anthesterion (Jan./Feb.):
    (no sacrifices)

Elaphebolion (Feb./March):
    (no sacrifices)

Mounikhion (March/April):
    (1) 1 goat, 3 sheep, and 1 ox,[84]
       + 1 sheep every other year,
       + whatever the *polis* provides[85]
    (2) 1 swine

Thargelion (April/May):
    (no sacrifices)

Skirophorion (May/June):
    (no sacrifices)

---

[84]Plus another οἶν ὁλόκαυστον, from which obviously no meat would be distributed, and two *khoiroi*.

[85]We learn of these victims only incidentally because the Salaminioi still had to pay for the firewood, etc. for their preparation (ξύλα ἐφ' ἱεροῖς καὶ οἷς ἡ πόλις δίδωσιν ἐκ κύρβεω[ν], line 87; according to Ferguson (1938, 67) ἐκ κύρβεων would refer to the so-called "Calendar of Nikomakhos," the recodification of the *polis'* sacrifices completed some time after 403; see further below, pp. 131-32. Since the purpose of the present calendar is to provide a record of the expenses to be paid for by the two branches of the Salaminioi out of rents, it naturally does not list victims provided by the *polis*.

The distribution of the sacrifices is odd, with no sacrifices at all in half the months of the year, though, as we will see shortly, there is some reason to believe that not all the sacrifices offered by the Salaminioi appear on the calendar, and some of these missing sacrifices may have been offered in the empty months.

Even more striking is the disproportionately large number of animals sacrificed at the first event in Mounikhion, six or seven including one ox, compared with the typical sacrifice of one swine per event elsewhere on the calendar; indeed the 119 dr. allocated to purchase the animals for this single event is one drakhma shy of three times the amount the Salaminioi allocated for any one of their other sacrifices. It is possible that the Salaminioi conducted the multiple sacrifices in Mounikhion for the benefit of a community larger than their *genos*, but this does not seem likely. Indeed, when the Salaminioi expected to consume, as part of this same event, victims purchased with funds from the *polis* (see further below), it is difficult to imagine them sharing with a larger community other victims bought with their own funds. More likely the Salaminioi were a very large *genos*, most of whose members attended the major event in Mounikhion while fewer attended the other sacrifices during the year.[86]

As to the frequency with which the Salaminioi sacrificed, information in the agreement which precedes the calendar shows that the calendar on the stele is only a partial one, limited to those sacrifices where the Salaminioi expended their own funds. The prefatory agreement also foresees two other sources of funds for sacrificial victims, public funds (20-21) and the *ôskhophoroi* and *deipnophoroi* (21-22; the *ôskhophoroi* and *deipnophoroi* are discussed below). The agreement specifies that the meat from both these sources was to be distrib-

---

[86]The arrangement of the calendar tells against a third possible explanation, that the sacrifices were spread out over several days (see above, note 83). Besides, such an arrangement would seriously inconvenience, and thus disadvantage, at least those Salaminioi (presumably the Salaminioi of the Heptaphylai) who lived at a distance from the shrine of the *genos* at Sounion where the sacrifices would take place.

uted raw (23-24). On at least one occasion, however, animals paid for by the *polis* were cooked (as part of the large sacrificial event in Mounikhion, for which the Salaminioi provided money for firewood[87]). There must therefore have been at least one other occasion beside the large event in Mounikhion when the Salaminioi purchased victims with funds from the *polis*, in order to explain the provision in the agreement that the Salaminioi would distribute raw meat from animals paid for with funds from the *polis*.

The *deipnophoroi* and the *ôskhophoroi* were women and young men who participated in the ceremonies of the Oskhophoria festival in Pyanopsion. Ferguson has argued that they (or rather, their *kurioi*) probably served a liturgic function, providing for sacrifices at the Oskhophoria from their own private resources.[88] Further, since the Oskhophoria was apparently the principal festival celebrated by the Salaminioi in which the *polis* also had a public interest, it is possible that the *polis* also supplied some of its own funds for the purchase of additional victims by the Salaminioi for this event,[89] and that this event was the one at which meat purchased with funds from the *polis* was distributed raw to the Salaminioi. Because of the Oskhophoria's associations with Theseus, Ferguson[90] dates the festival to Pyanopsion 6, the day on which, according to their calendar, the Salaminioi sacrificed a swine to Theseus (91 = item 1 under Pyanopsion in the chart above). The identification is possible, but it is far from compelling,[91] and it is likewise possible that the Oskhophoria and the

---

[87]See above, note 85.

[88]Ferguson (1938) 34. The *kurioi* of the *deipnophoroi* probably also supplied the loaves of bread whose division is described in lines 41-50 of the agreement.

[89]Despite the *polis'* interest in the Oskhophoria, there is no reason to believe that meat from victims sacrificed at this event was distributed to the population of the *polis* at large, any more than at the large event in Mounikhion at which victims purchased with funds from the *polis* were also sacrificed. See also below, pp. 131-32.

[90]Ferguson (1938) 27-28.

[91]Mikalson (1975) 68-69.

sacrifice to Theseus both occurred in Pyanopsion, but on two different days.

Finally, the calendar deals only with the joint sacrifices of the two branches of the Salaminioi supported by rents from the lands near the Herakleion. The two branches also collected separate rents on two other places, "the halê" and "the agora in Koilê,"[92] both of which supplied additional funds which the branches could use independently to fund other sacrifices of their own.

In sum then, the Salaminioi offered sacrifice on at least the eight occasions listed on the calendar, and almost certainly on an uncertain number of other occasions as well. Like the sacrifices on the Tetrapolis Calendar from Marathon, all these sacrifices would have been in addition to any other sacrifices the Salaminioi were eligible to attend as demesmen, etc. An interesting illustration of this is the sacrifice by the Salaminioi at the Panathenaia in Hekatombaion. We know that at the Panathenaia the *polis* sacrificed numerous victims, the meat of which was distributed, by demes, to all the citizens who came to the city on this occasion.[93] The sacrifice of the Salaminioi on this same occasion, presumably also in the city, provided the members of the *genos* with a second source of meat in addition to (and not instead of) that which they received from the *polis* through their demes.

Both the Marathonian Tetrapolis and the Salaminioi sacrificed victims sufficient to distribute meat on eight or more occasions annually. It is of course impossible, from the practice of these two political units, to generalize the sacrificial practice of all political units larger than demes and smaller than the *polis*, especially since the Marathonian Tetrapolis as a regional cult association and the Salaminioi as a *genos* are both somewhat atypical compared with tribes and trittyes, for which regrettably no similar calendars have survived intact. Still,

---

[92]On these places see Ferguson (1938) 54-55.
[93]For the distribution of meat at the Panathenaia see *IG* 2^2 334.15-16, 24-25.

such evidence as does survive is at least consistent with the view that these intermediate units sacrificed less often than the demes did,[94] but all sacrificed on more than one or two occasions annually. Since all Athenians belonged to at least tribe and trittys, and many also belonged to *genē*, phratries, regional cult associations *vel sim.*, the sacrifices of all these intermediate units must also be taken into account when considering the number of times each year a typical Athenian could participate in sacrifices at which meat would be distributed.

Besides the predictable events on the sacrificial calendars we know that the demes, tribes, etc. also sacrificed on special occasions to celebrate occurrences of particular importance to them. Thus, for example, we have a series of honorary decrees from demes and tribes in which the honorand is granted funds for sacrifice (εἰς θυσίαν). The amount granted is usually sufficient for the purchase of several sacrificial victims (e.g 100 dr. [*IG* 2^2 1186]; 50 dr. [*IG* 2^2 596, *IG* 2^2 1152 and probably also *SEG* 21.515]), and we must assume that after the honorands sacrificed the victims, they distributed their meat to the members of the deme, tribe, etc. which supplied the funds to purchase them.[95] This unexpected use of public sacrifice as a form of honor is an interesting index of the importance of public sacrifice and its attendant feasting in the socio-political life of the Athenians.

Finally we may consider the occasions upon which the *polis* sacrificed. It is important to distinguish here between two categories of sacrifices performed by the *polis*, one at which only one or two vic-

---

[94]Thus the fragmentary calendar in *IG* 1^3 246 (= *LSCG* 16), with two sacrifices in the single month of Thargelion, is more likely to be from a deme calendar than from a calendar of some larger unit.

[95]Other similar decrees are *AE* (1932), XPONIKA, 30-32 (50 dr.); *IG* 2^2 1198 (10 dr.); *AM* 66 (1941) 218-19, no. 1 (10 dr.). Even 10 dr. could be enough for one sheep or goat, especially if the wealthy honorand chipped in something of his own. For typical purchase prices for sacrificial victims see below, pp. 95-100.

tims were sacrificed, whose meat could be distributed to only a relatively small number of participants, and the other at which a sufficiently large number of victims was sacrificed to distribute meat to the general populace or to a significant portion thereof. The sacrifices of the first category, which were comparably frequent, include the routine sacrifices offered at the start of the *boulê*'s term (*eisitê(tê)ria*), those offered by the prytaneis before each meeting of the *ekklêsia* (or perhaps even daily), and those offered by the boards of generals, arkhons and similar officials at their meetings; meat from all of these sacrifices was usually shared only by the magistrates involved (bouleutai, prytaneis, generals, etc.).[96] The first group also includes the sacrifices on the so-called "Calendar of Nikomakhos," the recodification of the *polis*' "ancestral" sacrifices completed sometime after 403, where the typical victim, to judge from the surviving fragments, was a single sheep, and where the largest single offering appears to have been merely a pair of oxen.[97] The large sacrifices in the second

---

[96] Dem. 19.190 (on *boulê*, *prytaneis*, generals, and, σχεδὸν ὡς εἰπεῖν, all the *arkhai* offering sacrifice, and on the participants in the sacrifices sharing in joint banquets); cf. Antiphon 6 *Khor.* 45 and Dem. 19.190 (on *boulê* and *prytaneis*), Theophrast. *Char.* 21.11 (on *prytaneis*). The speaker of Antiphon 6 *Khor.* 45 says that he served as *prytanis* for every day but two of the prytany and sacrificed ὑπὲρ δημοκρατίας, indicating that he (and his fellow *prytaneis*) carried out a daily sacrifice "on behalf of democracy" during their prytany. Sharing in the meat of the victims sacrificed on these occasions could be considered a regular "fringe benefit," as it were, of office-holding in Athens.

[97] Even the pair of oxen would not have gone very far in a meat distribution open to the general populace. In point of fact, the two oxen were given to a more limited group, sc. the Gleontes (a pre-Kleisthenic tribe which evidently continued to be religiously important) for their sacrifice to Zeus Phratrios and Athena Phratria (*Hesp.* 1935, p. 21, no. 2, lines 44-51); I assume that the meat from the other sacrifices on this calendar were similarly distributed to other religious corporations involved in the respective sacrifices (cf. the mention of the Eumolpidai [*ibid.*, line 77], Pythaistai [*IG* 2^2 1357b.11], and Kerykes [*IG* 1^3 241.2.8]). Note also the three *trittoiai boarkhoi* at *IG* 1^2 845.6, 9-10 and 12 (on the *tritto(i)a* see above, note 50). The letters]μβεν hoπ[appear in another fragment (*IG* 1^3 240.26) but the restora-

category were comparably fewer, consisting primarily of the so-called *epithetoi heortai* (the meaning of this term will be explained below) all of which, as we shall see, involved a sufficient number of animals to allow for a wide distribution of meat. Since our concern in the present chapter is with the number of sacrifices and meat distributions in which an ordinary citizen might participate we will focus here exclusively on the sacrifices in the second category, understanding that the picture which we shall draw from our examination of the sacrifices in this second category would be modified only slightly for the typical citizen if we were to include the far smaller sacrifices (and more limited meat distributions) of the first category as well.

The *Dermatikon* Accounts (*IG* 2^2 1496, not in *LSCG*).[98]

Beginning in Poseideon (November/December) 334 and continuing at least until Elaphebolion (February/March) 330 the government at Athens maintained records for a series of Accounts called *to dermatikon*, detailing its income from the sale of the hides of victims[99] sacrificed at certain major festivals; *IG* 2^2 1496.68-151 contains the

---

tion hεκατό?]μβεν proposed by Dow (1941, 33) cannot be right since *the* hekatomb was sacrificed at the Panathenaia, one of the *epithetoi heortai*, as we shall see, and hence it could not be part of the calendar of "ancestral" sacrifices reedited by Nikomakhos. See also below, pp. 131-32, on the victims which the *polis* provided for the *genos* of the Salaminioi but whose meat was distributed only to the members of the *genos*.

[98]The text followed here is that of *IG* 2^2 1496.

[99]For the meaning of *dermatikon*, see Harpokrat. s.v. Lykourgos was in some way involved with these Accounts (Harpokration cites the word *dermatikon* from a speech of his entitled ἀπολογισμὸς ὧν πεπολίτευται; *IG* 2^2 333, containing the fragmentary text of a nomothetic law proposed by Lykourgos [cf. frag. *a* + *b*.14], mentions . . . τῶν θεῶν ἀργύριον [τ]ὸ ἐκ τοῦ δερματικοῦ γ[ενόμενον . . . [frag. *c*.23], but the exact context is uncertain). It is unclear whether Lykourgos began the practice of selling the hides to earn money for the public treasury, or simply rationalized a pre-existing practice and inscribed the result. I suspect that the latter is the case.

THE FREQUENCY OF SACRIFICE 49

surviving parts of these records.[100] The Accounts are arranged in four consecutive years (334/3, 333/2, 332/1 and 331/0). Within each year the festivals are also listed in chronological order, with each item containing the name of the festival, the festival officials from whom the money was received,[101] and the amount received.

The account for 334/3 begins only in Poseideon (instead of Hekatombaion, as in the other years), indicating that the policy reflected in this account was implemented after the year had already begun.[102] The end of the account of 331/0 has been lost, but it does not appear that there was originally enough room for the Accounts to continue beyond this year, at least not on the same stele. The inscription consists of four fragments, with the entries from Maimakterion through Pyanopsion of 333/2 lost between fragments *a* and *b*, perhaps some entries at the end of Skirophorion of 333/2 also lost between fragments *b* and *c*, the entries from Gamelion 332/1 through Hekatombaion 331/0 lost between fragments *c* and *d*, and the entries from Mounikhion to the end of the year in 331/0 lost at the bottom of fragment *d*. Despite these losses we can still reconstruct the annual cycle of sacrificial events which is repeated from year to year, since apparently every one of the festivals for which hides were sold occurs at least once on the extant portions of the Accounts. The surviving portions of the inscription have been badly damaged, but given the repetition of the

---

[100]The *Dermatikon* Accounts are in the rightmost of four columns on the front of the stele. The first three columns, of which only the last few lines survive, contain records of gold crowns dedicated on the acropolis and of gold crowns bestowed by the Athenians. The reverse of the stele appears to deal with the accoutrements of the *kanêphoroi* (on which see the decree of Stratokles quoted in [Plut]. *Vit. X Or.* 852B).

[101]Or less likely, the officials who delivered the hides which were subsequently sold.

[102]Line 67, just before the start of the *dermatikon* account for 334/3, contains a *kephalaion* of 42 T. 2,910+ dr. which is too large for a *dermatikon* account, and which therefore must refer to something else. Since no earlier *dermatikon* account precedes that of 334/3, we may conclude that the account for 334/3 is the first on this stele.

annual cycle, the names of sacrifices which are missing in one year can be restored with reasonably certainty by comparison with corresponding entries in the other years. The actual amounts obtained from the sale of the hides varied from year to year, and cannot be similarly restored.

The following chart lists the annual sacrifices on the *Dermatikon* Accounts and, where they survive, the amounts of money received from the sale of the victims' hides.

Sacrificial Events in the Dermatikon Accounts

Hekatombaion (June/July):

    (1) sacrifice to Eirênê   874 dr. [333/2][103]
                                                                  713 dr. [332/1]

    (2) Panathenaia   (see note[104])

---

[103]The Accounts also list a sacrifice to Ammon in 333/2 from which the victims' hides yielded 44 dr. 4.5 ob. The sacrifice is not found on the account for 334/3, which does not begin until Poseideon; it is missing, however, from the account of 332/1, which is otherwise complete for Hekatombaion (the entry for Hekatombaion 331/0 has been lost). The sacrifice is otherwise unknown (Deubner [1932] 223), and may be either a one-time event or, less likely, a biennial sacrifice which would have reappeared in Hekatombaion 331/0, for which the entry has now been lost. Since the money from the sale of hides sacrificed to Ammon was received from the *stratêgoi*, as was also that from the sacrifice to Eirênê, and since it was a relatively small amount, it is also possible that in other years the sacrifice to Ammon was included under the rubric of the sacrifice to Eirênê. See also below, note 112.

[104]The account for 333/2 lists two sources of income for the Panathenaia, the first restored by Kirchner as *hieropoioi* who provided 61 dr. 3 ob., and another source which Kirchner (*IG* 2^2 *ad loc.*) restores as ἐκ τῆς ἑκατόμβης; this second source provided an amount ending in 33 dr. 3 ob. preceded by space for probably three more digits (e.g. $Π^Δ$HH]ΔΔΔ⊢⊢⊢ = 733 dr.or XHH]ΔΔΔ⊢⊢⊢ = 1,233, both of which would fit the available space as printed in *IG* 2^2). In 332/1 only the *hieropoioi* entry appears (there is no space for a second entry for the Panathenaia); the amount which the *hiero-*

THE FREQUENCY OF SACRIFICE 51

Metageitnion (July/Aug.):
   (1) Eleusinia[105]   (amounts lost)

Boedromion (Aug./Sept.):
   (1) sacrifice to Dêmokratia   414 dr. [332/1]
   (2) Asklepieia[106]   1,000 dr. [332/1]

Pyanopsion (Sept./Oct.):
   (1) Theseia   1,183 dr. [332/1]

Maimakterion (Oct./Nov.):
                     (no sacrifices)

---

poioi provided has been lost. The easiest explanation of all this is that the 333/2 account broke down the proceeds from the Panathenaia into two categories (e.g. money from hides of animals in the great sacrifice and money from other animals awarded as prizes; see also below, pp. 70-72 with note 13 there, and Supplementary Note C) while the 332/1 account combined the two sources into one. See further below, note 112.

[105]The festival (*heortê*) is to be distinguished from the Mysteries, which are a different event (Deubner [1932] 91). On the basis of *IG* 2^2 1672, lines 258-62, it is usually assumed that the feast was not actually annual but rather both trieteric and penteteric, the trieteric celebrations probably falling on the first and third year of the Olympiad, the penteteric falling on the second (for sources and details see Mikalson [1975] 46). Simms (1975), however, has argued that the religious celebration (and hence, we might add, the sacrifice) was annual, while the agonistic events associated with the festival were trieteric and penteteric (Simms [1975] 269-70 with note 2 for evidence). I find Simms' argument persuasive, but even if the conventional view is correct and an Eleusinia occurred, in effect, only on three out of every four years, for convenience's sake we may still treat the festival here as an annual event.

[106]Usually called the Epidauria, to distinguish it from the Asklepieia in Elaphebolion.

Poseideon (Nov./Dec.):

(1) Dionysia τὰ ἐν Πειραιεῖ   311 dr. [334/3][107]

Gamelion (Dec./Jan.):

(1) Dionysia τὰ ἐπὶ Ληναίωι   106 dr. [333/2][108]

(2) sacrifice to Agathê Tukhê   160+ dr. [334/3]
                                    101 dr. 3 ob. [333/2]

Anthesterion (Jan./Feb.):

    (no sacrifices)

Elaphebolion (Feb./March):

(1) Asklepieia   291 dr. [334/3]
                                    235 or 325 dr. [333/2]

(2) Dionysia τὰ ἐν ἄστει   808+ dr. [334/3]
                                    306+ dr. [333/2][109]

---

[107]Besides the sum of 311 dr. which is received [παρὰ] | [βοων]ῶν (70-71) the account lists a second sum of at least 280 dr. [καὶ] τὸ περιγενόμε[νον ἀ]πὸ τῆ[ς] | [βο]ωνίας (72-73). On this entry, see below, pp. 109.

[108]Before the entry for the Dionysia τὰ ἐπὶ Ληναίωι of 333/2 there is another extremely fragmentary entry which contains the words τῆι Δαείρ[αι and the figure of 229 dr. 5 ob. (102-04). Kirchner (*IG* 2² ad loc.) places the sacrifice to Daeira in Gamelion (when there was a sacrifice to Daira in the calendar of the Marathon deme [*IG* 2² 1358.B.11-12]; see further the discussion in *SIG*³ 1069 [= *IG* 2² 1496] ad loc.), but the sacrifice could also have taken place at the end of Poseideon. In either event, it would appear that the proceeds from the sacrifice to Daeira were combined with the entry for either the Dionysia τὰ ἐν Πειραιεῖ or the Dionysia τὰ ἐπὶ Ληναίωι in the accounts for the other years. See further below, note 112.

[109]Thus in *IG* 2², but the figure is surprisingly low compared with that for 334/3 and those for other major festivals elsewhere on the calendar.

Mounikhion (March/April):

    (1) Olympieia   631 or 671 dr. [334/3]
                                                   500+ dr. [333/2]

    (2) sacrifice to Hermes Hêgemonios   (amounts lost)

Thargelion (April/May):

    (1) Bendideia[110]   457 dr. [334/3]

Skirophorion (May/June):

    (1) sacrifice to Zeus Sôtêr   1,050 dr. [334/3][111]
                                                           2,613 dr. [333/2][112]

---

[110] Ferguson (1944, 100-2) distinguishes between the *orgeônes* who participated in the *pompê* at the Bendideia, and the broader body of citizens (including those *orgeônes* who were citizens) to whom the meat from victims provided by the *polis* was distributed (the Thracian *orgeônes* would have paid for their own victims).

[111] Kirchner places a dot under the numeral for 50, indicating that the reading is uncertain.

[112] In addition to the 2,613 dr. received [παρὰ βοων]ῶν (119) there was also at least 100 dr. [ἐκ ..5...ω]ν παρὰ βοώνου (120, possibly funds allocated for the purchase of animals but not spent; cf. below, pp. 109), another entry [ἐκ....8....]ων παρ[ὰ ἱ]εροπο[ῶν] (121), and possibly yet one more item on the damaged edges at the end of fragment *b* and the start of fragment *c*. These various entries, like the sacrifice to Ammon in Hekatombaion (see above, note 103) and that to Daeira in Poseideon or Gamelion (see above, note 108), may reflect additional sacrifices which occurred only in 333/2. I am more inclined, however, to believe that the Athenians for some reason adopted a more detailed accounting system for 332/1, breaking down the sources of funds for the Panathenaia, for example (see above, note 104) and distinguishing *dermatikon* money from that allocated but unspent by the *boônai*, and that they used a more streamlined system in the other years, combining all funds relating to a single festival into a single item.

In contrast to the sacrificial events on the deme and other calendars examined earlier, the sacrificial events in the *Dermatikon* Accounts are spaced out more evenly throughout the year, with one or two sacrifices occurring in ten of the twelve months of the year; the two months without sacrifices are Maimakterion (October/November) and Anthesterion (January/February), which are also among the months with the fewest sacrificial events on the deme and other calendars. To judge from the hide-sale figures, however, the sacrifices in both Poseideon (November/December) and Gamelion (December/January) were quite small, and it would seem fair to say that the entire period from Maimakterion (October/November) to Anthesterion (January/February) was one of a relatively low level of activity, without the mid-winter surge which we see especially in Gamelion (December/January) in e.g. the Erkhia and Marathon deme calendars. Since, as we shall see, there is no reason to believe that any of these sacrifices was intended for a group smaller than the *polis* as a whole, the drop in sacrificial activity reflected in the *Dermatikon* Accounts from Maimakterion to Anthesterion may perhaps be explained as the result of winter weather, which could make it unpleasant for citizens to come from the outlying demes to the *astu* and the Peiraieus where the *polis'* major sacrifices would naturally be performed.

The sacrifices in the *Dermatikon* Accounts belong, I believe, to a category called "additional feasts" (ἐπίθετοι ἑορταί, or simply τὰ ἐπίθετα). Our most important source of information about these "additional feasts" is Isok. 7 *Areop*. 29, where Isokrates contrasts τὰς πατρίους θυσίας with τὰς . . . ἐπιθέτους ἑορτάς, αἷς ἑστίασίς τις προσείη. Isokrates also tells us here that the *patrioi thusiai* were funded with income from the rental of sacred properties,[113] in contrast to the *epithetoi heortai*, which should therefore be funded from a

---

[113] ἀπὸ μισθωμάτων, on which cf. Didymos Grammatikos *ap*. Harpokrat. s.v. Some commentators have been misled by Hesykh. s.v. who mistakenly interprets the expression as ἐργολαβοῦντες ("contracting out"; similarly Bekker, *Anec*. 207.6-13).

different source, presumably by direct allocations from the general budget.[114] These same two categories of sacrifices are mentioned by Aristotle (*Ath. Pol.* 3.3), who says that unlike the *arkhōn basileus* and the polemarkh, the eponymous arkhon has no role in the supervision of τῶν πατρίων (sc. ἱερῶν) but is concerned exclusively with τὰ ἐπίθετα. Aristotle's usage in particular seems to show that, in referring to sacrifices, *epithetos* was not simply an adjective used to describe newer sacrifices, but the technical term for a specific category of sacrifices which were perceived to be newer than, and contrasted with, the *patrioi thusiai*. I would argue further that the *patrioi thusiai* are those recodified in the so-called "Calendar of Nikomakhos," which, as we saw earlier, were too small for any public *hestiasis* (cf. Isok. 7 *Areop.* 29 quoted above), and that the *Dermatikon* Accounts record all but one of the large annual *epithetoi heortai* where meat was distributed to the citizens at large.[115]

Besides being large enough to provide enough meat for a public *hestiasis*,[116] all of the sacrificial events mentioned in the *Derma-*

---

[114]Cf. the threefold division of πρῶτον μὲν κατὰ τὰ πάτρια θύειν, ἔπειτα ἃ μᾶλλον συμφέρει τῇ πόλει, ἔτι δὲ ἃ ὁ δῆμος ἐψηφίσατο καὶ δυνησόμεθα δαπανᾶν ἐκ τῶν προσιόντων χρημάτων at Lys. 30.19, where the first and last categories of sacrifices appear to be the *patrioi thusiai* and the *epithetoi heortai* respectively (the middle term may refer to special *ad hoc* sacrifices, or it may refer to nothing in particular and was simply added to make the *epithetoi heortai*, which follow, appear superfluous and wasteful. Cf. also Suidas and Harpokrat. s.v. ἐπιθέτους ἑορτάς: τὰς μὴ πατρίους ἑορτάς, ἄλλως δὲ ἐπιψηφισθείσας, ἐπιθέτους ἐκάλουν (referring to Isok. 7 *Areop.* 29).

[115]Although the Accounts refer to *thusiai* ("sacrifices") and *heortai* ("festivals"), since both are *epitheta*, for convenience I have retained Isokrates' terminology of *epithetoi heortai* to describe both.

[116]As will be seen below, the amounts of money recovered from hide-sales reflect large numbers of animals sacrificed (see briefly below, pp. 62-63, and, with more detail, pp. 68-72); and even for those events where figures are missing from the Accounts, since the number of sacrificial animals was sufficiently large to justify the *polis*' interest in the sale of their hides, the victims probably also provided enough meat to require its distribution to the general citizen population. On the festal nature of *heortai* see further Mikalson

tikon Accounts appear to be no older than the arkhonship of Hippokleides (566/5), when the Panathenaia, the oldest of the festivals mentioned in the Accounts, seems to have been formally organized.[117] As for the other feasts mentioned in the Accounts, Pickard-Cambridge[118] dates the major development of the urban Dionysia to the period of Peisistratos, and Deubner[119] associates the Olympieia with the construction of the temple of Zeus Olympios begun by the Peisistratidai. The Dionysia τὰ ἐν Πειραιεῖ and the sacrifice to Zeus Sôtêr celebrated in the Peiraieus are both unlikely to be earlier than the development of the Peiraieus begun by Themistokles in his arkhonship in 493/2.[120] The Theseia was probably established in 475, in conjunction with Kimon's return of Theseus' bones from Skyros in that year. The Bendideia was established in a short time before 429/8.[121] The two Asklepieias cannot be earlier than 420/19 when the cult of Asklepios was brought to Athens (*IG* 2^2 4960.10-13). The sacrifice to Dêmokratia commemorates the expulsion of the Thirty in

---

(1982) 213-21.

[117]It is conceivable that the Panathenaia existed in some earlier form which was substantially reorganized in 556/5 when the festival took on the form known in later times, but whatever earlier form the festival may have had, there is no evidence that it included a wholesale distribution of sacrificial meat, and we should probably see in *Iliad* 2.550-1 (ἔνθα δέ μιν [sc. ’Αθήνη] ταύροισι καὶ ἀρνειοῖς ἱλάονται / κοῦροι ’Αθηναίων περιτελλομένων ἐνιαυτῶν) nothing more than a general reference to Athenians worshipping Athena (*pace* Davison ([958, 25], who takes these verses as a reference to an earlier version of the annual Panathenaia). For sources for the (re)organization in 556/5 see Ziehen (1949) col. 459; Shapiro (1989) 19-20. For a survey of views of the Panathenaia before 556/5 see Robertson (1985) 231-38, with notes 2 and 3.

[118]Pickard-Cambridge (1968) 58. More recently, Connor (1989, 7-16) has argued for an even later date of c. 501.

[119] (1932) 177.

[120]For this dating of the sacrifice to Zeus Sôtêr (part of the Dipoleia) see Parke (1977) 167.

[121]Garland (1992) 111. A *terminus ante quem* is supplied by the fragmentary appearance of her name in *IG* 1^3 383.143, the accounts of the Treasurers of the Other Gods for 429/8.

403,[122] and that to Eirênê was established only in 374 (Isok. 15.109). The Dionysia τὰ ἐπὶ Ληναίωι is certainly an ancient festival, as shown by the involvement of the *arkhôn basileus* (Arist. *Ath. Pol.* 57.1; cf. 3.3), but it is significant that while the *agôn* at this festival was supervised by the *arkhôn basileus* alone, the *pompê* was jointly supervised by the *arkhôn basileus* and *epimelêtai* (Arist. *Ath. Pol.* 57.1), indicating that the *pompê* was in fact a comparatively recent addition. Further, the *epimelêtai*, and not the *arkhôn basileus*, were responsible for selling the hides from the Dionysia τὰ ἐπὶ Ληναίωι (*IG* 2^2 1496.75), indicating that the large sacrifice and *hestiasis* was associated with the *pompê* and not with the *agôn*, as we would expect to be the case even without this evidence. We have no information about the foundation date of the Eleusinia, but again the festival (*heortê*) need not have been as old as the Mysteries from which it is to be distinguished.[123] Finally, we have no information on when the sacrifices to Agathê Tukhê and Hermes Hêgemonios began, but there is no reason to believe that they were especially old either.

In sum then, the founding dates of most of the sacrifices mentioned in the *Dermatikon* Accounts can be established at least in terms of *termini post quos*. All of these are to be dated to 566/5 or later. Further, there is no reason why any of the remaining sacrifices, whose dates cannot be similarly established, cannot be similarly dated to 566/5 or later.

With the exception of the five hundred she-goats (*khimairai*) sacrificed to Artemis Agrotera on Boedromion 6 to commemorate the

---

[122] Plut. *Mor.* 349F; the annual sacrifice is an iteration of the original sacrifice made by Thrasyboulos and his followers to Athena after their success in 403 (for which see Xen. *HG* 2.4.39), but it is unclear from Plutarch's language whether the annual sacrifice began immediately in 402 (as we should probably expect) or possibly some time later; see further Deubner (1932) 39.

[123] Cf. above, note 105. Simms (1975, 276-78) dates the (re)organization of the *heortê* to 600-468, with a preference for either 560-27 or 480-68, but his arguments are purely speculative.

victory at Marathon,[124] we have no evidence that the Athenians offered any large-scale *annual* sacrifices which are not mentioned in the *Dermatikon* Accounts.[125] Since the animals the sale of whose hides were recorded in the *Dermatikon* Accounts were almost certainly all oxen, the Accounts' omission of the hides from the goats sacrificed to Artemis is quite comprehensible.[126] We may therefore conclude that, with the exception of the goat-sacrifice to Artemis, the *Dermatikon* Accounts mention all the annual *epithetoi heortai*, and further that these *epithetoi heortai*, including the goat-sacrifice to Artemis, were the only annual events at which the Athenian *polis* sacrificed victims for a large-scale distribution of meat to which the average citizen would have access every year.[127]

---

[124]Xen. *Anab*. 3.2.12. It is certain that the meat from these goats was distributed to the citizens at large. At Aristoph. *Eq*. 659-662 the Sausage Seller tells how he proposed to increase the number of goats (*khimairai*) to be sacrificed to Artemis Agrotera. Since the context here has the Sausage Seller pandering to the Dêmos, the number of animals would be significant only if their meat was to be distributed to the *polis'* populace at large. A single goat would not provide that much meat for the general populace, but five hundred would.

[125]See below, Supplementary Note B.

[126]The πεντήκοντα αἰγῖδ[α]ς mentioned in *IG* 2² 333.c.11, are not part of a separate goat-hide account parallel to the ox-hide *Dermatikon* Accounts. *IG* 2² 333 is generally concerned with ornamentation (*kosmos*) for various cults; in this context the αἰγῖδας must be a kind of ornament associated with some cult, the identity of which is not clear due to the fragmentary condition of the inscription. Harpokrat. s.v. defines αἰγῖδας as nets woven ἐκ στεμμάτων, citing Lykourgos in his περὶ τῆς διοικήσεως (= frag. 24 Blass; see further Dindorf's comments *ad loc*.; this same fragment of Lykourgos is cited by *LSJ* for its definition s.v. αἰγίς 3 ["dress worn by priestess of Athena"], even though, at least according to Harpokration, Lykourgos meant something very different by the word).

[127]Cf. Isok. 7 *Areop*. 29 quoted above, p. 54. In this context it is interesting to note that we have independent evidence from other sources for meat distributions to the general populace of the *polis* at only two of the fifteen events listed in the *Dermatikon* Accounts, viz. at the Lesser Panathenaia, at which *IG* 2² 334 prescribes that the meat from the sacrificial victims is to be distributed τῶι δήμωι τῶι Ἀθηναίων . . . καθάπερ ἐν ταῖς ἄλλαις κρεανο-

As their name indicates, the *epithetoi heortai* were perceived as new sacrifices, "added on to" the body of older *patrioi thusiai*.[128] The newness of the *epithetoi heortai*, I would suggest, is not simply a matter of chronology however, for these events also represented an entirely new way of conducting religious sacrifice on the level of the *polis*,[129] with *hieropoioi* and other similar officials who were elected annually[130] in place of closed priestly corporations whose members served for life, and with large numbers of victims sacrificed so that their meat could be distributed to the citizen populace at large, and not merely to a chosen few. Given the "novel" character of the *epithetoi heortai*, it is not surprising that a conservative like Isokrates can fulminate against Athens' expenditures on these festivals to the neglect of the *patrioi thusiai*, and that he glorifies the "good old days," before the introduction of these "new" sacrifices, when country

---

μίαις (24-27), and the Asklepieia in the Peiraieus (= the Epidauria, in Boedromion) at which *IG* 2² 47 makes the *hieropoioi* responsible for the distribution of the meat (32-39; on the connection of the Epidauria with the cult of Asklepios in the Peiraieus see Garland [1987] 115). *IG* 2² 334 is roughly contemporary with the *Dermatikon* Accounts, while *IG* 2² 47 dates to the beginning of the fourth century.

[128] I emphasize the word *perceived* here. While we have relatively good information on the dates when various *epithetoi heortai* were introduced, we have no similar information for the introduction of any of the *patrioi thusiai*. What is important for our purposes, however, are precisely these perceptions.

[129] Since this "new" kind of sacrifice is the only kind we find on the deme-level it is tempting to see the *polis* adapting to its own use in the *epithetoi heortai* practices which were typical of the more communitarian demes. It must be admitted, however, that we really known nothing for certain about religion in the demes in the sixth century, when the earliest of the *epithetoi heortai* were established, and it is also possible that the demes mimicked the practice of the *polis*, either taking over the sacrifices of smaller corporations or establishing new ones, in either case to be administered by deme officials, and with the sacrificial meat distributed to the demesmen at large.

[130] At least in the fourth century. We have no way of knowing how they were chosen when the earliest of the *epithetoi heortai* were instituted in the sixth century, but it is *a priori* unlikely that they would have been hereditary priests serving for life, as was the case with the *patrioi thusiai*.

folk remained in the country content with their private resources (ἐπὶ τοῖς ἰδίοις ἀγαθοῖς) instead of coming down into the city to the *heortai* paid for from public funds (τῶν κοινῶν, Isok. 7 *Areop.* 52).

In addition to the *epithetoi heortai*, which we have seen were all annual, we also know from Arist. *Ath. Pol.* 54.7 that the Athenians celebrated five major penteteric festivals, viz. the mission to Delos,[131] the Brauronia, the Herakleia, the Eleusinia and the Panathenaia, to which a sixth festival, the Hephaistia, was added in 329/8.[132] The penteteric Eleusinia and Panathenaia were more elaborate versions of annual festivals,[133] both of which appear in the *Dermatikon* Accounts, an indication, as we have seen, that meat was distributed at both. A large number of oxen were purchased for the quadrennial mission to Delos (109 in 375/4: *IG* 2^2 1635.35-36); these were sacrificed not at Athens but on Delos,[134] for the benefit of the participants in the mission, the choruses which performed at the festival, and any other Athenian citizens who attended.[135] How many attended is uncertain, but the number must have been substantial in view of the number of oxen sacrificed. As for the three other pente-

---

[131] The text of the *Ath. Pol.* says that there was also a heptateric mission to Delos, on which see Rhodes (1981) 606-7 *ad loc.*

[132] On the Hephaistia see also Supplementary Note B.

[133] On the Eleusinia, see above, note 105.

[134] Note the entry for [κομ]ιδὴ . . . τῶν βοῶν, *IG* 2^2 1635.38; the Athenian government apparently even charged an export tax (πεντηκοστή) on the oxen, *ibid*.

[135] The island of Delos, and hence its festivals, were managed from Athens and in Athens' interest (note, for example, that *IG* 2^2 1635+, which contains the accounts of the Athenian Amphiktyones for Delos, was found at Athens, not on Delos); it is therefore unlikely that the meat from the sacrificial victims was distributed to anyone except Athenian citizens. For the Athenians' unwillingness to share with non-Athenians the meat of victims for which the non-Athenians had not paid cf. the ox (*IG* 1^3 34.41-42) or other foodstuff (*IG* 1^3 14.2-8) which the members of the Delian League were required to bring to Athens for their own consumption at the Greater Panathenaia in the fifth century.

THE FREQUENCY OF SACRIFICE 61

teric festivals mentioned in Arist. *Ath. Pol.* 54.7, while there is no evidence of large-scale sacrifices in the fifth or fourth century at either the Brauronia, the Herakleia or the later penteteric Hephaistia, it nonetheless seems likely that relatively large numbers of animals were also sacrificed at these festivals, as they were at the other penteteric festivals, and that the meat from these sacrificial victims was likewise distributed to the citizens who participated in and/or attended the festivals.[136]

These penteteric festivals, the events on the *Dermatikon* Accounts, and the sacrifice of 500 she-goats to Artemis Agrotera appear to be all of the *regular* occasions at which large numbers of victims were sacrificed and their meat made available to the general citizenry. In addition to these regular sacrifices, the Athenian *polis* also distributed meat from non-recurring *ad hoc* sacrifices, e.g. at the dedication of temples[137] or to celebrate military and political successes and other good news,[138] though we have no way of knowing how frequently such sacrifices occurred. In any event, the exaggerations of Aristoph. *Eq.* 654-662 suggest that when they did occur, the number of victims was substantial enough for a general distribution of meat to the citizen body as a whole.

---

[136]None of the purely penteteric festivals appear on the *Dermatikon* Accounts, which appear to be limited to annual feasts. In all events, since we know from *IG* 2^2 1635 that oxen were slain in connection with the mission to Delos and the mission is not mentioned in the Accounts, the absence of the other penteteric festivals from the Accounts cannot be used as evidence that these other penteteric festivals did not involve the sacrifice of large numbers of animals (even if the victims sacrificed in connection with the mission to Delos were slain on Delos we would still expect the revenue from the sale of their hides to be returned to the treasury in Athens). Note also that the penteteric Hephaistia was established after the Accounts were drafted.

[137]Cf. Supplementry Note B on what appears to be sacrifices and meat distribution in connection with a the dedication of the temple of Hephaistos.

[138]E.g. εὐαγγέλια [sc. ἱερά] . . . τεθύκαμεν, Isoc. 7 *Areop*. 10; εὐαγγελίων θυσίας, Aiskhin. 3 *Ktes*. 160 (cf. Aiskhin. 3 *Ktes*. 77); cf. Aristoph. *Eq.* 1320.

To return to the events on the *Dermatikon* Accounts, one would very much like to know exactly how many victims were sacrificed at these events, but the answer is not easily determined.[139] The different amounts raised by selling hides from the same event (e.g. the sacrifices to Eirênê and Agathê Tukhê) in different years indicates at least the possibility that prices for hides fluctuated from year to year.[140] Further, it would appear that our other sources provide us with but one figure that seems to be an equivalent-worth price[141] for a hide, viz. 3 dr. as the value of a swine's hide[142] (*IG* 2^2 1356.5-6 and 12-13, from the beginning of the fourth century). Two other inscriptions also give a range of from 2.5 to 4.5 dr. as the purchase price of a *diphthera*, i.e. of a finished skin to be used as an overcloak/jacket (2.5 and 3 dr.: *IG* 2^2 1673.47, probably from 327/6; *IG* 2^2 1672.104, from 329/8); allowing for the costs involved in tanning the skin, and something of a profit for the merchant who sold it, we might calculate the value of the raw skin (*derma*), this time probably of a sheep or goat, at between about 1.5 and 3 dr.[143] The two

---

[139]Isokrates' assertion that 300 oxen were sacrificed at these *epithetoi heortai* (Isok. 7 *Areop.* 29) is polemical and should not be taken as an accurate index of how many victims were actually slain.

[140]The difference from year to year could also be explained if a different number of victims was sacrificed in different years (on this possibility, see further below, p. 118). On the face of it, there is no reason why one explanation would be preferable to the other.

[141]I.e. a price that someone thought a hide was was worth, not an actual sale price.

[142]ἅπαντος εὐστὸ τελέο. *Heustos* ("singed") applies only to swine, contrasted with *dartos* ("flayed") which applies to oxen, sheep and goats (Stengel [1920] 112, note 21). This point was missed by Boeckh (1886) 97, who identified the victims as oxen. Boeckh appears to be the source, direct or indirect, of most statements about the price of hides.

[143]In *SEG* 21.527, the agreement preceding the Salaminioi Calendar provides the priest of Eurysakes with 13 dr. "in lieu of" a limb plus the hide (σκέλος καὶ δέρματος [35-36]; the translation of the genitive as "in lieu of" is that of Ferguson [1938] 6). Unfortunately since there is no way of telling how much of the 13 dr. represented the worth of the limb and how much the worth of the hide, *SEG* 21.527 cannot be used as evidence for the sales price

figures do not allow precise calculations about the sales price of hides in the *Dermatikon* Accounts of 334-30, particularly since the victims in the Accounts are all almost certainly oxen, not swine, sheep or goats. All the same, the various prices, that of the raw swine-skin in *IG* 2^2 1356 and those of the finished sheep- or goat-hides in *IG* 2^2 1672 and 1673, are close enough to each other to suggest that they are not wildly out of line, and they can thus give us some help by broadly indicating lower and upper limits of what might be possible, viz. a range of perhaps 1.5 dr. to 5 dr. for a swine-, sheep- or goat-hide (and certainly not less than 1 dr. and certainly not as much as 10 dr.) and a slightly higher range for a larger ox-hide, perhaps 4 dr. to 10 dr. (and most probably not 2 dr. and most probably not 15 dr.).[144] If we take this last figure of 10 dr. as the highest amount likely to be raised by the sale of one ox-hide, we can divide each of the figures in the *Dermatikon* Accounts by 10 to arrive at a *minimum* likely number of victims at each event, ranging from a low of 10 oxen sacrificed to Agathê Tukhê in 333/2 to a high of 261 oxen sacrificed to Zeus Sôtêr in 333/2. Again, it should be emphasized, these are *minimum* likely numbers which are will increase to the degree that we have overestimated the sales price of a single ox-hide.

These figures for the numbers of victims in the *Dermatikon* Accounts should be compared with those from the deme calendars discussed earlier, where the typical sacrifice is that of one or two sheep or goats, and where the largest number of animals sacrificed at a single event is five sheep (in Erkhia in Boedromion) or three sheep and an ox (in Marathon every other year in Mounikhion). Even the smallest sacrifices in the *Dermatikon* Accounts are thus substantially larger than the largest deme sacrifices for which we have any evidence, and clearly they must have been intended for a far wider population. Given the number of victims involved, the largest sacrifices in the Accounts could only have been intended for the citizen population

---

of hides.
[144]See below, Supplementary Note C.

at large, but the smaller sacrifices in the Accounts must also have been meant for the same general population of the *polis*, perhaps with the expectation either that fewer people would participate in the meat distribution or that portions would be smaller. Indeed, if the meat at these sacrifices were not distributed to the general citizen population, it would have to have been distributed to some sub-group of citizens, but it is difficult to imagine any sub-group of citizens large enough to consume even the minimum likely number of ten oxen which the *polis* provided for the sacrifice to Agathê Tukhê in 333/2, apparently the smallest number of victims sacrificed at any of the feasts in the *Dermatikon* Accounts. In the absence of any identifiable sub-groups to which the distribution could be made,[145] we must conclude that in every case the distribution was to the citizen body as a whole, or more precisely to any its citizens who chose to participate.

In sum then, the typical fourth-century Athenian citizen had access to meat distributed by the *polis* on at least sixteen occasions every year, the fifteen *epithetoi heortai* in the *Dermatikon* Accounts plus the sacrifice to Artemis Agrotera.[146] This is not to say that every citizen participated in every meat distribution provided by the *polis*, and it is probably safe to say that far more participated in those which were part of a larger event that featured spectacle (like the Panathenaia) or entertainment like the (Urban Dionysia), since events like these were more likely to draw citizens from outlying demes to the

---

[145] On the *orgeônes* at the Bendideia, see above, note 110.

[146] As noted earlier, the *polis* of Athens sacrificed animals to the gods on far more occasions every year than the *epithetoi heortai*, but on most of these other occasions the sacrifices were either of unconsumable victims such as the piglets at the Thesmophoria or of either a single animal or a small number which would have produced neither a significant number of hides for sale nor a significant amount of meat for distribution to the general population of the *polis* (on these smaller sacrifices see further above, pp. 46-48). On occasions when one or two animals were sacrificed, the hides were probably given as part of the *geras* to the officiating priest or priestess, and the meat was distributed to a necessarily smaller group of people (cf. also above, note 96).

THE FREQUENCY OF SACRIFICE 65

astu or the Peiraieus.[147] But while some Athenians may have chosen not to attend one public sacrifice or another, the point is worth emphasizing that, as far as we know, no citizen in good standing was excluded from any of these sacrifices, and every citizen could attend every one them, if he so chose, by virtue of his citizenship.

To conclude, among the praiseworthy features of Athens which Thucydides has Perikles include in the "Funeral Oration" are the contests and sacrifices (*thusiai*) which the Athenians celebrated for their own recreation throughout the year,[148] a statement which the scholiast glosses with the comment that the Athenians sacrificed on every day of the year save one.[149] The scholiast is certainly exaggerating, but the evidence which we have examined in this chapter strongly indicates that sacrifice was a frequent occurrence in Athens; and even if this evidence cannot tell us exactly how often the Athenians sacrificed, it can at least suggest some broadly approximate figures. Thus, if the sacrificial practices of Erkhia, Thorikos and Marathon are in any way typical of those of the other demes, we must assume that the typical Athenian could, if he chose, participate in perhaps twenty different sacrificial events sponsored by his deme during the year.

Besides being demesmen, the Athenians were also members of trittyes and tribes, and perhaps also of *genê* and phratries, each one of which would likewise have its own sacrifices. We have examined documents from two of these supra-deme units, the Tetrapolis of Marathon and the *genos* of the Salaminioi, both of which show a

---

[147]Cf. the remarks by Mikalson (1982) on the festal nature of *heortai*.

[148]τῶν πόνων πλείστας ἀναπαύλας τῇ γνώμῃ ἐπορισάμεθα, ἀγῶσι μέν γε καὶ θυσίαις διετησίοις νομίζοντες, Thuc. 2.38.1. Cf. Aristot. *Eth. Nik.* 1160ª18-29, which also associates sacrifices with relaxation and leisure (especially with the reading of Wilson (1902, 28), who brackets ἔνιαι . . . βίον [lines 19-23] as an interpolation, and makes the sacrifices those of tribes and demes).

[149]δι' ὅλου ἔτους θύουσιν οἱ 'Αθηναῖοι καθ' ἑκάστην, πλὴν μίας ἡμέρας.

pattern of perhaps ten additional sacrificial events per year. Even if both the Tetrapolis and the Salaminioi are atypical, we would still expect each supra-deme unit to sacrifice at least once and perhaps two or three times per year, and such minimal numbers on each level (trittyes, tribe, etc.) would still provide the typical Athenian citizen (who belonged to two or more of these intermediate units) with perhaps another five to ten sacrificial events beyond the twenty or so sponsored by his deme. Finally, the *polis* itself annually sponsored a further sixteen or more public sacrifices which were large enough for meat to be distributed to a significant number of citizens from the population at large. The sacrifices on all levels would thus provide a typical Athenian with the opportunity to participate in sacrifices and to receive a share of meat from the sacrificed animal on in the range of forty to forty-five different occasions every year, or, on an average, once every eight or nine days.[150]

Again, it should be stressed, these figures should be understood as approximations; but even with an error margin of $\pm 10\%$ (thirty-six or fifty sacrifices annually or, on an average once every seven or ten days) they are still broadly suggestive of how major a role public sacrifices with their attendant distributions of meat played in Athenian civic life throughout the year.

Of course not every citizen participated in every sacrifice of every political unit to which he belonged, and some sacrifices were likely to be better attended than others. Since the deme was the unit of political society with which the individual was most likely to identify, and since participation in deme sacrifices was an important way of manifesting that identification,[151] we would expect most citizens to attend many or all of their demes' sacrifices. Ties with the units above the deme were likely to be weaker, and one sign of this weakness is

---

[150]On the sense of the expression "in the range of" see above, pp. 5-6.

[151]So e.g. at Isaios 9.33 an outsider tries to pretend that he is a member of the deme by sharing in the distribution of meat, but is excluded by the demesmen; cf. also Dem. 57.46-47 where the speaker will be excluded from the deme's sacrifice if he is found not to be a citizen.

THE FREQUENCY OF SACRIFICE

the fact that these supra-deme units appear to have sponsored fewer sacrifices than the demes did. Weaker ties would naturally mean that fewer Athenians would attend sacrifices sponsored above the level of the deme unless there was some additional reason which prompted them to participate, like the introduction of a child into his phratry,[152] or the entertainment or spectacle of some of the *polis* events. Beyond this, we can easily imagine calculations of distance from home to the place of sacrifice, of other obligations including work, of the availability (or the lack) of other food including that from deme and similar sacrifices, determining who chose to attend which sacrifices and to participate in which distributions. All the same, when all levels of government are taken into account it would appear that public sacrifices were frequent enough in fourth-century Athens to be, at least potentially, a major source of meat for the average citizen.[153]

---

[152] When a child was introduced into a phratry his guardian provided a sacrificial victim in the eating of which all the *phratores* participated as a sign of their acceptance of the new member ([Dem.] 43.82); given the importance of this ceremony for establishing citizenship, one would expect that a substantial number of *phratores* attended.

[153] Which is not to suggest, however, that the meat from public sacrifice was a major component of the Athenians' diet, which, as we have seen (above, p. 2 with note 3 there), consisted primarily of grain products. On the amount of meat involved see below, Supplementary Note D.

2. SUPPLYING THE VICTIMS

In this chapter we shall consider several topics related to the supply of sacrificial victims, viz. the number of victims which the Athenian *polis* and its sub-units (demes, etc.) required annually for their public sacrifices, some aspects of the livestock-raising "industry" which supplied the victims, typical prices for victims, and the nature of the markets where these victims were bought and sold.

In what follows, it should again be emphasized, the figures we shall arrive at are intended to indicate a general range of probability, rather than the precise number of animals sacrificed.[1] Further, in order not to overstate our case, we shall focus on minima rather than maxima. Our goal then will be to establish broadly approximate *minimum* numbers for the total of victims sacrificed annually by the *polis* and its subunits in the latter part of the fourth century B.C., the period best documented in our sources. Despite their imprecision, approximate figures of this sort can still be of value since they give us at least a general sense of the number of animals involved annually in public sacrifice, and of the demands which sacrificing so many animals was likely to have placed upon the rural economy.

To begin with the Athenian *polis* as a whole, as we saw in the previous chapter the central government annually sacrificed large numbers of victims and distributed their meat to the general citizen public only at the so-called *epithetoi heortai* which, by the late fourth century, comprised the festivals and sacrifices listed in the *Dermatikon* Accounts of 334/3-331/0 (*IG* 2^2 1496) plus the sacrifice to Artemis Agrotera, which is not listed in the Accounts.[2] As we saw in the previous chapter, we can establish a likely *minimum* number for the

---

[1]The reader is especially referred to the remarks on the expression "in the range of" in the Introduction, above, pp. 5-6.
[2]See above, pp. 48-58.

victims sacrificed at each event listed in the *Dermatikon* Accounts by dividing the proceeds from the sale of hides of animals slain at that event by 10 dr., the highest likely price for a single ox-hide (the victims in the Accounts, it will be recalled, were all almost certainly oxen).[3] To allow now for variations in the total number of animals slain from year to year at a particular sacrifice or festival we shall use figures from the year which provides the lowest money amount for the sale of hides from that sacrifice or festival. This lowest amount divided by 10 dr., the highest likely price for a single hide, will thus provide a figure which we may safely consider as the *minimum* number for the oxen slain annually at that particular sacrifice or festival. The results of these calculations are given in the following chart. Figures for oxen have been rounded to the nearest whole; the dates in brackets are those of the year chosen as that with the lowest sales total (in drakhmai) for the sacrifice or festival in question.[4] A blank space indicates that insufficient information survives on the stone to calculate a minimum number of animals for the sacrifice or festival in question.

Estimated Minimum Number of Victims in Dermatikon Accounts

sacrifice to Eirênê [332/1]	71 oxen
Panathenaia	
Eleusinia	
sacrifice to Dêmokratia [332/1]	41 oxen
Asklepieia (Epidauria) [332/1]	100 oxen
Theseia [332/1]	118 oxen
Dionysia τὰ ἐν Πειραιεῖ [334/3]	31 oxen
Dionysia τὰ ἐπὶ Ληναίωι [333/2]	34 oxen[5]
sacrifice to Agathê Tukhê [333/2]	10 oxen

---

[3] Pp. 62-63.

[4] Sales totals for all years are given above in the table on pp. 50-53.

[5] Combining the victims for the Dionysia τὰ ἐπὶ Ληναίωι and the sacrifice to Daeira for this year (see above, Chapter 1, note 108).

Asklepieia [333/2]	24 oxen[6]
Dionysia τὰ ἐν ἄστει [334/3]	81 oxen[7]
Olympieia [334/3]	63 oxen
sacrifice to Hermes Hêgemonios	
Bendideia [334/3]	46 oxen
sacrifice to Zeus Sôtêr [334/3]	105 oxen
Total:	724 oxen

Too much of the stone has been lost to restore any figures for the victims slain at the Panathenaia or the Eleusinia or at the sacrifice to Hermes Hêgemonios. We have no other evidence for the number of victims slain at either the Eleusinia or the sacrifice to Hermes Hêgemonios, and speculation would be pointless. In the case of the Panathenaia, however, we know that one hundred oxen, the famous hekatomb,[8] were slain annually and that their meat was distributed to the general citizenry.[9] We also know from another inscription, IG 2^2

---

[6]Reading 235 dr., not 325 dr. since we are seeking the least possible figure.

[7]Using the larger figure of 808+ dr. [334/3] rather than 306+ dr. [333/2] (for the reasons for doing so see above, Chapter 1, note 109).

[8]Cf. the etymology of ἑκατόμβη < ἑκατόν + βοῦς. None of the hekatombs of less than one hundred animals attested in our sources (mostly literary, for which see Stengel [1912] col. 2787) is directly comparable to the hekatomb at the Athenian Panathenaia. Athen. 3D (ἑκατόμβην τῷ ὄντι θύσας καὶ οὐ ψευδωνύμως) implies that some (presumably Athenian) hekatombs were less than one hundred animals, but it is highly unlikely, except in dire circumstances, that the Athenians would skimp on the hekatomb of the Panathenaia, the most important of the *epithetoi thusiai*, and probably the most important feast in the civic religious calendar.

[9]We know from IG 2^2 334.8-16, that the first portions went to various officials (*prytaneis*, arkhons, etc.) and to the citizens who had participated in the procession, and that the remainder was distributed to the citizenry at large; see further the discussion of this inscription in Rosivach (1991) 430-42. It is unclear whether the preliminary sacrifice at the altar of Athena Hygieia (IG 2^2 334.8-9) was part of the hekatomb or in addition to it; since, however, we are concerned here with *minima*, I have included it in the hekatomb and not

334 (to be dated to c. 335/4), that besides the hekatomb, some time after 338/7 a supplement of 41 mnai was allocated for the purchase of further sacrificial victims for the Lesser Panathenaia,[10] a sum which should have been sufficient to purchase a minimum of 41 additional oxen.[11] It is quite likely that these additional oxen were purchased each year throughout the period of the *Dermatikon* Accounts (334/3-331/0), and perhaps continued to be purchased thereafter down to 320.[12] Finally, a further eight or nine oxen were distributed annually at the Lesser Panathenaia as prizes for the *purrikhê* dances (one

---

counted it separately.

[10] The allocation was funded from rental of land in Oropos which the Athenians received as a gift from Philip in 338/7 or shortly thereafter (Rosivach [1991] 436-39).

[11] The highest reliable amount found in our sources for a single ox is 100 dr., the amount budgeted for animals to be purchased as prizes for some of the contests at the Panathenaia. 41 mnai (= 4,100 dr.) divided by this maximum price of 100 dr. gives a minimum total of 41 oxen. For the price of 100 dr. for an ox see *IG* 2^2 2311.71-81, dated to the first half of the fourth century. There are two higher figures found in our sources, the apparently faulty 150 dr. for an ox in the Marathonian deme calendar (*IG* 2^2 1358 col. 2, line 8, on which see above, Chapter 1, note 68), and 400 dr. for single oxen in the accounts of the Eleusinian *epistatai* for 329/8 (*IG* 2^2 1672.290), a figure which is simply too far out of line with all the other figures to be considered normal. Ziehen (1896, 215, note 4) believes that the horns of the oxen were gilded, and that the 400 dr. included the price of the gilding, but such an explanation will not account for the unusually high figure of 30 dr. each for sheep and goat found in the same inscription [289]. Pritchett (1956, 256) explains the extraordinarily high prices of these animals as a consequence of special circumstances, viz. the famine of 330-326, but note the relatively normal sheep prices in *IG* 2^2 1673.62, probably from 327/6. It may be significant that *IG* 2^2 1672 says specifically [289] that the 30 dr. prices for sheep and goats—and presumably also the 400 dr. for oxen—were set by the *dêmos*, and were thus, apparently, not normal market prices; but it is, again, unclear why the *dêmos* would require these victims to be purchased at artificially high prices, if in fact this is what it did. Clearly the anomalous prices of *IG* 2^2 1672 are yet to be explained. See also the discussion on prices of victims below, pp. 95-99.

[12] The date of Athens' loss of Oropos in the Lamian War, on which see Wiesner (1939) col. 1174.

each for boys, youths and men), for first and second place in the *neôn hamilla* (three for the winning tribe, two for the second-place tribe), and at least for some time one for the winning tribe in the *euandria* contest.[13] The 41 additional oxen funded from the supplementary 41 mnai allocated to the Lesser Panathenaia sometime after 338/7 and the eight or nine oxen awarded as prizes added to the 100 animals in the hekatomb give a minimum total of 149 oxen sacrificed at the Lesser Panathenaia at the time of the *Dermatikon* Accounts. Adding these 149 animals to our previous total of 724 oxen sacrificed at other feasts in the Accounts, we obtain a figure of 873 oxen. Further, since the figure of 724 oxen did not include those sacrificed at the Eleusinia or at the sacrifice to Hermes Hêgemonios, the two *epithetoi heortai* for which insufficient data survive either in *IG* 2^2 1496 or elsewhere, the *minimum* number of oxen sacrificed by the *polis* at the major public holidays listed in the *Dermatikon* Accounts must have been greater—though by how much we do not know—than the recoverable total of 149 + 724 = 873 oxen annually.

Besides the oxen sacrificed at the events in the *Dermatikon* Accounts, the Athenian *polis*, as we have seen, also sacrificed 500 goats to Artemis Agrotera annually. There is, however, no evidence the *polis* sacrificed sheep or swine for distribution to the general citizenry.[14]

---

[13] *IG* 2^2 2311.71-82, from the first half of the fourth century; see also our discussion of this inscription in Supplementary Note C. On the contests see Ziehen (1949) coll. 483-86. There is no way of telling whether the prizes listed in this particular inscription were for a Greater or Lesser Panathenaia, but we do know that the pyrrhic dances (and we may presume the other contests) were a feature of the Lesser Panathenaia (cf. Lysias 21.4; Ziehen, *loc. cit.* says that the contests for *euandria* probably and the *neôn hamilla* certainly were absent from the Lesser Panathenaia but gives no reason for this assertion). By the time of the *Ath. Pol.* shields were awarded for the *euandria* contest instead of an ox (Aristot. *Ath. Pol.* 60.3).

[14] More accurately the *polis* may have sacrificed one sheep at the Panathenaia: Harpokration s.v. ἐπίβοιον (cf. Suid. s.v.), as emended, quotes Philokhoros as saying that if anyone sacrifices an ox to Athena, a sheep is to be

Given our concern for minimum figures, our earlier total of more than 873 oxen probably sacrificed annually at *epithetoi heortai* is likely to be on the low side, but it is not likely to be excessively so. The 500 goats sacrificed to Artemis Agrotera and the more than 873 oxen sacrificed at the other *epithetoi heortai* are thus a conservative but realistic estimate of the total number of animals sacrificed by the *polis*-government at the annual *epithetoi heortai* at the time of the *Dermatikon* Accounts.[15] Further, to the degree that the information in the Accounts is useful for the period before 338/7, 500 goats and more than 832 oxen would be a conservative estimate of the animals sacrificed by the *polis*-government at the annual *epithetoi heortai* in the immediately earlier period, before Athens allocated the supplementary 41 mnai for the purchase of additional sacrificial oxen at the Lesser Panathenaia. These figures, it should be noted, do not include the victims which the *polis* appears to have sacrificed at its six major penteteric festivals and at non-recurring *ad hoc* celebrations, albeit in numbers which cannot be estimated from available sources.[16] It will be recalled that, on the level of the *polis*, large-scale distributions of meat to the general citizenry took place only at the annual *epithetoi heortai* and at the penteteric festivals and *ad hoc* celebrations.

For the number of animals sacrificed annually by demes we must turn again on the three calendars from Erkhia, Thorikos and Marathon studied in the previous chapter. As we saw there, the total number of sacrificial occasions was roughly the same on all three calendars, and this consistency gave us reason to believe that, at least as far as the

---

sacrificed to Pandrosos, and a single sheep does appear in the procession on the north frieze of the Parthenon (slab IV); in any event, the amount of meat from a single sheep would be trivial compared to that from the hekatomb of oxen. On the *polis'* sacrifices with more limited distributions of meat see above, pp. 46-47.

[15] On Jameson's estimate of 1,400 to 1,700 oxen sacrificed annually (1988, 96 and 111) see Supplementary Note C.

[16] On the penteteric festivals and *ad hoc* celebrations see above, pp. 60-61.

frequency of sacrifices was concerned, the three calendars were reasonably representative of general patterns of sacrifice on the level of the demes. As to the total number of victims sacrificed, we must recognize at the outset that Erkhia, Thorikos and Marathon were only three of 139 demes, though all three were among the larger demes, and their combined population accounted for perhaps 4.2 to 4.5% of the total citizen population of Attika.[17] 4.2 to 4.5% is still a low sample for our projections, and the margin of error in those projections will be consequently higher; but again, it should be emphasized, our concern here, as throughout this study, is not with absolute numbers but with general patterns which the numbers we use will very broadly approximate.

There are further problems with using the three deme calendars which should also be mentioned here. First, the three demes sacrifice different combinations of animals,[18] a difficulty which we can overcome in part by combining into a single category sheep, goats and the victims labeled *teleoi* on the Thorikos Calendar.[19] Second, as we saw earlier, the Erkhia Calendar contains only annual sacrifices, but we have good reason to believe that there was also originally a second calendar which has now been lost, listing biennial sacrifices probably fewer in number than the annual sacrifices. Any projection based, in whole or in part, on the Erkhia Calendar will therefore tend to underestimate the total number of animals sacrificed annually throughout

---

[17]The population percentages are based on bouleutic representation (on which see above, pp. 6-8):

	original quota	% of 500	307/6 quota	% of 600
Erkhia	6/7	1.2/1.4	11	1.8
Thorikos	5	1.0	6	1.0
Marathon	<u>10</u>	<u>2.0</u>	<u>10</u>	<u>1.7</u>
TOTAL	21/22	4.2/4.4	27	4.5

[18]The choice of one kind of a victim instead of another may depend on such factors as perceived religious requirements, local taste, or the local availability of one kind of victim in contrast to another, knowledge of which would require more information than our sources can provide.

[19]On *teleoi* see above, Chapter 1, note 42.

Attika since the base does not include Erkhia's biennial sacrifices. This is less of a problem than it may at first appear however, since we are not seeking to establish the exact number of victims sacrificed but only to get a sense of the minimum number of animals involved; but it is still a problem since the minimum we determine may be misleadingly low. Finally, there is simply no way of knowing how typical Erkhia, Thorikos and Marathon were in terms both of each deme's financial resources and of its willingness to spend more or less of those resources on the purchase of sacrificial victims. Nonetheless, since the deme calendars are all we have, we shall have to assume, in the absence of evidence to the contrary, that a composite picture based on the number and kinds of victims sacrificed by the three demes will very broadly reflect general deme practice throughout Attika.

Listed below are the annual totals of victims sacrificed by our three demes. Lambs, kids and piglets have again been excluded since they were not the source of large-scale meat distributions; sheep, goats and the animals listed on the Thorikos Calendar as *teleoi* have all been combined into a single figure to compensate for the different ratios of these categories of victims in the three calendars, and no attempt has been made to adjust for the loss of the biennial calendar from Erkhia:

Annual Total of Victims Sacrificed by the Three Demes

	oxen	sheep, goats, *teleoi*	swine
Erkhia	0	39	0
Thorikos[20]	3	40	0
Marathon[21]	<u>6</u>	<u>27.5</u>	<u>1</u>
THREE DEME TOTAL	9	106.5	1

[20] The τρίτ[τοα in Mounikhion is treated as an ox, a sheep and a goat (see above, Chapter 1, note 50).

[21] Biennial sacrifices have been divided by two to give an annual average.

The single swine sacrificed by the deme of Marathon is too small a basis for any projection, but sheep and goats are sacrificed in all three demes, and oxen are sacrificed in two of the three; and both categories of animals are sacrificed in sufficient number to provide a meaningful basis for projecting the total number of these categories of animals sacrificed in Attika as a whole.

We saw earlier that the three demes accounted for approximately 4.2% of the total citizen population of Attika. Assuming, then, that the number of victims sacrificed by a deme was roughly proportionate to its population, we may use the figures in the deme calendars to project an initial grand total in the range of 214 oxen and 2,531 sheep and goats annually sacrificed by demes in Attika as a whole. However, since there were many more smaller demes (with bouleutic representation of one and two) than large demes, and since one would expect that smaller victims (sheep and goats) more often sufficed to meet the needs of these smaller demes, the total for oxen given here should probably be revised downward and that for sheep and goats upward, though it is impossible to say by how much.

To give a sense of scale to these figures, we may reflect that the citizen population of Attika was somewhere in the range of 27,500 adult male citizens,[22] for whom 2,531 sheep and goats sacrificed every year by the demes plus the 500 goats sacrificed by the *polis* to Artemis Agrotera would average out to approximately one sheep or goat per nine adult male citizens annually. Similarly, we have earlier calculated that the *polis* sacrificed more than 873 oxen annually at its *epithetoi heortai*, and an additional, undeterminable number at its major penteteric festivals and *ad hoc* celebrations. Ignoring for now the animals slain at the penteteric festivals and *ad hoc* celebrations we may combine the more than 873 oxen sacrificed at the *epithetoi heortai* with the 214 oxen sacrificed by the demes for a total of more than 1,087, which averages out to approximately one ox sacrificed by some government sponsor (either the *polis*-government or the demes) for

---

[22]For this figure see above, "Introduction," p. 6 and note 8.

approximately every twenty-five adult male citizens annually, or one ox for approximately every 26 adult male citizens if we exclude the 41 supplementary oxen purchased with the additional funds available after 338/7.[23] Again, it should be stressed, our calculations have been designed to produce probable *minima*. Thus the numbers of victims that were actually sacrificed are unlikely to be significantly lower than those given here, and they are quite likely to be significantly higher.

As we saw earlier,[24] in addition to the *epithetoi heortai* with their mass distributions of meat, the *polis* also sponsored numerous routine sacrifices whose meat was divided among smaller groups of citizens (viz. the sacrifices shared by *prytaneis*, *bouleutai*, etc., as well as the *patrioi thusiai* on the calendar reedited by Nikomakhos; and victims were also sacrificed throughout the year by tribes, phratries and other similar units between the *polis* and the deme. In all these cases, however, there is no reliable way of estimating how many victims were sacrificed,[25] just as there is also no way of estimating how many victims were sacrificed by individuals in private sacrifice.[26] But even if specific numbers are lacking, the combined totals of victims sacrificed by individuals and by units other than the demes and the *polis* at its major festivals must have been substantial, though probably not as large as the number sacrificed by the demes and at the *polis'* major festivals. Indeed, even if we limit ourselves merely to

---

[23] On which, see above, p. 88 and note 71.

[24] Above, pp. 46-47.

[25] While documents like the Marathonian Tetrapolis and Salaminioi Calendars could give us a sense of the frequency of sacrifice at this level (see above, pp. 36-46), they cannot help us to determine the number of victims sacrificed at this level either because, when we can estimate the size of the unit's population, the calendar is incomplete (e.g. the Tetrapolis Calendar); or, when the calendar is complete (the Salaminioi Calendar), there is no reliable way of estimating the population of the unit.

[26] Though at least in the latter case one would suspect that the sacrificial victims were more often smaller young animals (piglets, lambs and kids) which could be considered ordinary by-products of the animal-raising industry, as we shall see below, pp. 88-90.

the sacrifices for which we have quantifiable evidence, viz. those of the demes and the *polis' epithetoi heortai*, it is obvious not only that sacrificial animals were a major source of meat for the Athenian citizen body as a whole, but that the sale and purchase of so many animals was a major component of the economy of rural Attika in the fourth century B.C.[27]

In order to explore the place which the sale and purchase of sacrificial animals had in the rural economy and, ultimately, the rural social structure we may begin with some more general observations on animal raising in Attika, an activity about which it must be admitted that we know very little.[28]

---

[27] It also meant that there were a very large number of animals in Attika or otherwise accessible to the Athenians. As we shall see below (pp. 91-93), adult animals were probably not sacrificed before they reached the age of 3.5 to 4 years, and there is good reason to believe that they were not sacrificed until they were as old as 8 years (and, in the case of oxen, even older). If we assume conservatively that animals were slain at an average of 6 years of age, and allowing no margin for death by illness, accident, etc., there would have to be at any one time totals of at least 6,528 oxen and 15,186 sheep and goats in Attika or otherwise accessible to the Athenians merely to supply what we have estimated as the *minimum* requirements of deme sacrifices and the *epithetoi heortai*, to which should be added a proportionate number of animals for private sacrifices, routine sacrifices by the *polis*, sacrifices by other government units, etc., all this compared with an adult male citizen population of c. 27,500 at this time. Most of these animals were probably to be found in Attika itself, although some may also have come from herds in adjacent *poleis*. On animals brought in from outside Attika see below, Supplementary Note E.

[28] There is no comprehensive modern study of animal husbandry in Attika during the classical period. Most useful for now is Hodkinson's general survey of stock raising in classical and hellenistic Greece (1988), which contains much valuable information about stock raising in Attika. Boeckh (1886, *passim*) also provides much useful information, but not in any systematic or comprehensive way.

There is no evidence for publicly owned flocks and herds in Attika,[29] and it is therefore a reasonable assumption that all the sheep, goats, cattle and swine killed in public sacrifices were obtained from private individuals who bred and raised them.

Sheep and goats in small numbers were probably common, grazing unsupervised (or supervised by children) on non-arable land and on stubble and temporarily fallow fields,[30] but we do not hear about these animals in our sources, probably because owners of only a few sheep or goats would usually be farmers at the lower end of the social scale, the sort of people who rarely find their way into the sources.[31] Two or three animals would fill a farm family's need for milk and cheese, wool and an occasional victim for a domestic sacrifice,[32] but is is unlikely that the sale of these animals owned in

---

[29] At Aristoph. *Eq.* 1136 (ὥσπερ δημοσίους τρέφεις), the animals (βοῦς ἢ ταύρους ἢ ἄλλο τι τοιοῦτον εἰς θῦμα, schol. *ad loc.*) described as δημοσίους are probably recently purchased animals who are being "finished" in anticipation of an upcoming sacrifice, and not a public herd from which victims were drawn for state sacrifices. There is some evidence that the temple of Delos owned sheep while it was under Athenian administration, but this should be seen as reflecting previous Delian, not Attic practice. The evidence for Delos is found in the accounts of the Delian Amphiktyones of 355/4 (*IG* 2^2 1639) which contain the entry ψυκ]τὴρ ἀπὸ τῶν ἐρίων τῶν ἱερῶν προβάτων (17; cf. ψυκτῆρα ἀπὸ [τῶν ἐρ]ίων τῶν προβάτων, *IG* 2^2 1640.28 from the following year); the *psuktēr* would be a wine cooler apparently purchased with proceeds from the sale of the fleeces of sacred sheep.

[30] For the danger of free-ranging animals ruining grain plants in cultivated fields, cf. the analogy at Plato, *Lgg.* 639A.

[31] One example might be Aristophanes' Strepsiades, who is best understood as a comparatively wealthy version of a poor Attic farmer who keeps some sheep, his rustic life brimming with "bees and sheep (προβάτοις) and pressed olives" and himself smelling of "fresh wine and fig-drying racks and left-over bits of wool (ἐρίων περιουσίας)" (Aristoph. *Nub.* 43-50).

[32] Animals grazing on stubble and fallow agricultural land would also deposit dung to manure the fields between crops. The place of livestock in small-scale subsistence farming is summed up by Hodkinson (1986) 11:

> Livestock were able to feed on waste products such as prunings, vine and olive presssings and, besides non-agricultural pasture, to graze on fallow and stubble, thereby cleaning and manuring the fields and

small numbers would have gone very far toward meeting the continuing demand which we have seen for large numbers of sacrificial victims annually.

More typically, to judge from our sources, sheep and goats were raised in herds.[33] Such animals browsed on open land unsuited for cereals and other crops,[34] and for the sake of efficiency they were grouped together in herds so that a relatively large number of animals could be watched by a single herdsman. At Soph. *OT* 1135 the messenger says that he had shepherded a single herd on Mount Kithairon and that Oidipous' servant had pastured two (διπλοῖσι ποιμνίοις), a detail which suggests that a herd could be expected to contain something like a standard number of animals, and that herds that were significantly larger than the standard were divided into two units. In any event, the limited evidence which we have on the size of sheep and goat herds is fairly consistent. On the Attic Stelai recording the sale of property confiscated from the Hermokopidai, for example, we find an entry for 84 sheep καὶ ἔκγονα τούτον and a second for 67 goats καὶ ἔγγον[α τούτον] belonging to Panaitios;[35] Isaios 11.41 mentions property consisting in part of 60 sheep and 100 goats; and [Dem]. 47.52 speaks of a herd of 50 πρόβατα . . . μαλακά (therefore sheep[36]) seized, together with their (slave) shepherd, to satisfy an

---

performing an essential function in maintaining crop productivity. In this mixed-farming system modest numbers of livestock, small livestock in particular, represented a multi-purpose supplementary resource for peasant households, as well as an emergency store of food in times of famine."

On this symbiosis of animal husbandry and agriculture see further Hodkinson (1988) 41-51.

[33]This is the assumption, for example, at Aristot. *HA* 610^{b}20-611^{a}5.

[34]Thus the pasturing of animals is usually associated with mountains (e.g. Plato, *Tht.* 174E, *Tim.* 22D; at *Lgg.* 677B-C we are told that after the great flood only some shepherds and their herds survived since they had been up in the mountains).

[35]Pritchett (1953) VI.71-72 and 73.

[36]See below, note 67.

unpaid debt.[37] These numbers suggest that a single herd of sheep or goats generally consisted of between 50 and 100 mature animals plus their offspring.[38]

Besides herds of sheep and goats our literary sources also refer to herds of oxen (*boes*) and their herdsmen often enough to show that such herds must have existed in fourth-century Athens.[39] These references are almost always in general terms however, and we are much less well informed about specific details. None of our sources, for example, provide any information on the size of ox herds,[40] or even

---

[37]Following the pattern of the Attic Stelai quoted above I would assume that the figures given by Demosthenes and Isaios include only adult animals, to which should be added their young offspring.

[38]Isaios 6.33 mentions a herd of goats which were sold with their goatherd for 13 mnai = 1,300 drakhmai; comparison with the prices of sacrificial victims suggests that the herd was perhaps in the vicinity of 100 animals, but further precision is impossible since (a) the sale was a hurried one and the animals may well have been sold below their true market value, and (b) prices of sacrificial victims should not be directly comparable to those for animals with continuing productive lives. For comparison, at Dem. 47.52 fifty sheep, two slaves, various equipment and a bronze water jug are said to be sufficient to satisfy a debt of 1,313 dr. 2 ob. (cf. *ibid.* 64).

[39]Herds of cattle, e.g. Aristot. *HA* 575^{b}1-4, 604^{a}13, 611^{a}5-9; Plato, *Minos*, 318A; Dem. 19.265; βοῦς ἀγελαῖος, Antiphanes, frag. 133 E, line 3. Herdsmen, e.g. Eur. *Bakkh.* 714; Xen. *Mem.* 1.2.32; Plato, *Tht.* 174D. Hodkinson (1988, 50) suggests that these larger herds may have also supplied animals to smaller farmers needing replacements for their draft oxen.

[40]Unless perhaps the β[όε]ς τέτταρες καὶ μό[σχοι - - - on the Attic Stelai are such a herd (Pritchett [1953] VI.70). According to *IG* 2^2 351.15-18 the Plataian Eudemos contributed ([ἐπ]ι[δέδ]ωκεν) 1,000 ζεύγη in 330/29 for the construction of the Panathenaic stadium and theater, but these ζεύγη could not possibly be animals and are probably construction materials, as in *SIG*^{3} 245 l.35-42; cf. *IG* 1^3 386.23 (even at a modest 30 dr. an animal, 1,000 ζεύγη = 2,000 animals would represent 10 T., an extraordinarily large amount of wealth for anyone to possess; besides, given what we know about construction procedures in classical Athens, it is difficult to imagine how 1,000 pair of animals could be used effectively in this single building project, and one might also wonder what Eudemos did with these animals before he gave, or loaned, them to the Athenians).

the name of a single individual who actually owned a herd of oxen, and this paucity of information may well indicate that herds of oxen were rarer than herds of sheep or goats.[41] Oxen were also raised in pairs as draft animals,[42] but even if some of these animals may have become sacrificial victims at the end of their working days,[43] it is highly unlikely that by itself the population of these older draft animals could have been a sufficient source for the large number of sacrificial oxen Athens required annually.

We also find in our sources scattered general references to swineherds[44] and to browsing swine,[45] indicating that these animals were likewise sometimes raised in herds.[46] We would also expect that individual swine were raised in courtyards or pens even

---

[41] Cattle, sheep and goats can all graze on land which is unsuitable for agriculture, but sheep and goats, being smaller and more nimble, can graze in the steeper uplands where cattle cannot; sheep and goats will also eat vegetation that cattle will not. This combination of factors, rather than the higher per unit capital value of cattle vs. sheep or goats, will probably explain the predominance of sheep and goat herds compared with those of cattle.

[42] Thus the two pairs of *boe* (dual) on the Attic Stelai (Pritchett (1953) VI.68 and 69). Draft cattle are classed as *hupozugia*, together with horses and mules (Xen. *Oik.* 18.4); grazing cattle are classed as *boskêmata*, together with sheep, goats and swine (Xen. *HG* 6.4.29).

[43] On the possible sacrifice of working animals see below, Supplementary Note G.

[44] E.g. Plato, *Tht.* 174D; Plato Comicus, frag. 209 K-A; Aristot. *HA* 603^{b}5.

[45] E.g. Arist. *HA* 595^{a}31; swine are included with sheep and goats in τὰ . . . ἄλλα βοσκήματα (contrasted with cattle, Xen. *HG* 6.4.29).

[46] Cf. Xen. *Mem.* 2.7.6, where ownership of a large number of swine and cattle is taken as a sign of wealth. Outside Attika cf. Xenophon's chiastic description of the lands attached to his shrine at Skillos where (a_1) the pasture and (b_1) the wooded uplands were suitable for grazing (b_2) pigs and goats and (a_2) oxen and horses (Xen. *Anab.* 7.3.11).

though—surprisingly—there appears to be no unambiguous evidence for this.[47]

The herdsmen mentioned in our sources were usually slaves,[48] but hired labor was sometimes also employed.[49] Sheep and goat herds of the size our evidence suggests, the slaves and/or hired labor to tend the animals, and the necessary equipment for the herdsmen[50] together represent a substantial investment which would mark the owners of such herds as among the more well-to-do members of the community, typically large-scale agriculturalists[51] for whom large herds of animals were both an additional source of income[52] and,

---

[47] A speaker in Plato Comicus, frag. 27 K-A says that the other animals have been spared and only swine have been slaughtered (presumably in sacrifice: the fragment is from a play entitled *Heortai*) because, apart from their meat, swine are good for nothing except bristles, mud and the noise they make. The mud mentioned here may be that in a pig sty (so Edmonds [1957] 499, note a), but it could also refer to the ground dug up by rooting swine.

[48] This is the assumption at e.g. Xen. *Mem.* 1.5.2; cf. Isaios 6.33, [Dem]. 47.52, Plato, *Ion* 540C (βουκόλῳ . . . δούλῳ). At Plato, *Lgg.* 805E it is said that Thracians make their wives γεωργεῖν τε καὶ βουκολεῖν καὶ ποιμαίνειν καὶ διακονεῖν μηδὲν διαφερόντως τῶν δούλων (for which compare Eupolis, frag. 12 K-A from the *Aiges*: ἐπίσταμαι γὰρ αἰπολεῖν, σκάπτειν, νεᾶν, φυτεύειν [apparently a slave speaking]).

[49] Thus e.g. the shepherd ἐπὶ θητείᾳ πλάνης, Soph. *OT* 1026-29. The politician Phrynikhos was said to have been so poor (πένης) as a child that he tended sheep in the countryside (Lys. 20.11); this probably means that he was hired to watch some one else's flock, but it could also mean that he watched the family flock because his father was too poor to buy a slave or hire someone to do the watching (even if the statement about Phrynikhos is untrue, if could still be rhetorically effective if it reflected a common perception that only very poor people—or slaves—tended flocks).

[50] τὰ ἀκόλουθα τῆι ποίμνηι, [Dem.] 47.52.

[51] Evidence for large-scale Athenian agriculturalists also owning herds is discussed by Hodkinson (1988) 37.

[52] Xen. *Mem.* 2.1.28, 4.3.10; Aristot. *Pol.* 1258^{b}12-15.

like their extensive farm holdings, a visible sign of the wealth they already possessed.[53]

On a more modest level, most farm households probably raised one or more animals for their own immediate needs, but there is no evidence that the less wealthy also raised animals on a regular basis for the commercial market.[54] Individual farmers may have sold an animal or two from their domestic stock from time to time, but the absence of evidence for small-scale commercial animal raising makes it likely that larger enterprises of the sort described in the previous paragraph were the principal source of sacrificial victims for the open market in Athens during our period.

We shall consider below the nature of this market for sacrificial victims.[55] It should be noted here, however, that oxen, sheep and goats were apparently never slain simply for the sake of meat to be sold on the open market.[56] Rather these animals were always

---

[53] πολυπρόβατοι and πολυέλαιοι, Xen. *Vect.* 5.3; cf. Xen. *Mem.* 3.11.5, Dem. 19.265. At Xen. *Mem.* 2.7.6 the ability to maintain cattle and swine and still provide liturgies is taken as a sign of extreme wealth; in this last case at least the animals are seen as an expensive way of displaying wealth, not as a means of gaining more.

[54] Even if Phrynikhos tended his family's flock (above, note 49), the flock was not necessarily a commercial venture, and the animals could have been kept simply to serve the family's immediate needs.

[55] See below, pp. 101-6.

[56] Our evidence seems to indicate that swine were sacrificed less frequently than adult oxen, sheep and goats. The discrepancy may be a matter of taste in meat, but it is at least possible that in contrast to oxen, sheep and goats, swine may also have been slaughtered outside the framework of sacrifice, although the only evidence which I have found to this effect—and not very strong evidence at that—is Plato, *Rep.* 373C, where the luxurious *polis* is said to require *opsopoioi* and *mageiroi*, then *subôtai*, and then all the other kinds of *boskêmata*, if someone will eat them: the sequence suggests that eating the meat of swine tended by *subôtai* for the sake of luxury (and not in the context of sacrifice) falls somewhere in between eating the lesser cuts of meat obtained by *mageiroi* from sacrifices (on which see below), and slaying sheep, goats and oxen apart from sacrifice and just for their meat, a prospect which the text suggests is an almost unimaginable height of luxury. Dikaiarkhos

slaughtered for religious purposes and as part of a religious ritual, either public or private, an integral part of which was the distribution of the animal's meat to the participants.

As for the meat sold by butchers on the open market, we are never specifically told where it came from, but two lines of evidence lead to the conclusion that it was usually meat left over from a religious sacrifice.[57] First, when our sources speak of specific cuts of meat these cuts are always anatomical parts that could not be properly cooked as part of a normal sacrificial meal, e.g. feet, ears, snouts and liver (Alexis frag. 110.15-16 E) neck, tongue and spleen (Aristoph. frag. 520.4-7 K-A), or the animal's fat (Aristoph. *Eq.* 954, *Akhar.* 1102). Ribs (πλευρά, σχελίδες[58]) seem to have been particularly valued (e.g. Pherekrates, frag. 113.13 K-A; Hermippos, frag. 46.3 K-

---

(frag. 23 *FHG*) says that the *opson* at Spartan *sussitiai* was boiled swineflesh, but it is unclear both whether the swine had had first been sacrificed or simply slaughtered, and whether the Spartan *sussitia* is an appropriate *comparandum* for Attic practice.

[57]Berthiaume (1982, 64-67) simply assumes that *mageiroi* also slaughtered animals outside the framework of sacrifice in order to sell their meat directly on the open market. Since he also argues, quite properly, that any animal slain to be eaten had to be slaughtered in an appropriate religious manner, he is forced to distinguish between meat from victims slain as part of a religious sacrifice and that from animals slain simply to provide meat for the market, but the evidence he cites in support of such a distinction (67-69) is all later than our period and refers to places outside of Attika. In fact, for Attika in the fifth and fourth centuries the only unambiguous instance of slaying animals for their meat outside the framework of sacrifice is fictional, at Plato *Lgg.* 849D, where *mageiroi* dispose of meat (probably by selling it) to *xenoi*, *dēmiourgoi* and their servants, that is, significantly, to people who stand outside the inner circle of citizens and are thus excluded from sharing in sacrifices and their attendant meat-distributions which are typically the exclusive right of citizens. (Plato, *Euthyd.* 302A refers to the sale of live animals, not to their meat.) On the absence of evidence for butchers from vase paintings see Berthiaume (1982) 118, n. 15.

[58]Σχελίδες = βοὸς πλευρά, Suidas, s.v.

A; Aristoph. *Eq.* 362), presumably for the meat attached to the bone.[59] These various bits of meat (κρεᾴδια, less often κρέα) were often boiled in a *zômos*, the soup or broth which is often mentioned by our sources (e.g. Aristoph. *Eq.* 1178, frag. 606 K-A; Telekleides, frag. 1.8 K-A; cf. Theophrast. *Char.* 9.4). Finally, intestines, stomachs, and the like were used as casings for a variety of sausages and similar confections (e.g. Pherekrates, frag. 137.9-10 K-A; Aristoph. *Akhar.* 1119, *Eq.* 356). What is missing from this list, it should be noted, are the more substantial cuts of meat from chests, flanks, legs, etc. which could be most easily prepared, and were thus best suited for sacrificial purposes. The easiest explanation for their absence from our sources is that these better parts were always prepared and distributed to the participants at sacrifices,[60] while the odd parts

---

[59]Hermippos, frag. 63 K-A, line 6 speaks of πλευρὰ βόεια imported from Thessaly (with Kock's emendation for MSS. Ἰταλίας). If the reading is correct, this would require the meat to be preserved in some way, perhaps by salting as fish were. The economics of shipping salted beef ribs from Thessaly to Athens are, however, doubtful enough that the reading must be considered suspect.

[60]There are two exceptions to this statement in our sources. *IG* 1³ 244, a fifth-century calendar from the deme Skambonidai twice contains the entry "and sell the meat raw" (τὰ δὲ κρέα ἀποδόσθαι ὀμά, C.18-19, 21-22), where there was no sacrificial banquet and the uncooked meat of the entire animal (and not simply the odd parts) was sold, probably to butchers for resale to the public. Similarly at Theophr. *Char.* 22.4, in a slightly corrupt passage the Cheapskate (ἀνελεύθερος) also apparently sells the meat from the victim sacrificed at his daughter's wedding, except for the portion reserved for the priest; since the behavior of Theophrastos' Characters is always abnormal, if we have read this passage properly, it is strong evidence that at least some meat (presumably the better cuts) was in fact normally distributed to guests. The example of Theophrastos' Cheapskate also suggests the possiblity that other "cheapskate" Athenians may also have sold the meat distributed to them at public sacrifices, but such sales would have been contrary to the intent of the sacrifice, and in any event could not have been a major source of meat on the open market.

(feet, snouts, etc.) of the same sacrificial animals were later sold by butchers (and sausage-sellers) to the public.[61]

A second line of evidence leads to the same conclusion. On several occasions characters in different comedies describe fantasy feasts which they imagine either in some Golden Age in the past or in some ideal time in the future (e.g. the meals described by Krates, Telekleides, Pherekrates, Nikophron and Metagenes *ap*. Athen. 267E-270A; Aristoph. *Akhar*. 1097-1119, *Pax* 715-17, frag. 520 K-A; Hermippos, frag. 46 K-A). These fantasy feasts contain elegant versions of the ordinary daily fare of bread, fish, fowl, etc., as well as the meat-broth *zômos* and many of the odd parts of meat discussed in the previous paragraph, but we do not find in these fantasy meals anything that must be taken as the kind of meats usually consumed at sacrifices.[62] Now this is somewhat surprising since in the fantasies of comedy one would expect that anything would be possible. One would conclude that the absence of the more substantial cuts of meat from these fantasy feasts reflects a mind-set that associated such cuts exclusively with sacrificial meals, and the odd cuts with non-sacrificial ones. Further, if the more substantial cuts were consumed only as a part of sacrifices, there could have been no independent market for these cuts.

---

[61] At Aristoph. *Eq*. 300-2 the Paphlagonian threatens to denounce the Sausage-Seller to the *prytaneis* for possession of intestines (from sacrificial victims, τῶν θεῶν ἱερὰς κοιλίας) upon which the tithe has not been paid. The scholiast *ad loc*. offers two explanations: (1) that *mageiroi* were expected to give a tenth part of sacrificed victims to the *prytaneis*; (2) that the Paphlagonian means to denounce the Sausage-Seller for failure to pay the *eisphora* but he substitutes κοιλίας for οὐσίαν as more appropriate for a sausage-seller. The first explanation would support our argument that butchers like the Sausage-Seller sold the odd parts of sacrificed animals, but the second explanation is more likely to be the correct one.

[62] The κρέα mentioned at Aristoph. *Pax* 716-17 (ζωμὸν . . . χόλικας ἐφθὰς καὶ κρέα) and Metagenes, frag. 6.3-4 K-A ναστῶν καὶ κρεῶν ἐφθῶν τε βατίδων) could be the kind of meat normally distributed at sacrifice, but the sequence of items in both cases makes it more likely that κρέα refers to the odd cuts described above; similarly Alexis, frag. 27.5-7 E, Antiphanes, frag. 222.6-8 E.

Of course, if butchers did not sell substantial cuts of meat from non-sacrificial animals, this does not mean that *ipso facto* the meat which they did sell had to come from sacrificial victims, but economy certainly suggests that butchers sold the unused portions of sacrificial victims, not that they left unused the better portions of other animals and only sold the worse.[63]

In sum then, there is no evidence for animals being slain for their meat outside the framework of sacrifice; the meats available for sale from butchers appear always to be cuts that would be unsuited for sacrificial meals; and the fantasies of comedy seem always to associate private dining exclusively with these odd cuts. Each of these factors is most easily explained if we assume that animals were slain only for the purpose of sacrifice, and that only those parts of the animals unsuitable for sacrificial meals were disposed of by butchers on the public market.[64]

Although the focus of our study is on sacrificial animals and the meat they provided, it is important to understand that the animals we have been considering were not reared to maturity exclusively, or

---

[63]The butcher who sold these odd cuts is likely to have gotten them from the person who actually killed the sacrificial victim (or the butcher had killed the victim himself and now sold the odd parts left over from the sacrifice). Note that in addition to the hide and/or shares in the regular sacrificial meat, priests sometimes received some of these odd parts as perquisites or payment for their role in the sacrifice (so e.g. *IG* 2^2 1237.5-7 sets aside as *hiereôsuna* the victim's κωλῆν, πλευρόν, ὅς [= οὖς, ear] [cf. *IG* 1^3 250.34-35]; similarly *IG* 2^2 1356.10-11, 14-16, 18-19, 22-23 assigns ἐπὶ δὲ τὴν τράπεζαν the victim's κωλῆν, πλευρὸν ἰσχίο, ἡμίκραιραν χορδῆς [cf. *IG* 2^2 1359.8]; κωλῆ, τὸ πλευρόν, ἡμικραιρ' ἀριστερά, Ameipsias, frag. 7 E).

[64]We might also mention here that the flesh of animals which died of natural causes was apparently also eaten, though apparently with no great relish, if we may judge from Aristoph. frag. 714 K-A *ap.* Erotian, *Gloss. Hippocrat.* 82.8. (Erotian gives the name of the place where such meat was sold, but it is impossible to say whether such a market actually existed and, if it did, when.)

perhaps even primarily, for their meat.[65] Sheep were raised for their wool,[66] and Attic sheep were particularly known for the softness of their fleeces.[67] Since lactating ewes and she-goats produce more milk than they needed to nurse their young, these animals could also be raised for their milk; milk not immediately consumed was preserved in the form of cheese.[68] Further, since these animals will lactate for only a limited time after giving birth,[69] the animals had to reproduce annually in order to continue producing milk. The amount of land in Attika available for grazing was limited, and so herds had to be maintained at a relatively constant size by culling excessive animals. Because of the focus on reproduction for the sake of milk production, optimal use of available pasture required that most of the animals in a herd be female, though this requirement would be balanced out to some extent by the need for male animals to sacrifice

---

[65]In what follows I rely on contemporary evidence, notably Aristotle's *Historia Animalium*, whenever possible. Fecundity, lactation and the like can be affected by selective breeding, and the breeds raised in the fourth-centry Attika were different from modern, or even medieval ones. Similarly optimum herd size, composition, etc. are determined by economic and social concerns which differ over time and place; in particular, animal husbandry practices in fourth-century Attika must have been influenced by the demands of the system of public sacrifices studied here, demands not present in other times and places.

[66]In Attika goats were normally not sheared for their hair (Aristot. *HA* 606^{a}17 says that goats were sheared in Lycia as sheep are elsewhere, implying that goats were usually not sheared elsewhere). When sheep, goats and cattle died they could be flayed, but their hides were apparently thought of as a by-product of their death, not as a reason for raising them.

[67]Antiphanes, frag. 194.4 E. Cf. Athen. 219A (τινα τῶν 'Αττικῶν ἐρίων ἀλλ' ἐστὶ μαλακώτερα) which is likely to echo Athenaios' earlier literary sources and not his own contemporary reality). Note also the use of the adjective μαλακά, referring to their fleece, to describe the sheep at Dem. 47.52.

[68]Aristot. *HA* 522^{a}35-37.

[69]Ewes and she-goats gave milk for up to eight months, cows for less (Aristot. *HA* 523^{a}3-5).

to male gods.[70] Excess lambs and kids, particularly male ones, would be culled from the herd when still young, providing a ready supply of small sacrificial victims.[71] The economic aspects of sheep- and goat-raising are well summarized in two passages, the first the comic playwright Antiphanes (frag. 20 E) and the second from Xenophon (*Mem.* 2.7.13). In the first passage, the speaker says that of sheep he will eat only the inexpensive meat of a lamb which does not yet produce either wool or cheese, or of goats that of a kid which does not yet produce cheese. The meat of lambs and goats is inexpensive when compared with that of adult animals in their prime, whose ability to produce milk (and wool) make them too valuable for Antiphanes' speaker to kill. And in the second passage, Socrates describes a sheep who reminds its owner that it has provided him with "wool and lambs and cheese."

As noted earlier,[72] we are much less well informed about ox herds in Attika than we are about herds of sheep and goats, but it appears that Attic ox herds served primarily to supply replacement draft animals, especially for farmers but also for builders and other haulers.[73] To provide a margin of safety, prudence would dictate that more animals be raised to young adulthood than were actually required for work purposes or for breeding; as they matured, unneeded animals eventually had to be culled from the herd to make room for younger animals, and would thus be available for sacrifice.

---

[70]Male sheep are also better wool-producers than females. Males not needed for breeding purposes were probably castrated while they were still young. Besides being less troublesome, castrated sheep are also larger (Aristot. *HA* 632^{a}8-9), hence providing more meat than uncastrated ones do.

[71]For this optimal strategy (sc. high reproductive rates and predominance of adult females) aimed at milk and cheese production see Payne (1985) 229, and Jameson (1988) 88-89.

[72]Above, pp. 80-81.

[73]Cf. Plato, *Rep.* 370D-E; see also Jameson (1988) 97.

SUPPLYING THE VICTIMS

Piglets, up to twenty in a litter according to Aristotle,[74] were regularly sacrificed and eaten, and were in fact, apart from the swine's own meat, the principal product that swine produced.[75]

In different ways then, depending upon the type of animal, economic considerations suggest that the animals that were sacrificed and eaten were more likely to be either still too young to have cost their owner very much for their upkeep or old enough to have already provided him some other economic benefits in the form of milk, cheese, wool and offspring.[76] We have clear evidence for the sacrifice of young animals (lambs, kids and piglets, but not calves) from the sacrificial calendars discussed above in Chapter 1, but these same calendars also show that sacrifices of adult animals were far more common, at least in public sacrifices.

As to the age at which adult animals were sacrificed, we may consider the adjective *tele(i)os* which is often used to describe prime sacrificial victims.[77] As shown below in Supplementary Note A, this adjective refers to the animal's age as judged by the loss of its deciduous (baby) teeth. Both sheep and oxen complete the replacement of their deciduous teeth with permanent ones between 3.5 and 4 years of age. When this age is compared with a ewe's age of first service (between 12 and 18 months) and her period of gestation (5 months) it is clear that a ewe could have produced offspring and milk for two or more years before becoming *tele(i)os*. The same would be

---

[74] *HA* 573^{a}31-32; less precisely, *GA* 774^{a}15-25.

[75] On the uselessness of swine for anything but meat see Plato Comicus frag. 27 K-A paraphrased above, note 47.

[76] "For effective herd management today, with the emphasis on milk production and secondarily on meat, herdsmen cut out not only the majority of lambs and kids before they are a year old but also ewes and does past lactation (at six years) and rams and bucks from three or four to eight years," Jameson (1988, 101), citing a personal communication from H. Koster, whose University of Pennsylvania dissertation dealt with the ecology of pastoralism in the northeast Peloponnese.

[77] So e.g. Homer, *Il.* 1.66, 24.34; Aiskhyl. *Ag.* 1509; *SEG* 33.147; *SIG*^{3} 993.12-13.

roughly true of goats. In the case of cows the age of first service is somewhat later (between 14 and 22 months) and the period of gestation somewhat longer (9 months), but cows could still have reproduced at least once and possibly twice before they became *tele(i)oi*.[78] There is no reason to believe that animals were prevented from conceiving if they were eventually expected to be sacrificed or that animals who had not conceived were thought to make superior victims compared with those who had conceived (or vice versa).[79] On the other hand, the economic advantages which the animals' owner could derive from conception (viz. offspring and milk) would, if anything, make the encouragement of conception likely.

Further, it should be noted, the adjective *tele(i)os* described not simply an animal at the point in its life at which it had completely replaced its baby teeth with permanent ones, but any animal which had already gone through this process, whatever its age. In other words, a *tele(i)os* cow or ewe had to be at least 3.5 to 4 years of age, but could be older. According to Aristotle, ewes normally could conceive into their eighth year, sows into their fifteenth; goats might live for up to eight years and cows for fifteen, during most of which time they could also conceive, and thus also produce milk.[80] If we reflect on the value of these different animals while they were still alive,[81] it

---

[78]For the ages of first service, see below, Supplementary Note A, notes 11 and 12; for the periods of gestation see Arist. *HA* 573^{b}21 (sheep and goats) and *ibid.* 575^{a}25 (cows).

[79]When pregnant animals were required, as they sometimes were, for specific sacrifices it was for ritual reasons relating to the specific sacrifices intended to enhance agricultural fertility (so e.g. the βοῦς κυοῦσα for Gê at *IG* 2^2 1358.2.9 or the οἷς κυοῦσα for Demeter at *SEG* 33.147.44), and not because pregnant victims were generally superior to non-pregnant ones.

[80]Sheep to age eight, and to age eleven if well tended (Aristot. *HA* 546^{b}31-32); swine to age fifteen (*HA* 546^{a}14); goats can live to eight years, sheep to ten, though most live less (*HA* 573^{b}23-24); cows live to fifteen years (*HA* 575^{a}31). Aristotle does not provide information on how long goats and cows could conceive.

[81]Cf. Antiphanes, frag. 20 E paraphrased above, p. 90.

would seem that they were more likely to be offered for sale as sacrificial victims only late in their productive lives, after they had already provided their owners with a good return of offspring, milk and wool. And such older animals were natural candidates for sacrifice since the limited amount of land available for grazing meant that they had to be culled from the herds in any case, to make room for younger, productive ones.

It appears then that the principal focus of animal husbandry in Attika was not on the raising of animals to serve as sacrificial victims. Rather, these animals would have been raised primarily for their milk and the cheese made from it, for the offspring they bore, and, in the case of sheep, for their wool. On the other hand, if one may judge from e.g. the prescriptions for "finishing" animals[82] found Aristotle's *Historia Animalium*,[83] once these animals had served their other functions for an adequate length of time many, if not most, would be sacrificed and their meat eaten before they became too old.

As we saw earlier, oxen, sheep and goats were apparently never slain merely for their meat, but were always sacrificed as part of a religious rite, an integral part of which was the distribution of the victim's meat to those in attendance at the rite. The rite might be a private sacrifice in which the animal's owner slew the animal, especially a smaller, younger one, and distributed its meat to his family and friends. Such private sacrifices were probably not very frequent for small-scale subsistence farmers who kept only a few sheep or goats on the family farm; they were probably more frequent for the owners of the large herds which have been our principal focus here. The owners of the larger herds, however, would sell most of their animals to others to sacrifice: smaller, younger animals for others' private

---

[82]"Finishing" refers to the regime of special feeding used to increase the amount and quality of an animal's meat before slaughtering; for examples of these regimes see Aristot. *HA* 595^{a}19-22 (swine), 595^{a}22-23 (other animals), 595^{b}5-12 (oxen), 596^{a}24-27 (*probata*).

[83]And also from more general considerations of "economic rationality."

sacrifices,[84] and older, larger animals for the public sacrifices of the *polis*, deme, etc. In this sense the disposal of animals for sacrifice repeats on a smaller scale the general patterns of the rural economy as a whole, with small-scale subsistence farmers growing food and raising animals primarily for their own domestic use, and large-scale producers growing food and raising animals primarily for the open market to supply the needs especially of the non-agricultural *astu*.

In sum then, the raising and selling of animals for sacrifice was not an independent activity but was rather an integral part of a broader "industry" which supplied milk, cheese, wool, young animals for private sacrifice, and mature animals for public sacrifice. The money which an owner received for selling an animal to be sacrificed thus represented only a part, and perhaps a quite small part, of the total economic benefit which the owner derived from the animal during its lifetime. There is reason to believe, as we have seen,[85] that this market-oriented "industry" was dominated by those who raised animals in larger herds, with little or no place for those who raised them in twos and threes. And, as we have also seen,[86] those who owned these larger herds of animals were necessarily among the more well-to-do members of the community.[87]

---

[84]In some cases at least, when *mageiroi* were hired to cater a private sacrifice they, rather than their employers, supplied the victims, having purchased them in advance from the people who raised them (so e.g. the *mageiros* who brings with him the sheep for the sacrifice to Pan at Men. *Dysk.* 393; see also below, Chapter 3, note 2).

[85]Above, pp. 77-83.

[86]Above, p. 83.

[87]Hodkinson (1992) 53-57, argues that in the fifth century the cash demands of increasingly frequent liturgies, especially the trierarchy, as well as other taxes which fell on wealthy Athenians, caused them to turn to the production and sale of animal products as one way of raising the cash required of them; that there was also at this time a growing urban market for these products in the *astu* and in the Peiraieus; and that Athens' imperial ambitions sustained this system in the fourth century until the collapse of democracy at the end of the century. It is possible to argue with some of the details of Hodkinson's analysis, especially his emphasis on causality, but he is undoubt-

SUPPLYING THE VICTIMS 95

As to prices of these animals, some of the calendars studied above in Chapter 1 indicate amounts budgeted for the purchase of sacrificial victims, and similar budget entries are also found in the so-called "Calendar of Nikomakhos," the recodification of the *polis*' "ancestral" sacrifices completed sometime after 403. The following tables list the amounts budgeted for various sacrificial victims in surviving deme calendars and in the "Calendar of Nikomakhos." Calendars are arranged in chronological order, with dates given in square brackets;[88] M = male, F = female.[89]

Amounts Budgeted to Purchase Oxen for Sacrifice[90]

calendar[91]

Thorikos [430's]   40-50 dr.
"Nikomakhos" [after 403]   *[92]

---

edly correct about the interdependence of cash liquidity, animal husbandry and the urban market.

[88]Except for the date of the Thorikos Calendar (on which see above, Chapter 1, note 37), all dates are those of the calendar's most recent editors.

[89]The prices given here can be used to calculate the probable expenditures for sacrifices in calendars where the number and kind of victims are listed but prices are not given or have been lost. They may also be used, albeit with substantially less certainty, when only money amounts are given, to calculate the kind and number of victims probably purchased e.g. with the funds belonging to the deme of Plotheia (*IG* 1³ 258, dated by Lewis *ad loc.* to 425-413).

[90]See also Pritchett (1956) 255-57.

[91]Calendar of Nikomakhos (see above, "Abbreviations"); Marathon Deme and Tetrapolis Calendars = *IG* 2² 1358; Thorikos Calendar = *SEG* 33.147; Salaminioi Calendar = *SEG* 21.527.

[92]50 dr. are budgeted for βόε δύο / [λ]ειπογνώμονε at *Hesp.* 1935, p. 21, lines 50-51. The adjective *leipognômon* refers to an older animal, probably past the age when it can bear young, and hence of less value to its owner. On the adjective *leipognômôn*, see below, Supplementary Note A.

Marathon [c. 400-350]	90 dr.[93]
Salaminioi [c. 363/2]	70 dr.

Besides the amounts budgeted in these calendars, we also know that 5,114 dr. were spent on the hekatomb at the Greater Panathenaia of 410/9 (*IG* 1³ 375.7), for an average of 51.14 dr. per ox (on the reasonable assumption that the hekatomb consisted of 100 animals); 1 T. 2,419 dr. = 8,419 dr. were spent by Athens' Delian *amphiktyones* to purchase 109 oxen in 375/4 (*IG* 2² 1635.35-36), for an average of 77.24 dr. per ox; and 100 dr. were budgeted for the purchase of each ox to be awarded as a prize at the Panathenaia at some time between 400 and 350 (*IG* 2² 2311.71-81).[94] These figures represent a considerable range, the highest, 100 dr. for the Panathenaic prizes, being 2.5 times greater than the least, the minimum amount budgeted by the deme of Thorikos; and even if we confine ourselves to amounts actually expended, the average of 77.24 dr. spent on oxen by the Delian *amphiktyones* is 1.5 times greater than the average of 51.14 dr. spent for the hekatomb of 410/9.[95]

---

[93] On the entry βοῦς, followed by the figure 150 and an abraded space (*IG* 2² 1358.2.7) see above, note 11. There is also a βοῦς κύουσα (line 9) budgeted for Π^{Δ}ΔΔ[. . ., probably also 90 drakhmai.

[94] On the 400 dr. for a single ox at *IG* 2² 1672.290, see above, note 11. The prices for oxen on the Attic Stelai have been mostly eroded from the stone, but at Stele VI.68 traces survive to show that the sales price for two work-oxen was expressed by a single character, either Π^Δ (= 50 dr.) or H (= 100 dr.), of which Pritchett (1956, 257) chooses H, for a price of 50 dr. per animal. Similarly on the following line the price of two oxen is .ΔΔ; here Pritchett (*ibid.*) restores Π^{Δ}ΔΔ, for a price of 35 dr. per animal, but the restoration HΔΔ is obviously also possible, for a price of 60 dr. per animal. Outside of Attika but close to our time period, in *SIG*³ 1026, a sacrificial calendar from Kos from c. 300, directions are given to sacrifice a young cow (*damalis*) purchased foρ not less than 50 dr. (lines 6-8).

[95] The 5,114 dr. for the hekatomb of 410/9 and the 8,149 dr. spent on oxen by the Delian *amphiktyones* in 375/4 are the only figures we have for money actually expended to purchase animals of any sort, in contrast to the

Amounts Budgeted to Purchase Sheep for Sacrifice

calendar[96]	M adult	F adult/pregnant	ram[97]
"Nikomakhos" [after 403]	15 dr.	12 dr.[98]	17 dr.
Marathon [c. 400-350]	12 dr.	11/17 dr.[99]	12 dr.
Teithras [c. 400-350]		*100	17 dr.[101]
Erkhia [c. 375-350]	12 dr.	10/10 dr.	10 dr.
Salaminioi [c. 363/2]	15 dr.	12/12 dr.	

12 dr. are also allocated for a (possibly female) sheep and 17 dr. for a ram in an account from Eleusis apparently from c. 327/6 (*IG* 2^2 1673.62).[102] In Menander frag. 264 K a *probation* slain in a private sacrifice costs 10 dr.; despite the diminutive, the animal is almost certainly a "little sheep," not a lamb, but it is impossible to say wheth-

---

amounts budgeted for purchases in all our other figures.

[96]See above, note 91, to which add **Teithras Calendar** = *SEG* 21.542; **Erkhia Calendar** = *SEG* 21.541.

[97]The difference between a *krios* (ram) and a male *ois* (adult sheep) is probably that the latter is castrated, the former is not (van Straten [1987] 168-70).

[98]4 dr. are budgeted for an οἶν / λειπογνώμονα at *Hesp.* 1935, p. 21, lines 37-38; cf. above, note 92.

[99]Col. 1, line 28; 16 drakhmai at col. 2, line 12.

[100]Pollitt, the original editor, reads a figure of four drakhmai before the entry ’Αθηνᾶι ὄιν (*sic*) [_ _ _] (Pollitt (1961) 293, no. 1, A.8), but four drakhmai for an adult sheep seems impossibly low; Sokolowski (*LSS* no. 132) suggests οἶν [λειπογνώμονα] (on the adjective *leipogômôn*, see below, Supplementary Note A).

[101]This animal is called an οἶν ἄρρεν (*SEG* 21.542, A.5). Its higher price suggests that it is probably an uncastrated ram (see further above, note 97).

[102]On the 30 dr. for individual sheep at *IG* ^{2} 1672.289 see above, note 11. The figures for sheep have been completely lost from the Attic Stelai.

er the animal is male or female.[103] 7 dr. are allocated for a lamb in the Erkia Calendar.

Amounts Budgeted to Purchase Goats for Sacrifice

calendar[104]	M adult	F adult
Marathon [c. 400-350]	12[105]	
Erkhia [c. 375-350]	12	10
Salaminioi [c. 363/2]		10

5 dr. are also budgeted for a kid in the Erkhia Calendar. These are the only reliable figures for goats found in our sources.[106] The amounts budgeted for the purchase of sheep and goats are all relative-

---

[103] At Lysias 32.21 the speaker asserts that his opponent claimed to have spent 16 dr. on a "little lamb" (ἀρνίον) for the Dionysia, as an example of how he overcharged the estate of which he was guardian. If the speaker is telling the truth, 16 dr. is an inordinately high sum for a lamb, but the figures in the table of prices for sheep suggest that the animal was perhaps a male sheep or even a ram which the speaker misleadingly calls an *arnion*.

[104] See above, notes 91 and 96. *IG* 2² 1363 (from Eleusis at perhaps the beginning of the third century B.C.), budgets a total of 20 dr. for a goat to Pythian Apollo and τὰ ἐφ' ἱεροῖς, an older lamb (πρόγονος, on which see Hesykh. s.v.) and τὰ μετὰ το[ύ]του, a *trapeza* for the god and *hiereōsuna* (sic) for a priest (8-12), but it is impossible to tell how much of the 20 dr. were expected to be spent on the goat and how much on the other items.

[105] 15 dr. are budgeted for a τράγος παμμέλας at 2.18. The difference between a male *aix* and a *tragos* may be that the former is castrated (cf. the discussion of *ois* and *krios*, above, note 97), although either this difference or perhaps the animal's color could account for its premium price.

[106] On the figure of 30 dr. for individual goats in *IG* 2²1672.289 see above, note 11. On the Attic Stelai VI.73 the price of 67 goats is given as ...Δ; Pritchett's restoration (1956, 259) of [Π^HHH]Δ (= c. 10.6 dr. per animal) is a conjecture based on the prices of goats known from other sources, and is of no independent value.

ly consistent, particularly when compared with those budgeted for the purchase of oxen, suggesting that the market for sheep and goats was more stable than that for oxen, a point to which we shall return below. The higher prices expected to be paid for male animals should probably be explained not in economic terms,[107] but rather as a reflection of a traditional cultural bias in favor of males over females. Variations in the prices of rams and pregnant ewes are likewise inexplicable in strictly economic terms and probably reflect the particular values, principally religious, which the different purchasers placed on these animals.

Amounts Budgeted to Purchase Swine for Sacrifice

calendar[108]	adult	pregnant	piglet
"Nikomakhos" [after 403]			3
Marathon [c. 400-350]		20	3
Erkhia [c.375-350]			3
Salaminioi [c. 363/2]	40		3.5

Also at Aristoph. *Pax* 374 (produced in 421) one speaker asks another for 3 dr. to purchase a piglet to sacrifice at his initiation into the Mysteries; the context suggests that at this time 3 dr. was the standard price for this victim.

The number of swine mentioned on extant calendars is too small to serve as a representative sample. Enough piglets are sacrificed, however, to provide us with such a sample, and it is again significant that the anticipated prices for these animals are more or less the same on all of our calendars.

---

[107]Even though male animals, especially castrated ones, would usually yield somewhat more meat than female ones.

[108]See above, note 91.

Concerning these prices, it is probably meaningless to say that sacrificial victims were either "expensive" or "inexpensive," but we can at least get a sense of the relative value of these animals by comparing the prices paid for them with the cost of the foodstuffs (bread, wine, etc.) which made up an Athenian's normal daily diet.[109] By the mid- to late fourth century, an Athenian who purchased his food (rather than growing it himself) would probably have to spend about 2 ob. = 1/3 dr. a day to feed himself, if we may judge e.g. from the figure of 10 dr. per month (= 2 ob. a day) proposed by Demosthenes in 351 as *sitēresion* for a soldier who must purchase food while on campaign,[110] or from the 2 ob. per day paid by the Athenians as *trophē* to their adult *adunatoi*.[111] The prices paid for sacrificial victims certainly do not appear to be exceptionally high when compared with those paid for other foodstuffs, as reflected in these figures

---

[109] The stipends paid to citizens for various civic services (attending an assembly, sitting on a jury, etc. [for which see Aristot. *Ath. Pol.* 62.2]) are not helpful in reconstructing the cost of living since these stipends were really only monetary payments corresponding to the value which Athenian society placed upon these activities; the stipends were not full or partial replacements for wages lost when citizens participated in these activities, and hence *a fortiori* they were not equivalent to the daily cost of living for an individual or a family, as has sometimes been claimed. The notion of replacement wages would be quite out of place in an economy dominated by subsistence farming, where most citizens were not wage earners. Subsistence farmers might participate in government in slack periods, or they could rearrange their working schedules to accommodate their civic responsibilities, but they could not simply take off and leave work undone in the way e.g. an industrial worker might. See further Todd (1990) 168-69; and cf. Rosivach (1985) 53-55, for similar considerations affecting farmers rowing in the fleet.

[110] 10 dr. per month = 1/3 dr. per day, Dem. 4.28.

[111] *Ath. Pol.* 49.4, up from 1/6 dr. earlier in the century; see further Rhodes (1981) 570. Note also *Ath. Pol.* 62.2 for the supplement εἰς σίτησιν of 1/6 dr. given to the *prytaneis* (in addition to their pay of 5/6 dr.) and the 2/3 dr. given εἰς σίτησιν to each of the nine arkhons for himself, his herald and his flute-player (= 1/3 + 1/6 + 1/6?). The 2/3 dr. paid ephebes and the 1 dr. paid their trainers εἰς τροφήν (*Ath. Pol.* 42.3) must include salary in addition to simple maintenance (εἰς σίτησιν); cf. Rhodes (1981) 507.

for *sitēresion/trophē*, and they may in fact even be somewhat low. The 10 dr. paid for a ewe, for example, could also pay for ordinary foodstuffs for one soldier for a month or for thirty soldiers for a day but, whatever the size of the portions, it seems likely that the ewe herself would have provided meat for substantially more than thirty people.[112]

To consider the question of prices more broadly, in examining the tables given above one is struck by the contrast between the sums budgeted for oxen, which display a remarkable range, and the sums budgeted for sheep, goats and piglets, all of which are quite consistent from calendar to calendar over roughly half a century.[113] The relative consistency of anticipated prices for sheep, goats and piglets shows that there was little inflation (or deflation) in the market for these animals.[114] Perhaps more interestingly, it also seems to indicate that the market in these animals did not respond to supply and demand to any significant degree, but rather that the prices for these animals were in some way "fixed." Finally, the relative consistency of the anticipated prices for sheep, goats and piglets indicates that these prices were *per* animal, without regard to the amount of meat the animal could provide or to its quality.

The range of prices for oxen, on the other hand, suggests not merely that these latter prices were affected by supply and demand, but that they also reflected the differences in size and quality from one ox to another. As to this last point, note that the sums actually paid out for the Panathenaic hekatomb of 410/9 (*IG* 1^3 375.7) and for the oxen purchased by the Delian *amphiktyones* in 375/4 (*IG* 2^2 1635.35-36) average out to 51.14 dr. and 77.24 dr. per ox respectively. 51.14 dr. and 77.24 dr. are not normal fractions of drakhmai and obols, and

---

[112]See also Supplementary Note D.

[113]Swine are ignored in what follows since the base of the sample is too small to be of any use.

[114]Given the particular nature of the market for these animals to be discussed below, these price-series cannot be used as an index for overall trends in prices during the period in question.

the odd averages can be explained only if some animals cost more than others in the same lot. Similarly, an entry in the Thorikos Calendar[115] budgeting minimum and maximum amounts for purchasing an ox also indicates that, in contrast to the single specific prices of sheep, goats and piglets, the price of oxen was not fixed in advance, and that those purchasing an ox could bargain to strike the best deal they could, presumably depending on the availability of animals, their size and quality, etc.

In saying that the prices for sheep, goats and piglets were "fixed" I do not mean to suggest that there was some form of price control consciously imposed upon the market for these animals by governmental action. The explanation is, in fact, rather more complicated. We know that the various entities sponsoring sacrifices (the *polis* in its "ancestral" and routine sacrifices and the demes, phratries, etc.) required a fixed number of animals every year. The number of animals to be sacrificed in any given year would have been known in advance by those raising the animals because these sacrifices were "traditional," and thus not likely to vary from year to year, and because in many, if not all cases the number of victims required by the entity was published in calendars similar to those studied above in Chapter 1.[116] Under these circumstances, if producers raised only enough to meet the regular, anticipatable demand for animals, prices could remain relatively constant without external intervention in the form of price controls or price fixing. Such a scenario, however, requires a monopolistic market, or at least the absence of meaningful competition.

To pursue this point further, we should perhaps not even think of a single broad market for sheep or goats or piglets but rather of multi-

---

[115] SEG 33.147.28-30: βοῦ[ν μῆλατ]/τον ἢ τετταράκοντα δραχμῶν [μέχρι πε]ντήκοντα.

[116] Indeed it may even be that one of the reasons for publishing these calendars was to inform producers of anticipated demands and of the amounts budgeted, and hence the amounts the producers could expect to receive for their animals.

ple small closed markets, with the needs of each entity (deme, phratry, etc.) met by its own producer-suppliers who, once established, could easily continue indefinitely as the sole source of the entity's sacrificial victims, or at least as the entity's source of first recourse. Nor would the deme, etc. require a large number of producer-suppliers. The needs of even relatively large demes like Thorikos and Erkhia for sacrificial sheep and goats could probably be met with victims from as few as three to five herds, which could have been owned by even fewer producer-suppliers (since, as we have seen, a single owner could have owned multiple herds); and smaller demes may have required only one or two producer-suppliers.[117]

While we have no direct evidence for the system of closed markets described here, such arrangements would go a long way towards explaining the relative consistency of anticipated prices in the calendars we have been studying. The long-term arrangements with a few individual producers envisaged here are also not unlike e.g. the leases made by demes and other small units which rented out communally owned property for extended periods or even εἰς τὸν ἅπαντα χρόνον, provided certain conditions continued to be met.[118] Like the arrangements envisaged here, such leases ignore strictly economic considerations in favor of more social ones, or perhaps simply the comfort and convenience of long-term arrangements with people who are trusted because they are known.

---

[117]The figure of three to five herds is calculated as follows: A single herd of sheep or goats probably contained in the order of 50 to 100 animals (see above, pp. 80-81). If we assume that sacrificial animals were slain at about six years of age (a conservative estimate: see above, pp. 91-93 with note 81), a herd of 50 to 100 animals will remain constant in size if 8.3 to 16.7 animals are harvested annually (no account being taken for other forms of mortality). Both Thorikos and Erkhia required roughly 40 sheep and goats each year (see above, p. 75). At 8.3 to 16.7 animals per herd, the 40 animals required for sacrifices could be supplied by 2.4 to 4.8 herds.

[118]E.g. *IG* 2^2 2492 (forty years), *IG* 2^2 2496 (εἰς τὸν ἅπαντα χρόνον), *IG* 2^2 2497 (εἰς τὸ[ν ἅπαν]τα χρόνον), *SEG* 24.151 (εἰς τὸ[ν αἰεὶ χρόν]ο[ν]), *SEG* 24.203 (thirty years).

The relative consistency in the anticipated prices for sheep, goats and piglets may be contrasted with the broad range, noted above, of prices, anticipated and actual, for sacrificial oxen. Oxen were sacrificed only rarely by demes, phratries, etc., and the principal purchaser of sacrificial oxen was the *polis*, which required several hundred every year for its *epithetoi heortai*. Indeed, by our earlier calculations from the *Dermatikon* Accounts and other sources[119] it would appear that the sacrifices at the *epithetoi heortai* accounted for roughly four out of every five oxen sacrificed annually in Attika. As we shall see in greater detail in Chapter 3,[120] oxen for some, and possibly all the *epithetoi heortai* were purchased by *boônai* who were chosen annually and probably by lot, so that a different group of individuals dealt with the suppliers every year. Further, the number of animals required for even a single sacrifice was also so great that it could not have been met by a single supplier. With the large and anonymous *polis* dominating a single market for oxen and supplying the funds for most of the purchases, with multiple suppliers providing victims for the *polis'* large *epithetoi heortai*, and with the *polis'* purchasing agents changing from year to year, the market for oxen was unlikely to develop and/or maintain the kind of personal relationships between purchaser and supplier which I believe characterized the multiple smaller markets for sheep, goats and piglets purchased by demes, phratries, etc. In the absence of such relationships in the market for oxen, the size and quality of individual animals,[121] as well as supply and demand, could play a greater role, perhaps accounting for the greater variability

---

[119] Above, p. 76.
[120] Below, pp. 108-14.
[121] Note at Hermippos, frag. 36 K-A the speaker says that poor people (οἱ πενόμενοι) sacrifice lambs and skinny little oxen (βούδια), indicating that the poor quality of these animals made them attractive to poorer purchasers, and more generally that the price of sacrificial oxen was affected by their quality.

in the prices both anticipated and paid for these animals.[122] We may recall in this connection the role of traditional values noted earlier in the pricing of sheep and goats, with higher prices assigned to male animals compared with female. It is not surprising that such values affected prices in the more socially oriented markets of demes, phratries, etc., who sacrificed mainly sheep and goats, and that they were absent in the ox-market dominated by the *polis* where, significantly, there was apparently no difference in the prices for male and female oxen.[123]

A final note on the market for oxen: Most oxen were sacrificed at the *epithetoi heortai*, which were, as we have seen,[124] comparatively recent (sixth- to fourth-century) additions to the aggregate of sacrifices in Attika.[125] The *polis*-dominated oxen market described above was thus a more recent development than the more traditional markets in sheep, goats and piglets; and we should imagine this mar-

---

[122]The *polis* also purchased 500 goats annually for the sacrifice to Artemis Agrotera, but there is no sign that the purchase of so many animals each year had any effect on the structure of the goat market similar to the effect which its purchase of oxen had on the ox market. Of course even with its purchase of 500 animals the polis did not dominate the market for goats as fully as it dominated the market for oxen. All the same, the absence of any effect from the purchase by the *polis* of so many goats suggests that the principal variable in the market for goats (and also for sheep) was the ongoing personal relationships between purchaser and supplier within these smaller units rather than the purchasing power of the *polis*.

[123]Note, for example, that on the Marathon Calendar (*IG* 2^2 1358) oxen are to be sacrificed to the male hero Nekhos (?) (2.20) and to the female Athena Hellôtis (2.35). On the principle that male animals are sacrificed to male gods and female animals to female ones, Athena's *bos* must be female, the hero's *bos* male, but both are budgeted for the same sum, 90 dr.

[124]Above, pp. 54-57.

[125]For older sacrifices I am thinking particularly of those of phratries, *genê*, etc. The deme structure was formalized only with Kleisthenes at the end of the sixth century, but the demes and their sacrifices are likely to have adopted or adapted pre-existing local patterns of sacrifice, even if the specific occasions of sacrifice and the number of victims sacrificed may have evolved over time.

ket and the "industry" which supplied it both expanded *pari passu* with, and was stressed by, the introduction of each new *epithetos heortê* in a way that the more traditional markets in sheep, goats and piglets never were.

To conclude, as we saw earlier, it is most likely that the oxen, sheep and goats slain in public sacrifices came for the most part from comparatively large herds of animals which were raised at least as much for the milk, cheese, wool, etc. they provided as they were in order to serve as sacrificial victims. These large herds of animals were owned by wealthier members of the community, who would thus be the principal suppliers of milk, cheese, etc. for the general market as well as the principal suppliers of the victims sacrificed by the *polis*, demes, etc. In this rather simple sense then we may say that Athens' system of public sacrifice depended upon the wealthier members of the community who sold to the *polis*, demes, etc. most, if not all, of the victims they needed. Further, the particular nature of the traditional markets for sheep and goats, which we have considered above, also suggests a more subtle way in which the system of sacrifice on the level of deme, etc. depended upon a comparatively few wealthy individuals who could afford to function in these non-rational markets, and whose extra-economic interests could be well served by their participation in such markets. We shall return to this point in the next chapter when we consider the acquisition of victims.

3. ACQUIRING THE VICTIMS

Private sacrifices for family and friends usually required only a small animal like a lamb or a kid. Those wealthy enough to own flocks could always use one of these animals for sacrifice,[1] and even most small-scale farmers were likely to have a lamb or two available for a special occasion. City-dwellers and others without their own animals could apparently count on a supply of lambs being available for purchase in the agora, along with *mageiroi* for hire, if needed, to slaughter and cook them.[2]

For public sacrifices, there is no evidence that any Athenian public entity (*polis*, demes, etc.) owned its own flocks or herds.[3] At least on the level of the polis, there is also no evidence that victims were ever donated outright by individuals as an act of piety or civic-mindedness; the situation is a bit less clear-cut in the case of political units below the level of the *polis*, where, as we shall see,[4] there are at least grounds for suspecting that, in some instances, manifestations of *philotimia* in connection with sacrifices need not have been limited to outlays in cash to purchase victims, but may also have included contributions of the victims themselves.

It will become clear in what follows that the agents who purchased victims for the *polis'* large-scale sacrifices and, especially, the sources of funds for their purchases were quite different from the purchasing

---

[1] e.g. Eur. *El.* 494, where the old man brings a sheep from the flocks he tends as part of a meal for the "strangers" Orestes and Pylades (cf. 414); since the animal is still alive, we may assume that it will be sacrificed immediately before the meal.

[2] Cf. e.g. Men. *Sam.* 189-95. Similarly at Plautus, *Aulularia* 280-81 (a play based on a Greek model), we learn that *coqui* (= *mageiroi*) were hired in the *forum* (= *agora*) where two live lambs were also purchased (328) to be slain to celebrate a wedding (cf. 568).

[3] See above, p. 79 with note 29.

[4] Below, pp. 128-31.

agents and funding procedures of the demes and other units. We will therefore treat each separately, beginning with the purchasing and funding done by the *polis*.

As we saw in Chapter 1,[5] the sacrifices sponsored by the polis were divided into two groups, the *patrioi thusiai*, where any distributions of meat were quite small and limited to those directly involved in the ritual (priests, religious brotherhoods, groups of officials, etc.), and the *epithetoi heortai*, the "supplementary festivals" listed in the *Dermatikon* Accounts, where a comparably large number of animals was sacrificed and their meat distributed to the citizen population at large. We will have something to say below[6] about the funding of the *patrioi thusiai*, but since our principal focus is on those sacrifices where meat was available to the general citizen population, we will for now concentrate on the *epithetoi heortai*.

The victims for at least some, and probably all, of the *epithetoi heortai*, were purchased by the *boônai*. As their name indicates, the *boônai* ("ox-buyers") should be associated especially, if not exclusively, with the *epithetoi heortai*, since it was at these festivals that the largest number of oxen were sacrificed. In Demosthenes' speech against Meidias, delivered in 349, the speaker lists the offices to which the people had elected (ἐχειροτονήσατε) Meidias, viz. *mustêriôn epimelêtês*, *hieropoios* and *boônês* (Dem. 21.171). Assuming the accuracy of Demosthenes' statement that the *boônês* was an elected official, and building on a confused tradition found in Harpokration and Suidas,[7] Hiller von Gaertringen interpreted the office of *boônês*

---

[5]Above, pp. 54-55.
[6]Below, pp. 121-27.
[7]Harpokration and Suidas s.v. βοώνης say that the office was λαμπρόν because αἱ μέγισται ἀρχαὶ ἐπὶ τούτῳ ἐχειροτονοῦντο (Harpokration) or because στρατηγούς φασι βοώνας μάλιστα χειροτονεῖσθαι (Suidas). Harpokration's note may well derive from a (mis)interpretation of Dem. 21.171, while Suidas' note appears to combine the information found in Harpokration's note with some recollection of Khares' grand gesture in 356, when he

as a liturgy entailing a substantial outlay of the *boônês'* own money.[8] This, however, does not seem likely. First of all, of the two offices mentioned by Demosthenes together with that of *boônês*, the *mustêriôn epimelêtai* were elected by the people (Arist. *Ath. Pol.* 57.1), but the *hieropoioi* were chosen by lot (Arist. *Ath. Pol.* 54.6). Demosthenes is therefore guilty of some rhetorical looseness here, and there is no way of telling whether that looseness is limited only to the *hieropoioi* or whether it extends to the *boônai* as well. If Demosthenes misrepresented the selection of the *boônai*, and they were in fact chosen by lot and not elected, the office could not possibly have been liturgic; and as we shall see below,[9] there is reason to believe the *boônai* were in fact chosen by lot, not elected. Moreover, at *IG* 2^2 1496.72-73 the *boônai*[10] appear to have returned to the *polis* unspent funds which had been allocated to them for the purchase of sacrificial victims (τὸ περιγενόμε[νον ἀ]πὸ τῆ[ς] | [βο]ωνίας); if their office were liturgic, we would expect them first to have spent all of the money allocated by the *polis*, then to spend their own money, rather than spending their own money first and returning unexpended funds to the *polis*, as they appear to do in *IG* 2^2 1496. Finally, the number of feasts for which the *boônai* purchased victims (see below) would also make their office intolerable if they had to supply a substantial part of the funds themselves. We may conclude then that, whether the *boônai* were chosen by lot or elected, their office was not liturgic, and the funds which they spent were solely those allocated by the *polis* for this purpose. It is impossible to say why the board of *boônai* was created, but we can at least be certain that it was not intended as a device for supplementing state funds for major sacrifices.

---

sacked Lampsakos and Sigeion and sent the oxen which he had captured back to Athens to be (sacrificed, and their meat) distributed κατὰ φυλάς (schol. *ad* Dem. 3.31 [= no. 146a Dilts]); for the date see *PA* 15292.

[8]Hiller von Gaertringen (1897) coll. 716-17.
[9]Below, p. 111.
[10]See below, note 14.

The *boōnai* appear in inscriptions in the plural,[11] and thus as a typical Athenian board of officials, functioning collectively rather than as individuals. We do not know how many *boōnai* made up the board, but a number between three and ten would not be unreasonable.[12] As to their specific duties, we know that the *hieropoioi*[13] were charged, "together with the *boōnai*," with purchasing victims for the Lesser Panathenaia (*IG* 2² 334.17-18); the phrasing suggests that the *boōnai* were to assist the *hieropoioi* and functioned under their authority. In the *Dermatikon* Accounts (*IG* 2² 1496), *boōnai* were responsible for the sale of the hides of the victims sacrificed at the Dionysia τὰ ἐν Πειραιεῖ,[14] the Dionysia τὰ ἐν ἄστει,[15] the Asklepieia in Boedromion[16] and the sacrifice to Zeus Sōtēr.[17] Given

---

[11]The one exception to this is in the *Dermatikon* Accounts, *IG* 2² 1496.120: [ἐκ ..5..ω]ν παρὰ βοώνου. Since this is the only place where the Accounts speak of a single official rather than a group of officials in the plural, one may justifiably suspect an error on the part of the inscriber.

[12]Hansen (1980) 162.

[13]Some scholars, most recently Hansen (1980, 159 with note 19) call attention to the phrase τοὺς ἱεροποιοὺς τοὺς διοικοῦντας τὰ Παναθηναῖα τὰ κατ' ἐνιαυτόν at *IG* 2² 334.31-32 and conclude that these *hieropoioi* were a special board for the Panathenaia, distinct from the *hieropoioi kat' eniauton* mentioned in Aristot. *Ath. Pol.* 54.7. While the language of *IG* 2² 334.31-32 is unexpected (perhaps "those of the *hieropoioi* managing the annual Panathenaia") it does not seem an adequate reason to assume a separate board of ἱεροποιοὶ εἰς τὰ Παναθηναῖα, especially in light of the references elsewhere in *IG* 2² 334 to *hieropoioi* with no further specification (τῶν ἱεροποιῶν, 6; τοὺς ἱεροποιούς, 8; οἱ ἱεροποιοί, 17-18), and in the contemporary *IG* 2² 1496 (παρὰ ἱεροποιῶ[ν, 129).

[14]Line 70-71. The word [βοων]ῶν is restored, but this appears to be the only possible restoration, given the number of spaces in the text as printed in *IG* 2² (there certainly is not enough room for the genitive of *stratēgoi*, the magistrates in charge of the festival). Note also the following item, the payment of the surplus ἀ]πὸ τῆ[ς] | [βο]ωνίας (72-73).

[15]Lines 80-81.

[16]Line 133.

[17]88-89, 118-19, 133. Note also [ἐκ ..5..ω]ν παρὰ βοώνου (on which see also above, note 11). Apparently the *boōnai* were not responsible for the sale of the hides from the Panathenaia (see further below).

their name ("ox-buyers"), it is reasonable to assume that these *boônai* were also involved in the initial purchase of the victims whose hides they were now responsible for selling. It is also reasonable to assume that these *boônai* were the same as the *boônai* who purchased the victims for the Panathenaia, and that they also functioned here under the authority of the *hieropoioi* or other presiding officials, as they appear to have done in the case of the Panathenaia.

Curiously, even though the *boônai* are linked with the *hieropoioi* in the purchase of victims for the Panathenaia in *IG* 2^2 334.17-18, in the *Dermatikon* Accounts the *boônai* were not responsible for the sale of hides from the Panathenaia, at least in 332/1, when the task was assigned to the *hieropoioi* (*IG* 2^2 1496.129; the entries for the Panathenaia in the other years have been lost from the stone). This inconsistency would seem to confirm the hypothesis advanced above that the *boônai* functioned as assistants to the *hieropoioi*; in some cases the *hieropoioi* saw to the sale of the hides themselves, at other times they delegated the task to the *boônai*.[18] If the *boônai* functioned under the *hieropoioi*, who were chosen by lot, it would further increase the likelihood that the *boônai* themselves were similarly chosen by lot, and that their office was not liturgic in character.

It is noteworthy that the *boônai* are listed as selling the hides of victims from only some of the *epithetoi heortai* listed in the *Dermatikon* Accounts, while responsibility for the sale of hides from the other festivals was assigned variously to the *mustêriôn epimelêtai*,[19] the *stratêgoi*,[20] the *tou dêmou sullogeis*,[21] and the *hieropoioi*.[22] In

---

[18] Note in this regard that the *Dermatikon* Accounts are descriptive (telling what was done), unlike e.g. the various sacrificial calendars which are prescriptive (detailing what should be done).

[19] At the Dionysia τὰ ἐπὶ Ληναίωι (74-75).

[20] At the sacrifice to Hermes Hêgemonios (84-85, 115-16), the sacrifice to Eirênê (94-95, 127-28), at the sacrifice to Ammon (96-97), and at the sacrifice to Dêmokratia (131-32).

[21] At the Olympieia (82-83, 113-14). On the *dêmou sullogeis* see *SIG*^{3} 944, note 10.

the case of the Dionysia τὰ ἐν Πειραιεῖ it would appear that the *boônai* sold the hides in 334/3,[23] but the *stratêgoi* did so in 331/0, the only other date for which the entry for this feast is reasonably intact (144-45). It is possible that the *boônai* were associated with this festival only in 334/3, but—much as was the case with the Panathenaia—it is also possible that the *boônai* bought oxen for this festival throughout the period, and that in some years the *stratêgoi* (who were in charge of the festival) sold their hides, and at other times the *boônai* (who purchased the oxen) did so. As for the other festivals where the *boônai* are not mentioned, we have no way of knowing whether the officials who are identified as selling the victims' hides also purchased the victims, or whether the *boônai* were also involved, but if the *boônai* purchased victims but did not sell their hides in the case of the Panathenaia and apparently also of the Dionysia τὰ ἐν Πειραιεῖ, then it is at least possible that the *boônai* purchased the victims for all of the *epithetoi heortai* in the *Dermatikon* Accounts (presumably under the authority of the officials in charge of the festivals), even when they are not specifically mentioned there.

As we saw earlier, the *boônai* were probably chosen by lot, but whether chosen by lot or elected, they would have held their office for one year, as both categories of Athenian officials typically did. In either case, but particularly if they were chosen by lot, the membership of the board of *boônai* would change from year to year, with consequences for the ox-market such as we saw in the previous chapter.[24] This of course raises the issue of expertise, since as we also saw in the previous chapter,[25] prices for oxen were not fixed, and their purchasers appear to have bargained with their suppliers even over the purchase of individual animals. Since far and away most

---

[22] At the sacrifice to Agathê Tukhê (76-77), at the Asklepieia in Elaphebolion (78-79), at the Bendideia (86, 117), and at the Eleusinia (130).
[23] See above, note 14.
[24] Above, pp. 104-5.
[25] Above, pp. 101-2.

Athenian citizens were farmers, the odds were always good that some farmers with the necessary practical experience would be selected every year, and the Athenians appear to have been willing, in the interest of democracy, to tolerate the inexperienced, especially townsmen, whom the lot also threw up.

The earliest evidence for the *boônai* is the passage discussed above from Demosthenes' speech against Meidias delivered in 349 (Dem. 21.171). Of the epigraphic evidence, *IG* 2^2 1496 (the *Dermatikon* Accounts) covers the period from 334/3 to 331/0 while *IG* 2^2 334 on the Lesser Panathenaia probably dates to 335/4 and is almost certainly, like the *Dermatikon* Accounts, Lykourgan in date and inspiration. There is no way of telling how long the board of *boônai* remained in existence after 331/0, the latest date in the *Dermatikon* Accounts, and there is likewise no way of telling how long the board was in existence before Demosthenes' speech against Meidias in 349. *IG* 1^3 375, from 410/9, shows the *hieropoioi kat' eniauton* receiving funds for the purchase of the Panathenaic hekatomb of that year (6-7), but strictly speaking this is not inconsistent with the language of *IG* 2^2 334.17-18, which has the *hieropoioi* purchasing victims "together with the *boônai*" for the Panathenaia of 335/4, and it need not be seen as evidence that the board of *boônai* did not yet exist in 410/9. A scholion to Dem. 21.171 (= no. 584 Dilts) glosses ἱεροποιόν there as τὸν ἐπισκοποῦντα τὰ θύματα μὴ ἀδόκιμα καὶ πηρά, but it is quite possible that the scholion has migrated, and that it originally glossed βοώνην in the same passage. Finally, in *IG* 2^2 47, from the start of the fourth century, the *hieropoioi* are in charge of the *heortê* of the Asklepieia "in respect to the funds supplied by the *dêmos*" for the festival, with responsibility for the distribution of meat (31-39), but, again, this need not rule out a role for the *boônai* in the actual purchase of the victims.

To summarize our discussion of the *boônai*, it seems likely that in the 330's, at the time of the *Dermatikon* Accounts, the *boônai* purchased sacrificial victims for all of the *epithetoi heortai* in the Accounts.²⁶ Two earlier inscriptions, *IG* 1³ 375 and *IG* 2² 47, show the *hieropoioi* receiving funds in one case for the purchase of victims and in the other for the general superintendence of the festival which included the distribution of sacrificial meat; however, as we have seen, this financial role of the *hieropoioi* still leaves room for the *boônai* actually to purchase the victims under the general supervision, financial and otherwise, of the *hieropoioi*. And what is true of the relation of *boônai* and *hieropoioi* in the case of those festivals for which the *hieropoioi* were responsible will also be true of the relation of *boônai* to *epimelêtai*, *stratêgoi*, etc. in the case of those festivals for which these other officials were responsible. Our understanding of the role of the *boônai*, and particularly their subordination to the *hieropoioi kat' eniauton*, who were chosen by lot, makes it quite unlikely that the *boônai* were elected officials, despite Demosthenes' statement in his speech against Meidias (21.171). If not elected, the *boônai* must have been chosen by lot, with a totally new board of *boônai* chosen every year. Because they were chosen by lot, their office could in no way be liturgic, since there was no way the lot could assure the selection of men wealthy enough to provide the funds a liturgy would require. Rather, all of the victims purchased by the *boônai*, and thus all the victims sacrificed at *epithetoi heortai*,²⁷ were paid for with funds allocated for this purpose by the *polis*.²⁸

---

²⁶It is also possible that, despite their name, they also purchased the goats to be sacrificed to Artemis Agrotera, but we have no evidence for this.

²⁷This statement will be true even if *hieropoioi*, *stratêgoi*, etc., rather than *boônai*, purchased the victims at some of the other *epithetoi heortai* since there is no evidence that any of these other officials, even the elected *stratêgoi* and *epimelêtai mustêriôn*, were thought of as performing a liturgic function. In the case of the *hieropoioi*, who were chosen by lot, a liturgic function is impossible.

²⁸I believe this would also be true of the penteteric festivals, with the obvious exception of the mission to Delos, which the Athenian *amphiktyones* for Delos paid for from the rentals of the estates on Delos and Rheneia, and from interest on loans made by the shrine (for these expenditures see *IG* 2² 1635+.36-40, from 377/6).

ACQUIRING THE VICTIMS

We have surprisingly little evidence for the fiscal arrangements that supported the system of large-scale public sacrifices on the level of the *polis*. In a passage from the *Areiopagitikos*, which we have already discussed (7 *Areop*. 29), Isokrates contrasts the *patrioi thusiai* with the *epithetoi heortai*, saying that the former were funded ἀπὸ μισθωμάτων, i.e. from the leasing out of sacred lands, while the latter were celebrated sumptuously (μεγαλοπρεπῶς), but he does not say what the source of their funding was. In a somewhat tendentious passage from the speech against Timokrates (24.96-97) Demosthenes says that revenues from taxes secure τὴν διοίκησιν . . . τήν θ' ἱερὰν καὶ τὴν ὁσίαν (96; cf. διοικεῖται τὰ κοινά, 97), i.e. that the *polis'* ordinary expenses, both sacred and secular, were met by income from taxes (ἐκ τῶν τελῶν).[29] Demosthenes continues by saying that the proper payment of these taxes provides the money spent for meetings of the *ekkle^sia*, sacrifices, meetings of the *boulê*, the cavalry, etc. (τὰ εἰς τὰς ἐκκλησίας καὶ τὰς θυσίας καὶ τὴν βουλὴν καὶ τοὺς ἱππέας καὶ τἆλλα χρήματα, 97). Now the *thusiai* which Demosthenes says were funded from tax revenues cannot be the *patrioi thusiai*, which we know from Isokrates (7 *Areop*. 29) were financed by the leasing out of sacred lands, but must rather be those at the *epithetoi heortai*.[30] In other words, the costs associated with the *epithetoi heortai*, notably the purchase of sacrificial victims, were seen as ordinary recurring expenses, no different from e.g. the regular payments to citizens who attended meetings of the *ekklêsia* and *boulê*, and like

---

[29] This is a slight misstatement on Demosthenes' part since the *polis'* ordinary revenues also included fines and confiscations, and royalties from the exploitation of resources owned by the *polis*, notably contracts to mine the veins at Laureion. See further below, p. 120.

[30] The context makes it most unlikely that Demosthenes has in mind here either the routine sacrifices at meetings of the *boulê*, etc. (on which see above, pp. 46-47) or the extraordinary sacrifices on special occasions (on which, see above, p. 61), even though both of these would also have to be paid for out of ordinary revenues.

the expenditures for the *ekklēsia* and the *boulē*, they would have been paid out of the *polis*' ordinary budget.[31]

One would assume that, at least in the fourth century, decrees of the *ekklēsia* could allocate funds for special *ad hoc* sacrifices or for the first celebration of events meant eventually to become permanent, but that permanent fiscal arrangements for established events were usually spelled out in laws passed through the process of *nomothesia*.[32] This is the process we see reflected on a smaller scale in *IG* 7 4254.37-45, where a decree of 329/8 directs the *tamias tou dēmou* to provide funds for a sacrifice at a newly established festival in honor of Amphiareus for the current year, and directs the matter of permanent funding to be taken up by the *nomothetai* at their next meeting. In the case of the *epithetoi heortai*, one would also assume that the laws governing these festivals included among their provisions the specific number of victims to be purchased and/or the amounts to be allocated for their purchase at each event. We may perhaps see evidence of the effect of such provisions in the *Dermatikon* Accounts (*IG* 2^2 1496.72-73), where the *boōnai* returned some of the funds allocated for the purchase of victims for the Dionysia τὰ ἐν Πειραιεῖ, presumably because they bargained well and thus spent less than the total amount available to them to purchase the required number of victims. On the other hand, from time to time the amount of funds the *polis* could provide for the purchase of victims might fall short of the requirements of the law, and adjustments would have to be made to ac-

---

[31]We have evidence from the first century B.C. for a separate budget for sacrifices (ἡ ἱερὰ διάταξις) administered by its own treasurer (*IG* 2^2 1035.16-17; *IG* 2^2 3503.17-19), but there is no evidence for a separate budget for *ta hiera* in the fourth century. Indeed, the recapitulation διοικεῖται τὰ κοινά (Dem. 24.97) indicates that τὴν διοίκησιν . . . τήν θ' ἱερὰν καὶ τὴν ὁσίαν (Dem. 24.96) refers to a single account for both, and not to separate accounts for ἡ διοίκησις ἡ ἱερά and ἡ διοίκησις ἡ ὁσία, as argued by Schlaifer (1940) 233.

[32]Before the introduction of *nomothesia* similar arrangements would have been determined by the *ekklēsia* itself.

commodate the law's ideal requirements to the real variations in Athens' public income.[33]

That expenditures for the *epithetoi heortai* were part of the *polis'* ordinary budget will go a long way to explaining why we have so little evidence for their funding, since routine expenditures rarely make their way into either our literary sources or the epigraphic record, both of which are more often concerned with the extraordinary than the ordinary. Thus, for example, *IG* 2^2 334 (from c. 335/4) mentions the purchase of *additional* victims for the Lesser Panathenaia with 41 mnai in rentals from land newly acquired probably in Oropos,[34] but it says nothing about funding for the ordinary purchase of victims for the hekatomb, which presumably would have been included in the regular budget of the *polis*. From *IG* 1^3 375 we learn that in 410/9 the Treasurers of Athena transferred 5,115 dr. to the *hieropoioi kat' eniauton* for the hekatomb at the Greater Panathenaia of that year (6-7). Since no similar transfers occur in any of the other years covered by the extant accounts of the Treasurers of Athena[35] we must conclude that the transfer in 410/9 was an extraordinary occurrence, perhaps due to wartime exigencies, and that in other years the hekatomb was included in the *polis'* regular budget to be paid for out of ordinary revenues. The only example from the epigraphic record for ordinary funding of an *epithetos heortē* appears to be *IG* 2^2 47 (from the early part of the fourth century) relating to the cult of Asklepios, where funds ἐκ τõ λιθοτομε[ί]ο (30), presumably one of the rock-cuttings in the Peiraieus,[36] are to be used for the *prothumata* to

---

[33] On this point see further below, p. 118.

[34] Lines 16-17. See further Rosivach (1991) 436-39.

[35] In 415/4 funds were transferred from the Treasurers of Athena via the Hellenotamiai to the *athlothetai* (*IG* 1^3 370.66-68) and possibly in 406/5 directly to the *athlothetai* (*IG* 1^3 378.14), presumably for prizes at the Panathenaia but not for the hekatomb, in contrast to 410/9, when funds were directly allocated to the *athlothetai* but additional funds were also transferred to the *hieropoioi kat' eniauton* for the hekatomb (*IG* 1^3 375.5-7).

[36] On Attic quarries see further Ampolo (1982) 251-60.

Asklepios and for the construction of his temple (29-32), while the *hieropoioi* are "to manage the *hortē* in respect to what comes from the *dēmos*" (ἐπιμε<με>λεῖσθαι τῆς ἑ[ο]ρτῆς τὸ ἐκ τοῦ [sic] δήμο γιγνόμενον) in order that they might distribute as much meat as possible to the Athenians (32-35). Here τὸ ἐκ τοῦ δήμο γιγνόμενον (sc. ἀργύριον) would be the ordinary allocation for the *heortē*, contrasted with the revenues "from the quarry" which have been dedicated to the cult's *prothumata* and to the construction of the temple. The phrase τὸ ἐκ τοῦ δήμο γιγνόμενον also raises the possibility that despite the provisions of the relevant laws, the amount actually paid out for victims at the Asklepieia (and presumably also at the other *epithetoi heortai*) varied from year to year,[37] perhaps depending upon the amount of money the *polis* had available to purchase victims in a given year (or even at a given point in a given year).[38] Such variations in funding levels would mean that fewer animals might be purchased for a particular festival in one year than in another, and this could help to explain the differences we noticed earlier[39]2 in the *Dermatikon* Accounts, in the amounts received from the sale of hides of victims sacrificed at the same festival in succeeding years.

If funds for the *epithetoi heortai* were part of the regular budget of the *polis*, the normal procedure would be for the *apodektai*[40] to allocate funds either to the officials in charge of each festival and/or to the *boōnai* as needed to purchase sacrificial victims.[41] There is,

---

[37]The obvious exception to this would be the Panathenaic hekatomb where, by definition, 100 oxen had to be sacrificed.

[38]The task of adjusting outlays required by law to the realities of variable incomes probably fell to the *boulē* (Jones [1966] 103).

[39]Above, pp. 50-53.

[40]The *apodektai* were the officials who received state revenues from various sources and allocated them to the accounts of the officials who would spend them.

[41]That is presuming that the office of ὁ ἐπὶ τῆι διοικήσει did not yet exist (the office is not mentioned in Aristotle's *Ath. Pol.*, on which see Rhodes [1981] 516). If the office did exist, the *apodektai* would have given the official ὁ ἐπὶ τῆι διοικήσει the money he needed for his entire budget, and the

however, a tantalizing statement in a spurious decree[42] quoted in the manuscripts of Demosthenes' *de corona* (18.118) to the effect that when Demosthenes was in charge of the Theoric Fund he contributed an additional 100 mnai (= 10,000 dr.) of his own money to the spectators from all the tribes for sacrifices (ἐπέδωκε τοῖς ἐκ πασῶν τῶν φυλῶν θεωροῖς ἑκατὸν μνᾶς εἰς θυσίας). This statement could be easily dismissed were it not for the fact that a confused version of the decree is paraphrased in Ps.-Plut. *vit. X orat.* 846A, which says that Demosthenes paid from his own funds 100 mnai for repair of the city's fortifications (the spurious decree says he spent 3 talents [= 18,000 dr.] from his own funds on the fortifications) and that he contributed an additional 10,000 (dr.?) for θεωροῖς. Either the statement in the *vit. X orat.* draws on the spurious decree, or both draw upon a common source which seems to have said that when Demosthenes was in charge of the Fund he contributed (presumably on a single occasion) 10,000 dr. of his own money for the purchase of additional victims beyond the unknown number funded by an allocation from the Theoric Fund. We do not normally associate sacrifices with payments from the Theoric Fund, but the spurious decree in the *de corona* and the statement in the *vit. X orat.* at least open up the possibility that at some point responsibility for the administration of funds for certain sacrifices was assigned to the Theoric Fund,[43] its overseers receiving money from the *apodektai* and paying it out to the officials in charge of the festivals and/or the *boōnai* to purchase sacrificial victims; if the Theoric Fund did administer funds for sacrifices,

---

latter would then have disbursed the funds as needed to the officials in charge of the festivals and/or the *boōnai*.

[42] The decree as quoted must be spurious since it names the wrong arkhon, and there are differences in wording when the actual decree is quoted both by Demosthenes elsewhere in the *de corona* and by Aiskhines in his speech against Ktesiphon (Aiskh. 3).

[43] On the expanded role of the overseer(s) of the Theoric Fund in other areas of public finance during the middle third of the fourth century see Aiskh. 3 *Ktes.* 25, and more generally Rhodes (1972) 106-7.

the victims purchased with those funds are most likely to have been those slain at either some or all of the *epithetoi heortai*, where meat was distributed to the citizen populace at large.

Whether the monies to purchase sacrificial victims for the *epithetoi heortai* were or were not administered through the Theoric Fund, it is important to remember that they were paid out of the ordinary revenues of the *polis*, unlike some of the other expenses associated with some of these festivals (e.g. the costs of choruses at the two Dionysia) which were paid for by liturgies, and unlike the victims sacrificed at the *patrioi thusiai*, which were purchased, as we shall shortly see, with income from sacred lands rented out for this purpose.[44] Further, particularly in the fourth century, after the Athenians had lost the income from their empire, the ordinary revenues of the *polis* came, generally speaking, from only three sources, from rentals of resources owned by the *polis* (especially royalties from the Laureion silver mines), from taxes, and from fines and confiscations.[45] Some taxes were paid by non-citizens, notably the head-tax paid by metics and some portion of the taxes on imports and exports, and the rest were paid by citizens. As for the citizens, it was in the nature of the Athenian system that the tax burden fell most heavily on those most able to pay, namely the wealthier Athenians. This is most obviously true of extraordinary taxes like the *eisphora*, but it is also by and large true of the ordinary taxes, especially the indirect ones such as those on

---

[44] The "supplementary" oxen purchased for the Panathenaia out of "rentals" from Oropos were a late innovation in the funding of the Panathenaia, and probably in the funding of sacrifices in general. At any rate, there is no evidence for any victims at any of the other *epithetoi heortai* being purchased with funds from rentals; note also that even at the Panathenaia, the principal sacrifice (the hekatomb) was not financed through rentals but rather, apparently, from general revenues. On the "supplementary" oxen at the Panathenaia, see further the discussion above, p. 71 and note 10 there.

[45] On the regular sources of income for the Athenian state see generally Boeckh (1886) 372-468.

imports, since the wealthy were the ones most able to purchase the goods so taxed.⁴⁶ And the burden of fines and confiscations likewise fell predominantly upon the wealthy. On the other hand, it was also in the nature of the Athenian system that the more visible benefits of government, in the form of state pay, etc., accrued disproportionately to the poor,⁴⁷ if only because there were so many more of them. What was true of state pay and the like was also true of sacrifices, as the so-called Old Oligarch recognized. Wealthy people could pay for their own sacrifices but, according to the Old Oligarch, the poor, at least as individuals, could not; and so in Athens' democracy "the *polis* sacrifices numerous victims at public expense (δημοσίᾳ)," and thus with revenues derived to a large extent from the wealthy, "but it is the *dêmos*," and hence predominantly the poor, "who do the feasting and receive a share of the victims."⁴⁸ We need only add that when the Old Oligarch speaks of the *polis* sacrificing many victims (ἱερεῖα πολλά) to distribute their meat to the poor, he must have in mind primarily the *epithetoi heortai*,⁴⁹ since these were, as we have seen, the only annual events sponsored by the *polis* at which there were significant distributions of meat to the general citizen population.

Since our principal focus is on large-scale meat distributions we need not examine in too great detail the procedures for funding the *patrioi thusiai*, where, as we have seen, relatively few victims were

---

⁴⁶With import taxes, etc. the merchant may pay the actual tax to the *polis* or its agent, but he then passes on the cost of the tax to the purchaser in the form of a higher price, so that the burden of the tax ultimately falls not on the merchant but on the purchaser.

⁴⁷In contrast to the less visible benefits of safety, security and prosperity, which accrued disproportionately to the wealthy who had so much more to lose in their absence.

⁴⁸[Xen.] *Ath. Pol.* 2.9 (the passage is quoted in full above, p. 1).

⁴⁹And perhaps, but certainly to a lesser degree, both the penteteric festivals and the special *ad hoc* sacrifices discussed above, pp. 60-61.

sacrificed and their meat distributed to necessarily smaller groups, presumably those who participated in each sacrifice.[50] A few brief remarks will be in order, however, on how the funding of the *patrioi thusiai* differed from that of the *epithetoi heortai*.

Like the *epithetoi heortai*, the *patrioi thusiai* were also sponsored by the *polis*, but unlike the *epithetoi heortai* they were not paid for out of the general revenues of the *polis*. Rather, as we know from Isok. 7 Areop. 29, the *patrioi thusiai* were funded ἀπὸ μισθωμάτων,[51] i.e. from rentals of properties (*temenê*), usually farm lands but also apparently houses,[52] which were thought of as belonging to the gods whose cult was subsidized by income from their rents.

Even if these *temenê* were owned by the gods, they were still administered by the *polis*. We know from Aristot. *Ath. Pol.* 47.4-5 that the *arkhôn basileus* had the primary responsibility for renting *temenê*, subject to compulsory review by the *boulê*,[53] that rent payments were made to the *apodektai*, and that the public slave (ὁ δημόσιος) was responsible for record-keeping. Given the Athenian preference for boards over individual magistrates as a measure against corruption in financial matters, it seems improbable that a single individual chosen by lot, the *arkhôn basileus* in this case, would be given full responsibility, even under the supervision of the *boulê*, for the rentals of these public lands, and one might well suspect that e.g.

---

[50] See above, pp. 46-47.

[51] See also Supplementary Note F.

[52] There is some confusion of terminology here. Xen. *Vect.* 4.19 distinguishes between *temenê* and *oikiai*, but Aristot. *Ath. Pol.* 47.4 either combines both land and houses under *temenê* or simply ignores the houses. For the rental of houses, besides Xen. *Vect.* 4.19, cf. e.g. *IG* 2^2 1590, from 343/2, a fragmentary account of rentals of buildings belonging to Athena Polias (on the relation of this and related inscriptions to the *patrioi thusiai* see below, pp. 125-27).

[53] "The *basileus* brings in (*sc.* to the *boulê*) the rentals of *temenê*, having written them on whitened tablets" (εἰσφέρει δὲ καὶ ὁ βασιλεὺς τὰς μισθώσεις τῶν τεμενῶν ἀναγράψας ἐν γραμματείοις λελευκωμένοις, Aristot. *Ath. Pol.* 47.2).

the *pôlêtai* were also involved.⁵⁴ This, at any rate, is what happens in *IG* 1³ 84, our one detailed instance of a *temenos* rented by the *polis*. The inscription, dated 418/7, prescribes how the *arkhôn basileus* and the *pôlêtai* are to rent out the *temenos* of Kodros, Neleus and Basilê, and specifies that the rent is to be paid to the *apodektai* who will then hand it over to the Treasurers of the Other Gods κατὰ τὸν νόμον.⁵⁵ The phrase κατὰ τὸν νόμον (18) seems to indicate that it was the regular practice, at least at the time of this inscription, for the *apodektai* to hand over to the Treasurers of the Other Gods the monies paid in rent for all (or at least most) *temenê* administered by the *polis*; and, one would assume, the Treasurers of the Other Gods, in turn, disbursed the monies as needed to the appropriate priest or other official in charge of each *patrios thusia*. Indeed, seen in this light it would appear that one of the reasons for publishing the so-called Calendar of Nikomakhos and of its predecessors was to provide a detailed schedule of disbursements by the Treasurers⁵⁶ for the *patrioi thusiai*.⁵⁷ Since rent payments were customarily made in the

---

⁵⁴Thus Walbank (1991) 158.

⁵⁵Lines 11-18. This is actually an amendment to the main motion (5-7) where the *pôlêtai* are directed to contract for fencing the *hieron* of these deities; the purpose of the amendment is to transfer this task to the renter, who is to fence the *hieron* at his own expense, and not to alter the procedures for renting out the *temenos*, which had been described in short-hand terms in the original motion, with only the *arkhôn basileus* mentioned.

⁵⁶At the time the Calendar of Nikomakhos was codified the board of the Treasurers of the Other Gods had been combined with that of the Treasurers of the sacred monies of Athena. For the chronology, see below, note 59.

⁵⁷This of course raises the question of how the income from rentals was handled before the creation of the board of Treasurers of the Other Gods in 435/4. In the Calendar of Nikomakhos there are several rubrics introduced with the preposition ἐκ (ἐκ τῶν κατὰ μῆνα, ἐκ τῶν φυλοβασιλικῶν, ἐκ τῶν μὴ ῥητῆι and ἐκ τῶν σ[), which have often been interpreted as separate funds out of which specific sacrifices were financed (thus originally Hauvette-Besnault [1879, 71-72] in his *editio princeps* of *IG* 2² 1357), but it is difficult to imagine how or why separate funds continued to exist after the board of Treasurers was created in 435/4. Dow's alternative explanation (1959, 15-21), that the

ninth prytany (Aristot. *Ath. Pol.* 47.4) but funds to purchase sacrificial victims were disbursed throughout the year, it is understandable that the *apodektai* would deposit these funds with the Treasurers until they were needed.[58]

Although *IG* 1³ 84 is from the fifth century, it is quite likely that similar procedures were also followed in the fourth century, with the *pôlêtai* still working with the *arkhôn basileus* to arrange contracts for the renting of *temenê*, and with the *apodektai* receiving the monies from the rents and immediately handing them over to the Treasurers, who then disbursed them as needed. There is no reason to believe that these procedures were affected by organizational changes in the board of Treasurers in the late fifth and into the fourth centuries.[59]

If the *apodektai* did indeed hand over the income from rentals to the Treasurers, who then disbursed monies as needed for the *patrioi thusiai* in the manner described above, such a procedure opens up the

---

ἐκ-rubrics indicate the sources of law (i.e. earlier partial codifications), and not sources of funding, would eliminate the problem. It is also possible that separate funds once existed but were eliminated when the board of Treasurers was created, surviving only in fossilized form, as labels now indicating, as Dow would have it, the legal justification for the sacrifices in question.

[58] As noted below (pp. 131-32 with note 84), the *genos* of the Salaminioi received victims ἐκ τô δημοσίο (*SEG* 21.527.20-21); this, however, could simply be a shorthand reference to the whole system of public finance, including the Treasury of the Other Gods (which was controlled by the *dêmos*), and not a reference specifically to the current account of the *apodektai*.

[59] The Treasurers of the Other Gods and the Treasurers of Athena were combined in a single board in 406/5; the two boards were separated again probably in 385/4, and in 343/2 or a little earlier the Treasurers of the Other Gods disappeared and their administrative functions were assumed by the Treasurers of Athena (Ferguson [1932] 104-6); these Treasurers may perhaps have been again styled the Treasurers of Athena and the Other Gods (see below, note 63, on *IG* 2² 1590.2). For evidence of a role for the Treasurers in the fourth century, see the law quoted at [Dem.] 43.58 which speaks of those not paying rentals τῶν τεμενῶν τῆς θεοῦ καὶ τῶν ἄλλων θεῶν καὶ τῶν ἐπωνύμων, where the phrasing probably reflects the involvement of the Treasurers of Athena and the Other Gods in the process (the *temenê* of the *epônumoi* are a puzzle).

possibility that rent from leasing out the *temenos* of one god might be siphoned off to pay for sacrifices to other gods whose *temenos*-rentals had fallen in arrears or whose sacrifices were not supported by rental monies, or even that revenues in excess of sacrificial requirements might find their way into the general coffers of the *polis*. Something like this may well be what the speaker of Lysias 30.19-20 wishes to suggest when he says that the new sacrifices costing six talents allegedly added by Nikomakhos drained off funds which were thus not available for what the speaker considers the real *patrioi thusiai*, three talents' worth of which thus went unperformed, whereas without these six talents' worth of "new" sacrifices all of the "real" *patrioi thusiai* would have been performed and a surplus of three talents would still have accrued to the *polis*.[60] If this understanding of procedures associated with the *patrioi thusiai* is correct, then in sharp contrast with the *epithetoi heortai*, which were nothing but a drain on the general revenues of the *polis*, the *patrioi thusiai* were at least theoretically self-supporting, thanks to the system of *temenos*-rentals, even if from time to time the *polis*, which administered the system, may have had to step in to adjust accounts or make up shortfalls when renters fell behind in their payments.

IG 2^2 1590-91+, a series of fragmentary inscriptions dating from 343/2[61] and recently (re)published and studied by M. B. Walbank,[62] probably contained, before they were damaged, a complete record of all of the lands rented out to support the *patrioi thusiai*.[63]

---

[60] On Nikomakhos' "new" sacrifices see Supplementary Note F.

[61] Dated by the arkhôn's name in the first line of *IG* 2^2 1590. Walbank (1983, 227-28) sees the inscriptions in two series, the first, on a single stele, dated to 343/2, and the second, on four other stelai, representing a revision the first list in 333/2, but his argument is not persuasive.

[62] Walbank (1983) 100-35, 117-231. The texts of the leases are also republished in Walbank (1991) 179-84, 189-94.

[63] It is difficult to see what else they might be. The words [']Aθηνᾶς Πολιάδο[ς καὶ τῶν ἄλλων θεῶν, Walbank's tentative restoration of *IG* 2^2 1590.2, bring us back to the Treasurers of Athena and the Other Gods who had a role, as we have seen, in the receipt of rentals for the *patrioi thusiai*.

The inscriptions, as they stand, list for each lease the name of the god to whom the property belongs, a brief description of the property, the name of the renter and of his guarantor(s), and the amount of the rent. According to Walbank, of the 86 renters who can be identified, 15 definitely belonged to the liturgic class or were members of families prominent in public life; and an additional four were metics, at least two of whom belonged to families which later received citizenship, and possessed considerable wealth. Walbank was struck by the large number of renters who cannot be identified as rich or famous, and assuming that those who cannot be so identified must be poor, he speculated that the system of leases found in these inscriptions reflects a preference for the poor.[64] Given the spotty nature of our sources, Walbank's assumption that anyone who cannot be identified as either rich (i.e. as a member of the liturgic class) or famous must be poor is a very hazardous one. Indeed, with 15 renters out of 86 identified as rich or famous, the rich or famous already form a substantially higher percentage of the names in our inscription (17%) than they did in the adult male citizen population at large, where the 1,200 persons on the trierarchic register accounted for only 4% of the total adult male

---

Several of the gods whose sacrifices appear on the Calendar of Nikomakhos also appear in these inscriptions (Athena Polias [Walbank's lease no. 77], Herakles [leases nos. 31-37], Apollo [leases nos. 20-23] and Zeus, albeit not Zeus Olympios [leases nos. 23-26 and 43]); more generally, the gods on these inscriptions are almost exclusively the major sort found by and large in the Calendar of Nikomakhos, and not the local gods and heroes found on non-*polis* calendars. Walbank does not seem to have considered the possibility that the properties in these inscriptions supported the *patrioi thusiai*; rather he believes that the *polis* "took over . . . the property of cults that was *not* under the control of demes, phylai, or religious corporations or the like" (1983, 230) but, again, it is difficult to imagine what kind of land this might have been, belonging to a cult but not controlled by a religious corporation or the like.

[64]Walbank (1983) 224-25.

ACQUIRING THE VICTIMS 127

citizen population of c. 27,500.[65] Further, to the 15 renters identified by Walbank as rich or famous we should probably add at least the two metics whose families are later attested as wealthy, as well as an additional five citizens who are not otherwise known but who are wealthy enough to rent property for the substantial amount of 600 dr. or more per year,[66] for a total of 22 out of 86 (26%). Considering how incomplete our knowledge is of who was wealthy and who was not, 26% is a remarkably high figure, and it suggests that many of the other renters listed in our inscriptions might also be identified as wealthy if our knowledge were better. In effect, though it cannot be proven, one certainly has the impression that the properties leased out to support the *patrioi thusiai* were rented by the wealthier members of the community. Such an impression is consistent, as we shall see, with what we know about other leases whose income was used to support sacrifices.

Finally brief mention should be made of three other categories of sacrifices sponsored by the *polis*, the routine sacrifices offered by the *prytaneis*, arkhons, etc. as part of their regular meetings, the special *ad hoc* sacrifices offered on occasions of public celebration, and the penteteric festivals.[67] We have no evidence of how any of these categories was regularly financed,[68] but one would assume that the expenses of the routine sacrifices were included in the ordinary budget of the group in question, while the special sacrifices and the penteteric festivals (with the exception of the Mission to Delos) were probably

---

[65]For 1,200 (not all of whom were adult male citizens) on the trierarchic register see Dem. 14.16; for the figure of c. 27,500 for the total adult male citizen population see above, p. 6.

[66]Walbank's lease nos. 32, 46, 48, 72 and 73 (no. 30 is rented by someone who is already identified as rich). The figure of 600 dr. was obvious a threshold of some sort, since at and above this amount two guarantors were required instead of only one.

[67]For the routine sacrifices, see above, pp. 46-47; for the *ad hoc* sacrifices, see above, pp. 61; for the penteteric festivals, see above, pp. 60-61.

[68]But see above, p. 116 on *IG* 7 4254.37-45.

funded from general revenues in much the same way that the *epithetoi heortai* were.

To conclude this discussion of sacrifices sponsored by the *polis* it is worth emphasizing this last point, that of the sacrifices at which there were wide-scale distributions of meat, viz. the *epithetoi heortai*, and probably also the special *ad hoc* sacrifices and the penteteric festivals, all except the penteteric Mission to Delos were funded from the general revenues of the *polis*, and not from income derived from the leasing of public and/or sacred lands. On the level of the *polis* rentals supported only the *patrioi thusiai* at which significantly fewer animals were sacrificed and their meat distributed to restricted groups of citizens. This is in marked contrast, as we shall see, with the situation that prevailed in the demes, where the sacrificial budget depended to a large extent on rents. Unlike the demes, the *polis* did not have to rely on rents for its major sacrificial activity since it had other reliable sources of income, notably extensive indirect taxes, which the demes did not.

Moving on to sacrifices sponsored by governmental units other than the *polis*, we will consider first who purchased the victims for these sacrifices, and then the sources of funds for their purchases.

Generally speaking, wherever there are officials such as *hieropoioi* or *epimelêtai* to supervise a rite we would expect them to purchase the victims. Where such officials are absent we would expect the purchases to be made either by the priest who will conduct the rite, or by some official of the governmental unit sponsoring the sacrifice, e.g. the demarkh on the level of the deme.[69]

Normally these officials would purchase victims with funds from the deme, etc., but in contrast to the officials who used only the *polis*'

---

[69] For religious duties assigned to the demarkh see Whitehead (1986a) 127-28. See also below, note 77, on *IG* 2^2 1194+. For the *merarkhai* of *IG* 2^2 1203, see below, note 76.

money to purchase victims for its *epithetoi heortai*,[70] officials of these smaller units, as we shall see, sometimes either supplemented public funds or perhaps even provided for the victims entirely from their own resources. Of course, the officials who could afford to do so would necessarily be among the more prosperous members of the community. Their contributions could have been in the form of money used to purchase additional victims, but since at least some of Athens' wealthy owned herds of sheep and goats,[71] on occasion they may well have contributed the actual victims from their own herds. Especially in the case of the smaller units (demes, *thiasoi*, etc.) individual sacrificial events rarely required more than three or four animals, usually sheep or goats, (and sometimes as few as one or two),[72] which an owner could easily supply from his own herds at no great expense, particularly since there was no significant market for these animals except as sacrificial victims. To be sure, the owner would lose the milk and wool that the animal might have produced, but this loss could easily be make good if the contribution was anticipated and the owner of the herd culled fewer animals from the herd than he would otherwise normally do.[73]

In inscriptions the generosity of these benefactors is sometimes attributed to piety (*eusebeia*), but these same inscriptions also say that a donor has been φιλότιμος εἰς τὰς θυσίας,[74] or has sacrificed φιλοτίμως,[75] or more generally that they φιλοτίμως ἐπεμελήθησαν

---

[70]See above, p. 109.
[71]See above, pp. 80-83.
[72]Cf. the discussion of the deme calendars above in Chapter 1.
[73]As background to these observations see the discussion on the stock-raising industry above, pp. 78-94.
[74]*IG* 2² 1204 (a decree from the deme Lamptrai).
[75]*IG* 2² 1163 (a decree of the tribe Hippothontis) and *IG* 2² 1166 (a decree of the tribe Acamantis), both from the first half of the third century B.C.

τῆς θυσίας.[76] The adjective *philotimos* and the adverb *philotimôs* in these inscriptions are both a discrete indication that their honorands contributed some of their own resources for these sacrifices[77] and and explanation of why they did so, viz. to earn the recognition and gratitude of the demesmen, tribesmen, etc. who will have benefited from their generosity.[78]

It should be noted that the inscriptions praising individuals for their *philotimia* in subsidizing public sacrifices begin to appear only in the last third of the fourth century and are all erected by tribes,

---

[76] *IG* 2² 1199 (a decree of the deme Aixone honoring the *hieropoioi* in the temple of Hêbê); cf. καλῶς καὶ φιλοτίμως τῶν θυσιῶν ἐπεμελήθησαν καὶ τῶν κοινῶν, *IG* 2² 1203 (a decree of the deme Athmon honoring *merarkhai*), καλῶς ἐπεμε]λήθησαν καὶ φιλ[οτίμως τῆς τε πο]μπῆς καὶ τῆς κρε[ανομίας καὶ τῶν] ἄλλων πάντων, *IG* 2² 1255 (a decree of the *orgeônes* of Bendis), and similar language in *SEG* 2.7 (a decree of the deme Halimous honoring a demesman for sacrifices ὑπὲρ τοῦ δημάρχου), *SEG* 21.520 (a decree of the deme Teithras honoring *bouleutai*), *IG* 2² 1259 (*orgeônes* honoring two ἱστιά[τορ]ες [sic]) and *IG* 2² 1262 (*thiasiôtai* honoring their *epimelêtai*). The *merarkhai* of *IG* 2² 1203 may well be liturgists, but the honorand of *SEG* 2.7 appears to be a private citizen who has volunteered on his own initiative to see to sacrifices which were properly the responsibility of deme officials.

[77] This is seen quite clearly in *IG* 2² 1261, a decree of some *thiasiôtai* of Aphrodite, where one Stephanos is singled out for the *philotimia* he exhibited as *hieropoios* in the sacrifices he conducted μετὰ τῶν ἄλλων συνιεροποι[ῶ]ν (29-30). In *IG* 2² 1194+1274+, a decree of c. 300 of the deme Eleusis reedited by Threpsiades (1939, 178), the demarkh is honored for providing from his own resources for the deme's sacrifice to Dionysos (παρ' αὐτοῦ ἔθυσεν καὶ εἰς τοὺς δημότας πεφιλοτίμηται, 10-11); in this case the honorand, a member of a prominent local family, uses the occasion of his term as demarkh (to which he was elected by lot [λαχών, 7]) to feast the demesmen at his own expense and to receive in return, almost dynastically, the same right of *proedria* which his ancestors had received in their day (cf. 15-17).

[78] Note, for example, in *IG* 2² 1204 the citizens of Lamptrai honor an Akharnian for his generosity in funding sacrifices, etc. by voting him *ateleia* and a share of the sacrificial meats equal to that of the demesmen; put crudely, the honorand, Akharnian by birth, Lamptraian by residence, has used his money to gain acceptance in his deme of residence. Cf. also our earlier remarks on *philotimia* and private sacrifice on p. 10 and the literature cited there in note 5.

ACQUIRING THE VICTIMS

demes, *thiasoi*, etc., i.e. by units smaller than the *polis*. The lack of similar inscriptions from earlier in the century may be nothing more than an accident of loss and survival,[79] but it may also be part of a more general trend prefiguring the demise of egalitarian democracy, whereby the wealthy received progressively more visible credit for their contributions to the common weal, beginning with the smaller units like *thiasoi*, demes and tribes which were more vulnerable to this kind of economic pressure.[80]

As to regular sources of funds for sacrifices below the level of the *polis*, we have clear evidence of at least one occasion upon which the *polis* made provisions for a sacrifice by a smaller unit, and in this case it appears that the *polis* provided the actual victims, not simply the funds for purchasing them. The evidence is found in the Calendar of the *genos* of the Salaminioi,[81] where the *genos* budgets 10 dr. for firewood for sacrificing its own victims and "for what the *polis* gives ἐκ κύρβεων" (ἐφ' ἱεροῖς καὶ οἷς ἡ πόλις δίδωσιν ἐκ κύρβεω[ν] Δ, 87-88) at its major sacrificial event in Mounikhion. In the Greek, ἐφ' ἱεροῖς refers to sacrificing the victims listed in the preceding lines, which the *genos* will purchase from its own resources, as we can tell from the prices listed for these victims on the calendar; the relative

---

[79]Note, however, *IG* 2² 1140 (a decree of the tribe Pandionis from 386/5) in which a priest (*hiereus*) is given *ateleia* from tribal liturgies "because he had done right by the tribe" (δικ[αιοσ]ύνης ἕνεκα τῆς ἐς [τὴν φυ]λὴν). It is not immediately clear how the priest had done right by the tribe, but displaying exceptional generosity in the sacrifices for which he was responsible seems the most likely possibility (note also that the priest must have been wealthy to be subject to liturgic obligations, and he may well have held his office for multiple years or even for life). All the same, even though the priest is rewarded for being generous, and probably in the expectation that he will continue to be in the future, it is nonetheless noteworthy that at least at this point early in the fourth century the language of *philotimia*, with its more blatant implications of *quid pro quo*, is still absent from the inscription.

[80]On this point see further Whitehead (1986) 174-75.

[81]*SEG* 21.527. On this Calendar see further above, pp. 40-45.

pronoun οἷς is parallel with ἱεροῖς, and so must refer to other *hiera* which the *polis* "gives." The most obvious meaning of the verb "gives" (δίδωσιν) is that the *polis* provided the actual victims for the Salaminioi to sacrifice. Finally, as Ferguson has properly noted,[82] the expression ἐκ κύρβεω[ν] refers to "the laws of Solon," specifically to the calendar of *patrioi thusiai* which formed a part of that code, or more properly in the present case to the recodification of that calendar in the so-called Calendar of Nikomakhos. The agreement which precedes the calendar also refers to victims, ὅσα . . . ἡ πόλις παρέχει ἐκ τô δημοσίο, whose meat will be distributed raw to the members of the *genos* (20-24); as we saw earlier,[83] this cannot refer to the victims at the Mounikhion event, whose meat will be cooked, but must refer to victims at yet another sacrifice or sacrifices, presumably also *patrioi thusiai* performed by the Salaminioi on behalf of the *polis*. Two points are worthy of note: first, the funds used to purchase these victims are viewed as coming from the *polis'* treasury[84] (and not e.g. from rentals of specific lands dedicated to the support of these sacrifices); and second, though these victims are paid for by the *polis*, their meat will be shared out exclusively among the members of the *genos*.

On the Calendar of Nikomakhos we also find a list of victims to be sacrificed to gods associated with Eleusis, and then the entry Εὐμολπ[ίδαι] ταῦτα [θύοσιν].[85] If the restoration is correct, the entry would indicate that, like the *genos* of the Salaminioi, the *genos* of the Eumolpidai also offered sacrifices on behalf of the *polis*, that the *polis* provided the victims for these sacrifices and that, if we may judge from the sacrifices of the Salaminioi, in all probability only the mem-

---

[82]Ferguson (1938) 67.
[83]Above, pp. 43-44.
[84]Τô δημοσίο is the genitive of τὸ δημόσιον, the treasury (*LSJ* s.v. III.c), not of ὁ δήμοσιος, the public slave (*LSJ* s.v. II.a). See further above, note 58.
[85]*Hesp.* 1935, p. 21, no. 2, lines 73-74.

bers of the *genos* shared in the meat of these victims.[86] The remains of the Calendar of Nikomakhos are quite fragmentary and we have only a small portion of the original text; the possibility therefore remains that if the *polis* provided victims for *patrioi thusiai* performed on its behalf by the Salaminioi and by the Eumolpidai, it also provided victims for *patrioi thusiai* conducted on its behalf by other *genē* as well.

Given the antiquity, real or perceived, of the *patrioi thusiai*, it is understandable that at least some of these sacrifices would have been performed by kinship units, notably *genē*, which were, or were perceived to be, of comparable antiquity. Conversely, there is every reason to believe that the newer territorial units, viz. the Kleisthenic tribes[87] and demes, did not perform any of the *patrioi thusiai* on the recodified Calendar of Nikomakhos. As to sacrifices not on the Calendar of Nikomakhos, there is no reason to believe that the *polis* would be interested in any sacrifices performed by the newer territorial units, and absent that interest, the *polis* would be unlikely to contribute to their support. The argument must be stated in this *a priori* fashion since documentation for units other than the demes is almost non-existent, but even in the case of the demes, where documentation does exist, there is no evidence that the *polis* ever contributed anything, in the form of either animals or money, to the demes for their sacrifices.[88]

Generally speaking then, apart from the sort of voluntary contributions discussed above, it would appear that the sub-*polis* units had only two ways of funding their sacrifices, by imposing compulsory liturgies on their more well-to-do members and by transfers from the

---

[86]On these points see further Healey (1984, 135-41), drawing upon his 1961 Harvard dissertation (repr. 1990), especially pp. 160-62.

[87]In contrast to at least one of the old "Ionic" tribes for whom the *polis* also supplied victims (Γλεόντων φυλῆι, *Hesp.* 1935, p. 21, no. 2, lines 35, 47).

[88]Whitehead (1986) 180.

general revenues of the unit. While some deme liturgies were common, notably *khorēgiai* at the rural Dionysia,[89] the evidence for liturgies in support of public sacrifices is very limited. Demosthenes lists the feast which he provided for his fellow tribesmen (εἰστίακα τὴν φυλήν, 21.156) together with multiple *khorēgiai*, implying but not proving that the *hestiasis*, like the *khorēgiai*, was also liturgic. On the deme level, the speaker of Isaios 3.80 says that a wealthy man was expected to feast the women of his deme at the Thesmophoria and τἆλλα ὅσα προσῆκε λῃτουργεῖν ἐν τῷ δήμῳ, though λῃτουργεῖν may be used metaphorically here.[90] *IG* 2^2 1203, a decree of the deme Athmon, honors *merarkhai*, who may be liturgists, for the *philotimia* they displayed in their supervision of *thusiai*. Finally, Dow[91] has shown that the sacrificial victims listed on the calendar from the deme of Erkhia (*SEG* 21.541) are distributed into the five columns in such a way that the total expenditures in each column are approximately the same, and he has argued that the purpose of this distribution is to allocate the deme's sacrificial expenses in an equitable manner among five deme liturgists.[92] All in all, this is not a great deal of evidence, and it suggests that while compulsory liturgies may have played some role

---

[89]Whitehead (1986) 152 with notes 13 and 14.

[90]The *hestiasis* in Theophrast. *Char.* 10.11 and the meat distribution at Menander, *Sik.* 183-85 both appear to be a private sacrifices to which the members of the deme are invited, not public liturgies imposed by the deme (on Theophrast. *Char.* 10.11 see above, Chapter 1, note 4).

[91]Dow (1965) 194-95; (1968) 182.

[92]Dow (1965, 97-98; 1968, 182-83) believes that all of the sacrifices on the calendar had originally been funded by *gennētai* who could no longer afford, or were simply unwilling, to do so; and that with the legislation which stands behind the calendar the deme assumed the responsibility for these sacrifices, allocating the funding for them among five liturgists. This may perhaps be the case, but it is far more likely, as Whitehead (1986, 174-75) has argued, that the Erkhians had once paid for the sacrifices out of common deme funds but were now forced to turn to wealthy liturgists, much like other contemporary fourth-century demes which "faced with a chronic fiscal shortfall," resorted at this time "to the resources of individuals to pay for what had once come out of general community monies" (*ibid.* 175).

in the funding of sacrifices in some units below the level of the *polis*, the role was extremely limited.

As we saw earlier, on the level of the *polis* the major sacrifices, the *epithetoi heortai*, were funded, either directly or indirectly, by allocations from the ordinary budget of the *polis*. Without a doubt, sacrifices by political units below the level of the *polis* were similarly funded by allocations from the ordinary budget of the unit in question. In fact, of all the activities carried on by these units, most cost little or nothing to perform, and of those activities which did require money to be spent (on honorary crowns, inscribing decrees, etc.) the funding of sacrifices probably consumed the lion's share of the ordinary budget of every one of these units.[93]

The question then arises: where did these units get the money for their ordinary budgets? Since we know virtually nothing about the fiscal arrangements for any of these units except the demes, of necessity we will limit ourselves to some observations on the financing of demes, and assume, not unreasonably, that the other units below the level of the *polis* followed more or less the same pattern of funding which we shall identify in the case of the demes.

As we saw earlier, taxes were probably the principal source of income in the regular budget of the *polis*. There is also some shadowy evidence for taxation by demes, but the opportunities for most demes to tax anything other than the property of its citizens (which the Athenians were generally reluctant to tax) must have been fairly limited, and in any case such taxation could not have raised much money for the demes, or we would certainly have heard more about it

---

[93] See further Whitehead (1986) 163-64. There is a suggestive illustration of this in *IG* 1^3 258, a list of *kephalaia* preceding a decree from the deme of Plotheia. The exact interpretation of the *kephalaia* figures is uncertain (capital to be lent out? income from loans or other sources?), but whatever the figures represent, the total of the *kephalaia* associated with various religious expenses (including sacrifices) is 21 times as large as that associated with the office of demarkh (on this inscription see further Whitehead [1986] 165-69).

from our sources.[94] Rather, the bulk of a deme's revenues consisted of rents paid on land and other properties which the deme owned or controlled, and of interest on loans of funds also under its control.[95] Compared with taxes, whose yield could vary widely from year to year, rentals and loans, particularly long-term ones, were relatively safe and predictable sources of income, and thus exactly the sort needed to meet, year after year, the fixed expenses of e.g. the deme's sacrificial calendar. And although it is difficult to quantify, the amount of land and/or capital controlled by the demes must have been substantial if it was able to support, by and large, the demes' need for sacrificial victims as indicated in the extant sacrificial calendars.[96]

We know relatively little about the loans made by demes, and substantially more about the land and other properties which they leased, thanks in particular to several inscriptions containing actual leases and other relevant information. The observations which follow

---

[94]On the general subject of deme income see Whitehead (1986) 150-60; on the evidence for taxation by demes see *ibid.* 150-52.

[95]On loans see Whitehead (1986) 158-60. On leases in general see 152-58; on the legal aspect of leases see also Behrend (1970); on the social dimensions of leasing see further below, pp. 138-42, and Osborne (1988) 281-92.

[96]Haussoullier (1884, 78-79) asserts that the *egktêtikon* tax and loans were the most important sources of revenues for the demes, and that rentals were of comparatively little importance. These assertions are based in turn on several assumptions, viz. that there were a large number of Athenians not living in their native demes, and hence liable to the *egktêtikon* tax levied on non-demesmen who owned property and/or resided in the demes; that demes did not control much land, and what they did control was not always of the best quality; and that when the deme leased lands, it leased them to people so poor that they would be unable to pay their rent in the event of a poor harvest. None of these assumptions is justified: there is also no warrant to assume that the *egktêtikon* was collected in all or even most demes (Whitehead [1986] 76, note 38); the amount of land controlled by demes was in fact quite substantial; and as we shall see below, pp. 138-40, the properties controlled by the demes were usually leased to wealthy men, not to poor ones.

are, strictly speaking, applicable only to leases, but given the sociopolitical structure of the demes and the nature of their financial needs, it is not at all unlikely that these observations will also be generally applicable *mutatis mutandis* to deme loans as well.

On the one hand, the sacrifices sponsored by the demes were, with rare exceptions, similar to the *polis' epithetoi heortai* in that the victims' meat was distributed not to a select group but to the deme's citizen population at large.[97] On the other hand, the demes' sacrifices were similar to the *polis' patrioi thusiai* in that the funds for the sacrifices came from rentals. Further, as we saw earlier, the individual properties controlled by the *polis* may have been thought of as "owned" by specific gods but they were leased out by the *polis* through its *arkhôn basileus*, not by the agents of the god's cult; and the income from these leases did not go directly to the god's cult but to the *polis*, which then allocated it as needed to support the cult of individual gods. Similarly in the case of the demes, there appears no instance of an *epimelêtês*, priest *vel sim.* renting out property that will be used to support a sacrifice sponsored by a deme.[98] Rather leases are always made by the deme, and even when rents from a particular piece of property are dedicated to the upkeep of a specific cult, the income from the lease does not pass directly to the ministers of the cult but is channelled through the deme. Thus, for example, in *IG* 2² 2493 (dated 339/8) οἱ δημόται of Rhamnous[99] rent out [τὸ τέμεν]ος τὸ τῆ|[ς θ]εοῦ τὸ ἐν Ἑρμει (3-5) with the rent to be paid apparently to the demarkh (13-15); in *IG* 2² 2498 (dated 321/0) *Peiraieis* set out the conditions upon which they will rent "Paralia and Halmyris and the Thêseion and τἄλλα τεμένη ἅπαντα" (1-3); and in *SEG* 24.151 (dated mid-fourth century) from the deme of Teithras, the Τειθρα]σίους

---

[97] And on occasion even to individuals who were not citizens of the deme; see Whitehead (1986, 205-6) for the limited evidence for this.

[98] The property controlled by *epimelêtai*, etc. in the *rationes centesimarum* inscriptions belongs to private cult associations, not to the demes.

[99] For the identification of the deme as Rhamnous see Jameson (1982) 66-74.

rent τὰ χωρία and the lessees pay the rental every year to the Τειθρασίο[ι]|[ς] (29-32).[100] Again, in *SEG* 28.103, a decree of the deme of Eleusis dated 332/1, the income from stone-quarrying rights in the deme are dedicated to the deme's sacrifice to Herakles ἐν Ἀκριδι (19-23) and are to be paid out for that purpose by the demarkh (31-33), but the demarkh is directed to provide 10 dr. "from the *prosodos* of the god" for the inscription of the decree (49-51); the rents may be dedicated to the god but they are paid to the demarkh, and the same deme assembly which decided to dedicate them can also direct the demarkh to use some of them for routine administrative purposes. Note also that in the so-called *rationes centesimarum* inscriptions (*IG* 2^2 1594-1603+), properties controlled by demes and villages are listed separately from property controlled by private cult associations,[101] and the former are always described as belonging to the deme or village, not to the gods who were thought to own them, showing that the territorial units administered these properties, determined to whom they were to be leased and presumably also received the rents and decided how those rents would be spent.

As to who rented the demes' properties, our evidence is extremely limited, but it is striking how many individuals of wealth and/or prominence appear as lessees in the limited record. Of the fifteen individuals who can be identified in leases and similar documents[102] as

---

[100]For other leases specifying that the lessor is the deme see *IG* 2^2 1176+ (rented by Πειραέας, 16); *IG* 2^2 2492 (rented by Αἰξωνεῖς, 1); *IG* 2^2 2496 (rented by Κυθηρίων οἱ μερῖται, 8—the *meritai* were apparently officials of some sort in the deme Kythêr(r)ios—); *IG* 2^2 2497 (rented by ὁ δῆμος ὁ Π[ρασ]ιέων, 1-2). Cf. also *IG* 2^2 2490, apparently an agreement by the trittys Epakreis (Ἐπακρέων τριττύο[ς], 8) to let out a χω[ρίον (5).

[101]I.e. voluntary groupings of worshippers (*thiasôtai, orgeônes*, etc.) in the service of a particular god or gods. For the organizational principle of the listing see Lewis (1973) 191-93.

[102]*IG* 2^2 2492 (Aixone), *SEG* 28.103 (Eleusis), *IG* 2^2 2496 (Kytheros), *IG* 2^2 1176+ (Peiraieus), *IG* 2^2 2497 (Prasiai), *IG* 2^2 2493 (Rhamnous), *SEG* 24.151 (Teithras), *SEG* 24.152 (Teithras).

lessees of deme properties two belong to families listed in Davies' *Athenian Properties Families*;[103] two more, who do not meet Davies' criteria, were nonetheless individuals of local prominence and substance;[104] and finally three more were wealthy enough to pay hefty rents of 600 dr. or more per year.[105] Thus, seven out of fifteen lessees (47%) can be identified as wealthier Athenians.[106] This number is already significant, but it is very possible that some, and perhaps all, of the remaining lessees were also wealthy who cannot be identified as such only because we lack the sources to do so.

This pattern of wealthier lessees is not confined to deme properties. As we saw earlier,[107] 26% of the lessees of lands let out to fund the *polis' patrioi thusiai* could be identified either as members of the liturgic class, as politically active, or as renting properties for an annual rent of 600 dr. or more, with the number of wealthy likely to be even higher if our sources were better. And the same is also true of the lessees of the properties in the so-called *rationes centesima-*

---

[103] Melesias Aristokratou, son of *PA* 1916 (*IG* 2^2 1176+); Kirrias Poseidippou, son of *PA* 12132 (*IG* 2^2 2497).

[104] Moirokles Euthudemou (*SEG* 28.103), on whom see Ampolo (1981) 190-204; and Hierokles, the previous lessee of the land in *IG* 2^2 2493, on whom see Jameson (1982) 66-74.

[105] Aristophanes Smikuthou, and Oinophon Euphiletou (both in *IG* 2^2 1176+), and Xanthippos in *SEG* 24.151, whose rent is transcribed as I.H..H (16), which is probably 900 dr. (Π^HH[HH]H). For the significance of 600 dr., recall that among the leases of properties supporting the *polis' patrioi thusiai*, those with annual rents of 600 dr. or more required two guarantors (see above, note 66).

[106] To whom should probably be added an eighth, Arethousios Aristoleo (*IG* 2^2 1176+), who paid an annual rent of 500 dr. The property leased in *SEG* 21.644 comes with *skeuē* that includes 4,000 vine-stakes and 800 of what appear to be wine casks (16-20), suggesting that this too was a substantial piece of property, and therefore likely to have been let to someone able to pay a rather high annual rent.

[107] Above, p. 126-27.

rum,[108] where of the 398,076 dr. worth of transactions which survive on the stones, 37% either involved individuals who can be identified as members of Davies' Athenian Propertied Families, or dealt with (probably multi-year) leases of 2,500 dr. or more; and again the number identified as wealthy would probably be even higher if our sources were better.[109] In sum, while we might assume *a priori* that poor landless tenants were the most likely to lease public properties,[110] in point of fact many, if not most, of the individual lessees of Athenian public properties were wealthy, and certainly in aggregate most public property was leased by the well-to-do.

It is easy enough to imagine why at least demes and similar units rented their properties to the well-to-do. As Jameson has rightly pointed out,[111] demes *et al.* let out their properties not to make a profit but to obtain a sure and constant source of funds for their cult activities, especially sacrifices, the financial demands of which remained more or less the same from year to year;[112] and in support of this first purpose, to insure continual occupation by tenants who would keep up their properties and maintain their value. This desire for an assured source of funds will go a long way toward explaining why most extant leases are either for a very long term or perpetual (εἰς τὸν ἅπαντα χρόνον).[113] It will also explain why so many

---

[108] For the argument that the transactions reflected in the *rationes* were, despite their language, rentals and not sales, see Rosivach (forthcoming).

[109] For the calculations see Rosivach (forthcoming). The one surviving phratry lease, for land belonging to the Dualeis (*IG* 2^2 1241), has an annual rent of 600 dr., indicating that its lessee, Diodoros Kantharou, was also well-to-do.

[110] So e.g. Finley (1973) 95.

[111] (1982) 72.

[112] Recall the fixed routines of the sacrificial calendars and the relative constancy of prices noted above (pp. 94-99), especially for sheep and goats, the victims most commonly sacrificed.

[113] *IG* 2^2 2492: 40 yrs.; *IG* 2^2 2493: 10 yrs.; *IG* 2^2 2496: εἰς τὸν ἅπαντα χρόνον; *IG* 2^2 2497: εἰς τ[ὸν ἅπαν]τα χρόνον; *IG* 2^2 2498: 10 yrs.; *SEG* 24.151: κατάπαξ; *SEG* 24.152: καθάπαξ. *SEG* 21.644 is also probably εἰς τὸν ἅπαντα χρόνον, since it refers to payments by the lessee's *ekgonoi* (8-9).

properties were leased to the more well-to-do members of the community, since the well-to-do had the resources, as their poorer brothers did not, to weather bad harvests and similar calamities and still pay, year after year, the rents the demes *et al.* required to fund their annual calendar of sacrifices.

Why, on the other hand, did the wealthy rent these publicly owned lands? Two inscriptions, *SEG* 28.103 and *IG* 2^2 1176+ suggest that at least part of the motivation was *philotimia*, the willingness to expend one's own funds for the common good in return for recognition by one's fellow citizens, the same impulse which we have seen[114] sometimes moved demarkhs *vel sim.* to subsidize deme sacrifices from their own resources. In SEG 28.103 the demesmen of Eleusis show their gratitude to their fellow demesman Moirokles, who has leased the local quarry, by voting him a foliage crown "because he takes care that their income be as great as possible;" and in *IG* 2^2 1176+ the demesmen of the Peiraieus similarly vote crowns both to the four men who leased the local theater and to a fifth who arranged the lease, which yielded 300 dr. more than anticipated (25-33).

A third inscription, however, *SEG* 24.151 suggests something very different. Here the demesmen of Teithras lease a *khôrion* to Xanthippos "because he has been a good man concerning the common interests of the deme" (ἐπε[ι]δὴ Ξ|[ανθί]ππό[ς] ἐστι ἀνὴρ ἀγαθὸς περ[ὶ] τ[ὰ κ]οινὰ τὰ [Τε|[ι]θ[ρασ]ί[ων], 6-8)—Xanthippos is rewarded for his other acts of *philotimia* by being granted the lease to this land. If Xanthippos' lease is a reward, then at least in this case it must be economically advantageous to have such a lease. And if in this case, then perhaps also in some or even most other cases, the lessees could expect to derive economic advantage from the properties they leased. Certainly in the case of the properties leased by the *polis* to support its *patrioi thusiai* we must assume that the lessees' primary motivation in leasing was strictly economic, the hope of turning a profit, since there

---

[114]Above, pp. 129-30.

was little chance that they would get much recognition for what, on the scale of the *polis*, were comparatively unimportant services rendered. Within the small world of the deme, however, most people would know who rented the deme's properties, and since the deme depended on the rents from these properties, and probably worried that they would not be rented at all, the demesmen might well be prepared to thank those who rented them, even if the lessees were making a profit from it.[115]

---

[115] Andreyev (1974, 43) states that "this type of land leasing is more in keeping with patriarchal traditions, the privileges of citizens and mutual collective aid." This is probably true from the point of view of the deme which, as we have seen, sought an assured source of funds rather than maximum economic advantage, but it undervalues the importance of economic motives on the part of the lessees. Jameson (1982, 73-74) is closer to the mark, at least on the level of the demes, when he says "On both sides the religious and social aspects may have been at least as important as the strictly financial."

CONCLUSION

Of necessity this study has ranged rather widely and discussed numerous subordinate topics. It will therefore perhaps be useful at this point to draw together the principal points of our argument.

The sacrificial system which we have been studying is in fact two separate but related systems, one serving the needs of the *polis* and the other serving the needs of the multiple political units below the level of the *polis*. The latter system is best documented on the level of the demes, but the limited evidence which survives for other sub-*polis* units is by and large consistent with the assumption that these units participated in the same system as the demes did.

To take this latter system first, funds for sacrifice were raised primarily through the leasing out of properties dedicated to the upkeep of cult activities; however, these properties were controlled by the civilian officials of the unit (demarkhs, etc.), not by religious officials directly associated with the cults, and the rents on the properties were paid to the civilian government which then allocated funds as needed for religious purposes, notably to purchase sacrificial victims and to pay for the miscellaneous expenses (e.g. firewood) involved in sacrifice.

To a large extent this system relied upon the more well-to-do to rent the properties, since they were the ones most likely to be able to pay the rents even if the properties failed to turn a profit in a given year. The multi-year terms of many leases likewise show that the demes *et al.* rented out their properties with an eye toward guaranteed income over the long haul rather than maximum immediate economic benefit. Since the system required the lessees to rent these properties voluntarily, the leases must also have been such that the lessees could expect to derive some benefit therefrom. Part of that benefit was in the form of gratitude publicly expressed by the demes *et al.*, but such gratitude does not exclude the possibility, and indeed the probability, that the lessees also derived real economic benefits from the exploitation of the leased properties.

Within this sub-*polis* system the principal animals sacrificed were sheep and goats. Large numbers of these animals were required every year for the many sacrifices offered by demes, tribes, *genê*, phratries, and the like. Indeed, the need for these animals was so great that the demes *et al.* could not depend on small-scale farmers who raised their animals in twos and threes, but had to turn to people who raised animals on a large scale in herds. Owning herds of sheep and goats was a sign of wealth, and understandably so since, given the capital investment required, only the more well-to-do could afford to own herds.

The sheep and goats in these herds were not raised for their meat to be sold on the open market, there being no market for meat apart from the sacrificial system. Nor were these animals raised primarily to be sold as sacrificial victims. Rather, it appears they were raised principally for the milk and wool which they produced, and for cheese which was made from their milk. Only animals which are nursing their young produce milk. To insure a continuing supply of milk, these animals must bear offspring as often as possible. However, the amount of land available for grazing was limited, and so herds had to be maintained at relatively constant size by culling excess animals, both the very young and those which had already had productive lives. In effect, the animals, both young and old, which were sold for sacrifice were, by and large, animals which would have to be culled in any case. The possibility of selling surplus animals as sacrificial victims conferred economic benefits upon their owners, who could not have otherwise sold these animals in the absence of any other market for their meat; it also benefited the purchasing demes *et al.* who were able to set relatively low prices for the animals, again because there was nowhere else for the suppliers to sell them. Furthermore, by buying their sacrificial animals from large herds the purchasers were able to deal with relatively few suppliers, with whom they could develop customary relationships similar to those implied by long-term leases,

CONCLUSION 145

with the corresponding advantage of an assured source of supply to meet predictable annual needs.

As we saw from our study of sacrificial calendars, the effect of all this was to provide an opportunity, for those citizens who wished to take advantage of it, to obtain portions of meat at no cost to themselves on numerous occasions throughout the year. These distributions of meat may not have been of great importance to the wealthier members of the community who also had access to meat from private sacrifices, but they could be important from an economic, and perhaps even from a purely nutritional point of view, for those who were too poor to sacrifice, or to sacrifice often, on their own. In effect, the system relied in different ways upon the resources of the more well-to-do to benefit principally the poorer members of the community.

To speculate on the origin of this system, it may well go back to a more archaic period where Attic society was dominated by local "big men." These "big men" would have owned herds of sheep and goats principally as symbols of wealth, but they would also have sacrificed some of these animals at appropriate times and distributed the meat to their dependents as a way of cultivating their loyalty, much as even in the fourth century deme magnates sometimes shared their private sacrifices with their neighbors as a way of buttressing their own local importance. At some point the demes and similar units replaced the "big man" as the distributor of sacrificial largess to their members, something which they were able to do only after they had acquired an independent source of funds in the form of *temenê* which they could rent out. There is no way of knowing how the demes and similar units acquired the *temenê*, but it is at least possible that the core of their holdings were originally cult lands controlled by priestly families, *genê*, etc., which were brought under the control of the demes *et al.* at the same time that they were expanding their own religious role to the detriment of the "big men." The "big men" now lost the credit for the meat distributions, but the system of sacrifice which permitted these distributions still relied to a large degree upon them and their successors, the wealthier members of the later communities. These wealthier individuals benefited economically from their support of the system, and eventually, by the late fourth century, they began to recover some of the prestige as well.

Broadly speaking, the *polis* sponsored two very different kinds of sacrifices, the *patrioi thusiai* ("ancestral sacrifices"), and the *epithetoi heortai* ("additional feasts") and similar events.[1] In the *patrioi thusiai* the victims were most often sheep and goats purchased with the income from the leasing out of sacred properties. The *patrioi thusiai* can thus be seen as an extension, on the level of the *polis*, of the sub-*polis* system we have just described, with the significant reservation that unlike the sacrifices of the sub-*polis* units, the meat from the *patrioi thusiai* was not distributed to the general population of the sponsoring unit (in this case the *polis*), but was limited to smaller groups which had some religiously sanctioned right to offer sacrifice on behalf of the *polis* and to share in this meat.

Most important among the second kind of sacrifices sponsored by the *polis* were the *epithetoi heortai*. As their name indicates, the *epithetoi heortai* were viewed as newer sacrifices compared with the *patrioi thusiai*, and were in fact part of a quite different sacrificial system. In this second system meat was distributed to the *polis*' citizen population at large, and was thus available for whoever wished to share in it. The occasions for sharing were frequent enough. By the time the system was fully established in the fourth century there were sixteen annual *epithetoi heortai*, as well as penteteric festivals and special *ad hoc* sacrifices, which were also part of the same system.

---

[1] For the sake of completeness we should add as a third category the routine sacrifices carried out by arkhons, *prytaneis*, etc. In the case of these routine sacrifices the distribution of meat was restricted to the magistrates involved (though in democratic Athens all citizens were at least potentially eligible for office, and thus for sharing in the sacrifice), but the victims were purchased from the general revenues of the *polis*, as were those of the *epithetoi heortai*.

CONCLUSION

While mainly sheep and goats were sacrificed at the *patrioi thusiai*, oxen were usually sacrificed at the *epithetoi heortai* and similar events; goats were sacrificed only at the festival of Artemis Agrotera, and sheep were never sacrificed. The number of oxen required by the *epithetoi heortai* and similar events was too great to be met by a relatively few suppliers in the sort of "customary" market that characterized the sub-*polis* system of sacrifice; instead, economic concerns dominated in the sale and purchase of oxen, with bargaining on the part of both purchasers and suppliers.

The sacrifices of the *epithetoi heortai* and similar events were funded not from rentals of sacred properties but from the ordinary revenues of the *polis*, which revenues, in the fourth century, came primarily from indirect taxes, the burden of which fell disproportionately on the more prosperous members of the community. In this sense the *epithetoi heortai* and similar events can be seen as one means (along with payment for public office, etc.) by which the egalitarian Athenian *polis* used the resources of the more prosperous for the benefit of the community at large, and thus especially for the poor. Significantly, since the funding of these larger *epithetoi heortai* was indirect (in contrast to e.g. liturgies, or even the *eisphora*), it was difficult for the wealthy to claim credit for the benefits which their taxes conferred on the community, credit which went to the democratic *polis* instead.

Finally, this study has emphasized some economic and social aspects of public sacrifice which have received less attention in previous studies of Athenian religion. This emphasis should not, however, be understood as a claim that these economic and social aspects were paramount in the minds of the Athenians who offered these sacrifices, or that the religious dimensions of their sacrifices were unimportant to them.

SUPPLEMENTARY NOTES

A. AGE TERMS FOR ANIMALS

ἄβολος· ὁ μηδέπω ἐκβεβληκὼς τοὺς ὀδόντας [ἵππους ἤγουν ὁ] πῶλος. καὶ γνώμων ὁ ὀδούς, ὅτι ἀπὸ τούτου ἡ ἡλικία γνωρίζεται τῶν πώλων τε καὶ μόσχων. τριάκοντα γὰρ μηνῶν γινόμενοι ἐκβάλλουσι τοὺς πρώτους ὀδόντας· εἶτα, ἐνιαυτοῦ παρελθόντος, τοὺς δευτέρους· καὶ μετ' ἄλλον ἐνιαυτὸν τέλειοί εἰσιν οἱ τεττάρων ἡμίσους ἐτῶν. ἀφ' οὗ καὶ λειπογνώμονες καλοῦνται οἱ μηκέτι διὰ τῶν ὀδόντων γνωσθῆναι δυνάμενοι (*Etymologicum Magnum* s.v. ἄβολος).

The Greeks used the teeth of maturing domestic animals to determine their age, but there is no accurate modern account of how they did so, or of the language which they used in this regard.[1] This appendix first briefly explains how teeth can serve as indicators of an animal's age, and then discusses a variety of terms which the Greeks used to describe an animal's age on this basis.

As we conceive it, horses, cows, sheep, etc., like humans, have two sets of teeth in their lifetime, a first, smaller set composed of incisors and premolars (their deciduous or "milk" teeth), which is complete within a few weeks of birth, and a second, larger set (their permanent teeth) composed of replacements for the deciduous incisors and premolars plus additional teeth, canines and rear molars, which fill out the larger mouth of a maturing animal. The Greeks seem to have conceived of the process somewhat differently. In their mind, the animal had a single set of teeth, some of which fell out and were replaced by others as the animal matured; the canines and rear molars which we consider part of the second, permanent set of teeth the Greeks considered as the part of the original set which was not replaced.[2]

A. AGE TERMS FOR ANIMALS:

[1] The most recent discussion of age terms is by Hansen (1973), drawing upon his 1969 Harvard dissertation (repr. 1990) 117-26. For Hansen's view on the meaning of *leipognômôn* see below, note 18.

[2] This way of looking at things can be seen very clearly in Aristotle's discussion of horse's teeth at *HA* 576ᵃ612 translated below.

The process of replacement is gradual, with new teeth pushing out old ones at regular and predictable intervals over two or more years until the permanent set is complete. The age of an animal can thus be determined with a high degree of accuracy by counting how many of its deciduous teeth have been replaced by permanent teeth and comparing this with the ages at which these teeth are normally replaced in this sort of animal. Thus, for example, a horse typically replaces its first four incisors (one upper and one lower on each side of the mouth) at 2.5 years; a horse with only these four permanent incisors will be between 2.5 and 3.5 years, the age at which the second group of four incisors is replaced; a horse with eight permanent incisors will be between 3.5 and 4.5 years, the age at which its third and final group of four incisors is replaced.[3] Of course this method of determining an animal's age will work only as long as its permanent set of teeth is incomplete. Once the set is complete, an accurate determination of the animal's age is no longer possible by this method, and all one can say is that e.g. a horse is at least 4.5 years of age.

The foregoing example follows Greek practice in ignoring an animal's premolars and counting only its incisors, as can be seen in e.g. Aristotle's discussion of the ages at which a horse loses its teeth (HA 576^{a}6-12):

> [A horse] has forty teeth. It loses (βάλλει) its first four teeth at 30 months, two uppers and two lowers; when a year passes, it loses (βάλλει) in the same manner four teeth, two upper and two lower; and again, when another year passes, the other four in the same manner. When four years and six months have passed it no longer loses (βάλλει) any teeth.

The intervals given by Aristotle are the same as those for a horse's incisors (cf. the previous paragraph), and not those for pre-molars, which are replaced at 2.5, 3 and 4 years.[4] Further since Aristotle specifies that at each

---

[3]The ages given here are taken from Frandson (1986) 314, table 19-2. Comparable figures for cows are: first incisors 1.5-2 yrs., second incisors 2-2.5 yrs., third incisors 3 yrs., fourth incisors 3.5-4 yrs.; comparable figures for sheep are: first incisors 1-1.5 yrs., second incisors 1.5-2 yrs., third incisors 2.5-3 yrs., fourth incisors 3.5-4 yrs. (Frandson, *loc. cit.*). Frandson adds (312) that "[t]his time of eruption or breaking through the gums by the teeth is probably the most accurate aid to determining the age of animals, when no accurate records are available."

[4]Fransdon (1986) 314, table 19-2.

of the three intervals four teeth are lost, two upper and two lower, for a total of twelve, he must be counting only the deciduous incisors and not the deciduous premolars.[5]

The verb βάλλειν and related words are used to describe the loss of deciduous teeth which will be replaced by permanent ones. This is the sense, for example, of ἐκβάλλειν in *EM* s.v. ἄβολος quoted above, and of βάλλει in Arist. *HA* 576ᵃ6-12 also quoted above.

Βάλλειν and related words are not used to describe the loss of permanent teeth. The adjective δευτεροβόλος describes an animal that has lost its second group of deciduous incisors, not its permanent teeth (so e.g. in Apsyrtos, *Hipp. Berol.* 20.4: ἐν τῇ πωλικῇ ἡλικίᾳ πρωτοβόλος ἢ καὶ μέλλων λαβεῖν τὸν δευτεροβόλον).[6]

The teeth the loss of which indicates age are called *gnômones*, as in *EM* s.v. ἄβολος quoted above. Xen. *Eq.* 3.1-2 can thus contrast the condition of an older animal, ὁ . . . μηκέτι ἔχων γνώμονας, with ὁπότε δὲ ἡ νεότης σαφής. Arist. *HA* 577ᵃ21 says that the last group of deciduous teeth which animals lose (the fourth in the case of the asses of which he is speaking) are their *gnômones*, but the language of the lexicographers suggests rather that whatever deciduous tooth was being lost was a *gnômôn* at the time it was being lost (ὁ ἀποπίπτων ὀδούς, Pollux 1.182; τὸν βαλλόμενον ὀδόντα, Hesykh. s.v. γνῶμα and Suidas s.v. κατηρτυκότα).

An animal whose deciduous teeth have all been replaced with permanent ones is said to be τέλε(ι)ος as in *EM* s.v. ἄβολος quoted above.[7] Τέλε(ι)οι

---

[5]The same intervals are also found in *EM* s.v. ἄβολος quoted above. There is also an alternative—and less accurate—Greek tradition that the first set of incisors was replaced at 2.5 years, the second set at 4 years, and the third and final set at 5 years. This tradition is found in e.g. Apsyrtos, *Hipp. Berol.* 95.1; *Geopon.* 16.1.12-16; and, in Latin, in Varro, *RR* 2.7.2-3. It is noteworthy that even in this alternative tradition the deciduous premolars are ignored and only the deciduous incisors are counted.

[6]Cf. also Pollux 1.182 quoted in the next note below.

[7]Plato, *Lgg.* 834C similarly describes horses as ἀβόλοις . . . μέσοις . . . τέλος ἔχουσι (cf. Pollux 1.182: οὕτω γὰρ Πλάτων τοὺς δευτεροβόλους ὀνομαζομένους). See also Hesykh. s.vv. κατηρτυκώς and λειπογνώμων; Eustath. 1404.59 f.

(cattle, sheep, etc.) often appear as sacrificial victims,[8] where the adjective indicates only their age,[9] not their ritual purity.[10]

Both cattle and sheep are *tele(i)oi* (i.e. they have a complete set of permanent teeth) normally at 3.5 to 4 years, which gives a general sense of the age at which these animals were sacrificed. This age should be compared on the one hand with life-expectancies of up to 15 years for cattle (Arist. *HA* 575ᵃ31-32) and 10 years or less for sheep (Arist. *HA* 573ᵇ23-24), and on the other hand with ages of first service of 14 to 22 months for cows[11] and 12 to 18 months for ewes.[12] The ages of first service are particularly significant since they show that these animals could have produced offspring and milk for two or more years before being sacrificed.

The intransitive perfect of the verb καταρτύειν is also used to describe an animal which is "thoroughly furnished" (sc. with teeth), as in Bekker, *Anec.* 1.105.25-26 (κατηρτυκέναι ἐλέγοντο οἱ μηκέτι βόλον ἔχοντες ἵπποι, citing Euripides' *Aiolos*), Hesykh. s.v. κατηρτυκώς, and Eustath. 1404.59 ff. quoted below.[13]

Finally, etymologically the adjectives λειπογνώμων and ἀπογνώμων describe an animal which has lost its *gnômones*, i.e. one which has replaced all its deciduous incisors with permanent ones (ἀποβεβληκὼς πάντας τοὺς

---

[8]So e.g. Homer, *Il.* 1.66, 24.34; Aiskhyl. *Ag.* 1509; *SEG* 33.147 (discussed below); *SIG*³ 993.12-13.

[9]Note also the contrast between τέλε(ι)α and γαλαθηνά at e.g. Hdt. 1.183; cf. *IG* 2² 1359.6-7, 1356.6-7, *SIG*³ 1015.31-32; cf. also the discussion of the terms for animals at different ages at Eustath. 1625.33 ff., derived from Aristophanes of Byzantion's περὶ ὀνομασίας ἡλικιῶν.

[10]*LSJ* not withstanding, the only time τέλε(ι)ος describes a sacrificial victim which is "perfect . . . entire, without spot or blemish" is in the rather special context of Aristotle, frag. 101 Rose *ap.* Athen. 674F (οὐδὲν κοβολὸν προσφέρομεν πρὸς τοὺς θεοὺς ἀλλὰ τέλεια καὶ ὅλα, from Aristotle's *Symposium*). Oddly this passage is not cited among the illustrations in *LSJ* s.v. for the definition "perfect . . . without blemish."

[11]Frandson (1986) p. 419, table 26-1. According to Aristot. *HA* 575ᵃ23-25, intercourse resulting in conception is generally agreed to be possible at the age of two years, but in fact it can happen as early as 12 months in some cases and usually at the age of 20 months.

[12]Frandson (1986) 419, table 26-1.

[13]Hesykh. s.v. ἄβολος mistakenly identifies κατηρτυκώς and ἄβολος, but the text may be corrupt. Suidas s.v. ἀβολήτωρ καὶ ἄβολις and s.v. κατηρτυκότα incorrectly identifies it with γνώμων.

ὀδόντας καὶ μὴ ἔχων δι' οὗ γνωσθῇ, Hesykh. s.v. ἀπογνώμων). In *EM* s.v. ἄβολος quoted above, λειπογνώμονες are identified with τέλειοι, and we read similarly in Eustathios (1404.59 ff):

τὰ τέλεια ἐπὶ πλείστων γενῶν καὶ κατηρτυκότα λειπογνώμονα καλεῖται διὰ τὸ μηκέτι ἔχειν τοὺς γνώμονας καλουμένους.[14]

There are grounds, however, for believing that ἀπογνώμων and λειπογνώμων are not simply synonyms for τέλε(ι)ος. The appearance of both τέλεον and λειπογνώμονα on the deme calendar from Thorikos (*SEG* 33.147) shows that the two terms were not identical, at least in Attic usage.[15] More importantly, as sacrificial victims λειπογνώμονες cost less than ordinary animals,[16] indicating that they were also, for some reason, worth less. The explanation may lie in some other entries in the lexicographers. In Hesykh. s.v. λειπογνωμων we read:

ὁ μηκέτι βόλον ἔχων. ὁ δὲ τέλειος καὶ γεγηρακώς, μὴ ἔχων γνωρίσματα τῆς ἡλικίας.

While an ox or a sheep, for example, becomes τέλε(ι)ος at 3.5 to 4 years (when it has replaced its last deciduous incisors with permanent ones), it will remain τέλε(ι)ος for the rest of its life. Therefore in the passage from Hesykhios quoted here, τέλε(ι)ος is not identical with γεγηρακώς, but γεγηρακώς is a particular subset of τέλε(ι)ος viz. an aged τέλε(ι)ος; and, according to Hesykhios here, the animal which is λειπογνώμων is both τέλε(ι)ος and aged besides. Similarly we read in Suidas s.v. ἀβολήτωρ καὶ ἄβολις:

καὶ ἀπογνώμονας τοὺς ἀπογεγηρακότας οἷς ἐλελοίπει τὸ γνώρισμα,

and in Pollux 1.182:

---

[14]Similarly *ibid.*, citing Aristophanes of Byzantion: καὶ 'Αττικήν τινα δωδεκηδα θύεσθαι λεγομένην λειπογνώμονα οἷον τελείαν though it is unclear whether the words οἷον τελείαν are Aristophanes' or merely Eusthathios'.

[15]Τέλεον: lines 11, 21-22, 22, 26, 27, 37, 40-41; λειπογνώμονα: line 34.

[16]On the so-called Calendar of Nikomakhos (*Hesp.* 1935, p. 21, no. 2) only 50 dr. are budgeted for βόε δύο [λ]ειπογνώμονε (lines 50-51), and 4 dr. are budgeted for an οἶν λειπογνώμονα (lines 37-38), the latter to be compared with a standard price of 12 dr. for a female sheep and 15 dr. for a male one elsewhere on the calendar. On the deme calendar from Teithras (*SEG* 21.542) Sokolowski (*LSCG*, no. 132) restores ⊢⊢⊢⊢ 'Αθηνᾷ οἶν [λειπογνώμονα], though perhaps here we should read [Δ]⊢⊢⊢⊢ for an ordinary sheep instead.

οἱ δὲ γεγηρακότες ἀγνώμονες καὶ λειπογνώμονες.

If we understand that, in common usage, the animal which was λειπογνώμων was not only τέλε(ι)ος but also γεγηρακώς, i.e. that it was not at its prime but past it,[17] we may also have the key to explaining why, as sacrificial victims, λειπογνώμονες cost less than τέλε(ι)οι. In ancient Athens, as we saw in Chapter 2, sheep, goats and cows were raised primarily for their milk and, in the case of sheep, their wool, but not for their meat. The shorter life remaining for older animals compared with younger ones, and their consequently lower value as potential milk- and wool-producers, will explain the relatively low prices to be paid for them as sacrificial victims.[18]

---

[17]Cf. Eustath. 1627.10 ff. (commenting on the ἀρνειοί in *Od.* 9.239): τρίτη δὲ ἡλικία εἶναι δοκεῖ ὁ ἀρνειός, τέταρον δὲ μετ' αὐτὸν ὁ λειπογνώμων οἷς (citing Ister 334 F 23 for the sequence ἄρνα, εἶτα ἀμνόν, εἶτα ἀρνειόν, εἶτα λειπογνώμονα). For Eustathios, in this context ὁ ἀρνειός is τέλειος; cf. Eustath. 49.35 ff. Note also γνώμας λειπομένα σοφᾶς (Soph. *El.* 474), where the language is apparently meant to recall the adjective λειπογνώμων, and where the context shows that the meaning is closer to "effete" than to "in one's prime."

[18]Hansen (1973, 328) comes to the very different conclusion that these lower prices indicate that the *leipognômones* were in fact very young animals in their first few weeks of life, who had yet to grow any teeth (so too, more recently, "avant la première dentition," Daux [1983, 155]; similarly in van Straten [1987, 166-67, 168]); and Hansen further argues (1973, 328-32) that the adjective *leipognômôn* was used to describe any animal without age-indicating teeth, either because it was too old or because it was too young, even though he can cite no instance (other than the calendars, as he interprets them) where *leipognômôn* is used to describe a very young animal ("No ancient scholar seems to have realized the ambiguity of λειπογνώμων," [331]). Hansen's argument that the *leipognômones* on the Calendar are young animals follows from his unsupported assumption that the Athenians would not sacrifice older animals that had lost most of their market value (". . . it would be ridiculous to assert that the Athenians sacrificed animals so old or so inferior that they had only one-fourth of their normal market value," [328]). It is, however, risky at best to assume that we really know what victims the Athenians would and would not consider appropriate to sacrifice to certain gods, especially in the present case when Hansen assumes that the Athenians would not sacrifice older animals but all the evidence says that this, and only this, is what *leipognômones* were. It is also a bit provincial to assume that economic values were paramount for the Athenians, and we should at least entertain the possibility that ritual motives which we do not understand could account for the choice of these older animals. Note also that *leipognômôn* is always used with nouns describing older animals (*bous, ois, hus*), and not the younger calves, lambs and piglets we would expect if Hansen were correct.

B. THE SACRIFICES IN *IG* 1³ 137 AND *IG* 1³ 82

The sacrifice to Apollo in *IG* 1³ 137 (from the fifth century) appears to be in recognition of some specific service supplied by the god (ἐπ]ειδὲ ἀνεῖλεν ἑαυτὸν ἐχσεγετὲ[ν . . 6 . . | . . 8 . . ʼΑθεναίο]ις, 4-5); the attendant meat-distribution is therefore almost certainly a one-time occurrence and not a recurring event. A second inscription, *IG* 1³ 82 (dated to 421/0 by the arkhon's name in line 3) mentions the distribution of the meat from three oxen to metics (25-26), implying an even greater distribution of meat to the citizens. This very fragmentary inscription also mentions the god Hephaistos (17), the festival of the Hephaistia (33), and the altar of Hephaistos (38), and because of this it has often been assumed that this inscription contains regulations for the annual Hephaistia, in which case the inscription would be evidence of another annual occasion upon which a large enough number of victims was sacrificed for meat to be distributed to the citizens at large. The inscription is, however, more likely to be a description of the elaborate arrangements for celebrating the dedication of the temple of Hephaistos and Athena Hephaistia (the so-called "Theseion"), and the conduct of the annual feast was probably far more modest[1]. The word πεντετερίδι occurs twice in *IG* 1³ 82 (6, 32-33); line 6 is too fragmentary to establish any context for the first use, but in lines 32-33 the *pentetêris* appears to be contrasted with the Hephaistia. The logical inference is that the *pentetêris* in question is the Greater Panathenaia,[2] to which perhaps the torch-race was now added by this legislation. In any event, the *pentetêris* cannot be the penteteric Hephaistia which, as we know from Aristot. *Ath. Pol.* 54.7, was established only in 329/8.

B. THE SACRIFICES IN *IG* 1³ 137 AND *IG* 1³ 82:
[1]For the dating of the dedication, cf. *IG* 1³ 472, the accounts for the ἀγαλμάτοιν ἐ[ς τὸ] hεφαίστιον [472.2], dated 421/0-416/5.
[2]So Ziehen (1906) 52.

C. THE VALUE OF OX HIDES

We have seen above[1] that there is reason to believe that ox-hides such as those whose sale is recorded in the *Dermatikon* Accounts of 334-30 had a value in the range of 4 to 10 dr. Some check of this figure may perhaps be provided by the *Dermatikon* Account's two entries for the Panathenaia of 333/2, the first listing hides sold for 61.5 dr. and the second listing hides sold for 1,233 dr.[2] The first group of hides, which were sold for 1,233 dr., would be from the traditional hekatomb of 100 victims + the additional victims purchased with 4,100 dr. newly available, as we learn from *IG* 2^2 334. At 7 dr. a hide, the mid-point between our upper and lower limits of 4 dr. and 10 dr., 1,233 dr. would represent the sale of 176 hides = 100 from the hekatomb + 76 purchased with the additional 4,100 dr. 4,100 dr. ÷ 76 = 54 dr. per ox, which, though low, is still well within the range of attested prices for oxen, as we have seen in detail in Chapter 2.[3]

The first of the two entries for the Panathenaia of 333/2, 61.5 dr., divided by 7 dr. per hide = 8.8 victims. As suggested earlier,[4] these hides could well be from the animals offered as prizes in some of the contests. *IG* 2^2 2311, from the first half of the century, contains the following list of prizes (71-81):

	νικτήρι[α]	71
H	παισὶμ πυρ[ρι]χισταῖ(ς) βοῦς	
H	ἀγεννείοις πυ[ρ]ριχισταῖς βοῦς	
H	ἀνδράσι πυρριχισταῖς βοῦς	
H	εὐανδρίαι φυλῆι νικώσει βοῦς	75

C. THE VALUE OF OX HIDES:

[1] Pp. 62-63.

[2] The larger of the two figures restorable for the second entry from the Panathenaia; see above, Chapter 1, note 104.

[3] Above, pp. 95-96. Recall that in our discussion of these supplementary oxen (above, p. 61) we used the *maximum* figure of 100 dr. in our calculations since our goal was to determine the *minimum* number of animals sacrificed; the actual number of animals sacrificed was probably higher than this minimum, and their purchase price less than the maximum.

[4] Chapter 1, note 104.

Η	φυλῆι νικώσει βοῦς	
ΔΔΔ	λαμπαδηφόρωι νικῶντι ὑδ[ρία]	
	νικτήρια νεῶν ἁμίλλης	
ΗΗΗ	τῆι φυλῆι τῆι νικώσε[ι]	
ΗΗ	κ[α]ὶ εἰς ἑστίασιν	80
ΗΗ	τῆ[ι δε]υ[τέ]ραι β[όες δύο]	

The text is not without its problems. The entry on line 76 appears to be a partial duplicate of the previous line (it cannot be the prize for the *lampadēphoria* since this is the *hudria* in line 77). The entry ΗΗ seems to have been inscribed first in error on line 80 and then correctly on line 81. *IG* 2² 2311 thus appears to list ten *boes* awarded as prizes. Now we know that instead of an ox, by Aristotle's day (*Ath. Pol.* 60.3), and thus also probably by the time of the *Dermatikon* Accounts, shields were awarded as prizes for *euandria*. The remaining eight *boes* awarded at tt the Panathenaia are close to the 8.8 victims we calculated above as the source of the hides sold for the first entry for the Panathenaia of 333/2 in the *Dermatikon* Accounts.

There are of course many debatable points in this argument, but the correlations of the numbers in both entries with other figures derived from outside the Accounts (*IG* 2² 334 for the second entry, *IG* 2² 2311 for the first) would appear to suggest both that our interpretation of the two entries for the Panathenaia is, in broad outline, correct and that our mid-point figure of 7 dr. is at least within the general vicinity of what an ox-hide sold for at this time.

Recently Jameson (1988, 107-112) has also argued for a sales prices of 6-7 dr. per hide for the *Dermatikon* Accounts. Briefly, Jameson begins with the prices for wheat and for ox hides in the *Edict of Diocletian*, calculating that the *Edict* valued an ox hide at 1.17 times the cost of a *medimnos* of wheat, and suggesting further that the conditions which account for this ratio were also present, broadly speaking, in the fourth century B.C. Using the wheat:hide ratio of 1:1.17 and a standard figure of 5 dr. for a *medimnos* of wheat, he then calculates that hides would have sold at between 6 and 7 dr. each at the time of the Accounts. Finally he assumes a figure of 10,000 dr. in sales for the complete year of 335/34 on the basis of a seven-month total of 5,099+ dr. still extant on the stone, and concludes that the *Dermatikon* Accounts for this year represent a sale of hides from between 1,400 and 1,700 full-grown cattle. Jameson himself recognizes that his argument rests on two assumptions, that the ratio of value of wheat to cattle and that of animal to hide were roughly the same in the fourth century B.C. as it was at the time the *Edict of Diocletian* at the start of the fourth century A.D., and although he provides some suggestive supporting material, the assumptions themselves remain unproven. Jameson's annual figure of 1,400 to 1,700 oxen is substantially larger than the *minimum* figure of 724 argued for above in Chapter 2,[5] based as it is on a substantially higher estimate of total annual revenues (10,000 dr. vs. a reconstructed minimum of 7,240[6]) and on a lower figure for the value per hide (7 dr. vs. a realistic maximum of 10 dr.), and it probably represents the *maximum* number of animals sacrificed annually at the *epithetoi heortai* as our figure of 724 represents the *minimum*.

D. HOW MUCH MEAT?

Although the typical size and meat yield of ancient animals were different from those of modern ones, figures for modern animals can suggest, albeit very broadly, a sense of scale. Drawing on a variety of studies of contemporary nomadic economies, chiefly in Africa, Dahl and Hjort propose an average cold dressed weight of 100-120 kg. per animal for cattle slain in abattoirs, with a figure probably somewhat higher for animals slain in the field for ritual purposes; 15-20 kg. per animal as the normal meat yield of pastoral goats; and a range of 10 to 25 kg. per animal for the meat yield of sheep depending on breed and local conditions.[1] If we assume a standard meat yield of somewhat less than 50% of live weight these figures given by Dahl and Hjort are roughly comparable to those for estimated live weights of animals from the Middle Helladic to Dark Ages at Nichoria in Southwest Greece given by Sloan and Duncan, 200 kg. for small cows, 40 kg. for sheep and 60

---

[5]Pp. 68-72.

[6]Using the lowest money amounts given for each event over the four-year cycle of the *Dermatikon* Accounts rather than calculate the proceeds from any single year.

D. HOW MUCH MEAT:
[1]Dahl and Hjort (1976) 163-67 [cattle], 203 [goats], 202 [sheep].

kg. for goats, based on their archeological sample and on the known live weights of comparable species,[2] although one should add that estimating live weight from skeletal remains is necessarily imprecise.[3] In particular, "finishing" an animal can add substantially to its meat yield without significantly altering its skeleton.[4]

Unfortunately there is no way of telling how far this meat went since we do not know what the size of a typical portion of meat was a public sacrifice, nor whether the size of portions varied from event to event.[5] We also do not know whether the portions were intended only for the adult male citizens, or also for their wives, children and other dependents; and if the latter, whether or not the portions varied according to the number of dependents shared in them.

E. ANIMALS FROM ABROAD

Even in the absence of evidence it is not unreasonable to assume that some of the animals Athens needed were acquired from herds pastured in neighboring states in upland regions immediately adjacent to Attika, but such acquisitions were likely to be on a limited *ad hoc* basis and not part of a

---

[2] Sloan and Duncan (1978) 76.

[3] By way of comparison, a modern commercially raised North American bovine with a live weight of 1,000 lbs. will yield a bit less than 500 lbs. of meat, and a "lamb" with a live weight of 100 pounds will yield a bit over 45 lbs. of meat (carcass to live weight ratio: Romans and Ziegler [1977] 433, fig. 13.3 [bovine]; 492, fig. 14.3 ["lamb"; the "lamb" is 9-10 months old, the age at which these animals are usually slaughtered in the U.S.A.]; meat yields from carcasses: *ibid.* 306-7, table 11.8 [bovine]; 332, table 11.12 ["lamb"]).

[4] For Greek evidence for "finishing" see above, Chapter 2, note 82.

[5] Even for sacrificial events where we know both the number and kind of victims and the population of the unit (e.g. a deme) we are still be unable calculate the size of portions since we can never be sure what percentage of those eligible to participate in the *kreanomia* actually did so (or were expected to); indeed, it is very likely that at least the percentage of those actually participating varied from year to year.

regular system of exchange. In any event, for the fourth century at least we have no evidence of a regular import trade in animals brought into Attika from elsewhere: the *mêla* of Hermippos, frag. 63 K-A, line 17 are apples, not sheep; at Dem. 26.167, the sheep which Meidias brought back from Euboia when he was trierarch were for his own use [ὡς αὐτὸν], as were the vine-poles, etc. he also brought back, and not for sale; on the ζεύγη at *IG* 2² 351, line 18, which Pritchett[1] sees as evidence for large herds in Boiotia supplying Athenian needs see above, Chapter 2, note 40.

In the fifth century, Athens required her colonies[2] and allied cities[3] each to bring a *bous* to the Greater Panathenaia. On these occasions the representatives of the colonies and the allied cities participated in the Panathenaic *pompê*,[4] and they, and possibly others from their cities present in Athens, presumably shared in the distribution of meat which followed.[5] Since it is unlikely that the representatives of the colonies and allies consumed by themselves all the meat from the animals their cities provided, these animals would thus have been an additional source of meat for the Athenians themselves at the Greater Panathenaia.[6] Similarly Hodkinson[7] has speculated that overseas estates owned by wealthy Athenians may have supplied some of the animals required for sacrifice during the heyday of the empire in the fifth century.[8] With the collapse of the empire, however, sources which depend-

---

E. ANIMALS FROM ABROAD:

[1](1953) 255.
[2]Schol. Aristoph. *Nub.* 386; cf. *IG* 1³ 46.15-16.
[3]*IG* 1³ 71.57; cf. *IG* 1³ 34.41-42.
[4]*IG* 1³ 71.57-58.
[5]Cf. the earlier *IG* 1³ 14.3-4, which appears to require the allied city of Erythrai to bring *sitos* to the Greater Panathenaia and distribute at least some of it to Erythraians present in Athens at the time.
[6]Significantly, the Athenians were prepared to punish allies who failed their obligation to bring a *bous* to the Greater Panathenaia (*IG* 1³ 34.41-42), probably not because they were concerned about the loss of meat, but because they saw the allies' participation in the festival and its *kreanomia* as an important religious expression of the political status the Athenians had imposed upon them, virtually making the allies, as it were, an extension of the Athenian community.
[7]Hodkinson (1992) 57.
[8]However, when Thucydides (2.14.1) describes the Athenians in 431 transporting *hupozugia* and *probata* to Euboia and the nearby islands to protect them from the Peloponnesian invaders the implication is that, like the *hupozugia* which would be required to work the fields after the invaders had left, the *probata* were only temporari-

ed on the existence of the empire disappeared, and in the absence of evidence for a regular trade in animals we must conclude that in the fourth century, the focus of our study, Athens' need for sacrificial victims was met primarily by herds in Attika, with perhaps some animals also supplied from herds in adjacent states.

F. NIKOMAKHOS' "NEW" SACRIFICES

Given the polemical nature of Lys. 30.19-20 it is impossible to say with any certainty exactly what "new" sacrifices Nikomakhos added to the Calendar, and *a fortiori* why he added them. My own view is, briefly, that the system of *temenos*-rentals was badly disrupted by the Peloponnesian War, particularly in its closing years after Sparta had established a base at Dekeleia, and that as a consequence of this, a large number of *patrioi thusiai* had to be funded instead out of the *polis*' general revenues; that when the Athenians added the new *epithetos heortê* in honor of Dêmokratia in 402 or shortly thereafter[1] to commemorate the expulsion of the Thirty in 403, they paid for it be reallocating the monies they had been using as substitute funding to support *patrioi thusiai*, anticipating that the *temenos*-rents for the *patrioi thusiai* would be quickly restored now that the war was over; that the *temenos*-rents were not restored as quickly as anticipated, leaving some *patrioi thusiai* un- or under-funded; and that the speaker of Lys. 30 is trying to blame this all on Nikomakhos, who, for all we know, may have played a significant role in the events leading to the creating of the sacrifice in honor of Dêmokratia.[2] If this understanding of events is correct, the speaker of Lys. 30 seeks to mislead his audience by exaggerating the amount of money involved (perhaps the six talents of expenditures allegedly added by Nikoma-

---

ly removed with the expectation that they would return as soon as the Peloponnesians were gone.

F. NIKOMAKHOS' "NEW" SACRIFICES:
  [1]See above, Chapter 1, note 122.
  [2]For Nikomakhos' democratic credentials see Robertson (1990) 74-75.

khos and the three talents of unfunded *patrioi thusiai* are actually multi-year cumulative totals, not those for just one year), and especially by attributing the new sacrifice to Dêmokratia to Nikomakhos *qua anagrapheus* (cf. ἀναγράψας, 19; ἀνέγραψε, 20). By thus fudging some important distinctions the speaker is able to imply that the temporary situation caused by the war was permanent, and that the sacrifice to Dêmokratia will henceforth be included in the *patrioi thusiai*—which it was not—, to be funded in the future, as it presently is, by funds that would otherwise be used for the *patrioi thusiai*—which is not the case, since the *patrioi thusiai* will eventually be funded again from *temenos*-rentals.[3] For a rather different view of Nikomakhos' "new" sacrifices see Robertson (1990) 67-75, although Robertson is certainly correct in his more general argument that the work of Nikomakhos and his fellow *anagrapheis* did not involve a re-edition of the entire corpus of Attic law.

G. SACRIFICING WORKING ANIMALS

From a strictly economic point of view it seems *a priori* unlikely that the Athenians would not regularly slay and eat the meat of their working oxen at the end of the animals' useful lives; and if they did slay these animals, they must have slain them as they slew all oxen, sheep and goats, viz. in sacrifice, either public or private. In a frequently cited passage, however, Ailianos (*VH* 5.14) says that it was a *nomos* . . . *Attikos* not to sacrifice (θύειν) a βοῦν ἀρότην καὶ ὑπὸ ζυγὸν πονήσαντα σὺν ἀρότρῳ ἢ καὶ σὺν τῇ ἁμάξᾳ since καὶ οὗτος εἴη γεωργὸς καὶ τῶν ἐν ἀνθρώποις καμάτων κοινωνός, and Varro (*de re rustica* 2.5.3) describes the ox as *socius hominum in rustico opere et Cereris minister*, adding *ab hoc antiqui manus ita abstinueri voluerunt, ut capite*

---

[3]For the intentional confusion cf. Isok. 7 *Areop.* 29 which similarly juxtaposes the *epithetoi heortai* and the *patrioi thusiai* in a way that suggests, without actually saying so, that money spent on the former would not be avilable to spend on the latter.

sanxerint si quis occidisset; qua in re testis Attice, testis Peloponnesos.[1] Now Aratus (*Phaen.* 132) says of the men of the Bronze Age: πρῶτοι δὲ βοῶν ἐπάσαντ' ἀροτήρων. The scholion to this verse explains: ἀσεβὲς γὰρ ἦν ἀρότην βοῦν φαγεῖν· πρῶτοι δὲ οἱ 'Αθηναῖοι ἐγεύσαντο τῶν τοιούτων βοῶν, ἐπεί ποτε βοῦς θυσίας ἀγο<μένης πόπα>νον κατέφαγεν.[2] The scholion, it will be noted, describes two periods of time, the first the same as that described by Ailianos and Varro, when the Athenians did not sacrifice working oxen, and a second, later time, when they changed their former practice and began to sacrifice working oxen and eat their meat. In other words, the scholion, when read together with the verse of Aratus it explains, may be taken to mean that once upon a time the Athenians did not sacrifice working oxen, but now they do. Note also that the scholion says that they do so with no qualification, i.e. they do so regularly and not only on special occasions.

To pursue this point further, the detail in the scholion that the Athenians began to eat the meat from working oxen after one of the animals ate the ritual cake called *popanon* points to the strange ritual of the Bouphonia at the Dipolieia, when the sacrificial ox was not slain until it had eaten the food set out on the altar of Zeus Polieus; after the ox was slain the slayer fled, and the ax used to kill the ox was formally tried for murder in a court of law.[3] It is quite clear from Porphyry's account (*abst.* 2.29) that the animal slain in the Bouphonia was a working ox.[4] Parke (1977, 165), following Deubner (1932, 172), interprets this sacrifice of a working ox at the Bouphonia as repayment for a successful agricultural year.[5] It is possible, however, that the Bouphonia with its ritual trial played a rather different role, assuming, as

---

G. SACRIFCING WORKING ANIMALS:

[1] Cf. Columella, *de re rustica* 6 praef. 7. The case against sacrificing working animals has been made most recently by Jameson (1988, 87-88), principally on the basis of Ail. *VH* 5.14; Jameson notes, however, that there was probably no outright ban on the use of working animals in sacrifice (*nomos* in the Ailianos passage is "custom," not "law"), and he grants that such animals may have been consumed privately by the poor.

[2] For the text see Schöne (1909) 477.

[3] The details of the ritual are in Paus. 1.24.4, 1.28.10 and in Porphyr. *abst.* 2.29-30, the latter based on Theophrastos' περὶ εὐσεβείας (= frag. 18 in Pötscher [1964]).

[4] See further Durant (1986) 49-50.

[5] Somewhat similarly Burkert (1983) 42-43.

it were, the onus of similar animal deaths, specifically the deaths of all working oxen slain in sacrifice. Understood this way, the Bouphonia could be seen as assuring the Athenians that it was now alright to slay and eat these animals at other times during the year, despite the services the animals have rendered and despite the close ties between man and working beast. Note that in Porphyry's aetiology of the rite a response from the Pythia directs the Athenians to repeat the original sacrifice, and to eat the meat of the slain animal and not hold back (γευσαμένοις τε τοῦ τεθνεῶτος καὶ μὴ κατασχοῦσιν, abst. 2.29.3).[6] Whatever the origin of the Bouphonia may have been,[7] the later perception of the rite, as we have reconstructed it here, is consistent with the view that Athenians regularly sacrificed working oxen and ate their meat at the end of the animals' useful lives.

H. TAXES FOR RELIGIOUS PURPOSES

Besides rentals there are also some scattered examples of special taxes for specific religious purposes. From the fifth century, *IG* 1^3 138, dated to before 434, legislates a head tax on *hippeis*, *hoplitai* and *toksotai* for the benefit of Apollo; according to Jameson (1980, 224), the cult is probably that of Apollo Lykeios, and the head tax would pay for the repair and upkeep of the god's *temenos* mentioned in lines 15-17, viz. the Lykeion, which served as an exercise ground for Athens' land army. Also from the fifth century, *IG* 1^3 8, dated 460-50, details a toll on ships anchoring at Sounion, apparently to fund cult activities there. From the fourth century, *Hesperia* 5 (1936) 393-413, no. 10, a *pôlêtai*-inscription from 341/2-339/8, also mentions a τέλος τῆς πεντεδραχμίας τῆς τῶι Θησε[ῖ] (lines 134-35) and τέλους τῆς [δραχμῆς

---

[6]On the translation of μὴ κατασχοῦσιν see Bouffartigue and Patillon (1979, 211-12), who add, "Le dieu invite les futurs consomateurs du boeuf à avoir bonne conscience, ce qui est très important."

[7]And it could well have been quite different from the way the rite was understood in historical times; cf. Simon (1983) 11-12.

τ]ῶι Ἀσκληπιῶι (lines 142-43), but upon whom and how these taxes were levied, and to what purpose, is all quite uncertain.[1]

Schlaifer (1940, 233-35) also argues from two very fragmentary fifth-century inscriptions, *IG* 1³ 133 and *IG* 1³ 130, that the cults of the Anakes and of another god, perhaps Zeus Sôtêr, in the Peiraieus were supported by specific taxes on users of the port. As to the latter, Schlaifer's interpretation of *IG* 1³ 130 depends on an extraordinarily daring restoration of ὅπος ἂν τὸ [. . . 28 . . .]ω οὖν ἐι τôι ἱερôι to include a reference to the *hieron* of Zeus Sôtêr; Lewis (1960, 190-94), who critizes Schlaifer's restoration, see the money mentioned in the inscription not as going to the maintenance of some cult but rather as funding the construction of a shrine to Apollo Delios. On the other hand, Schlaifer may well be correct about *IG* 1³ 130, which appears to deal, at least in part, with the handling of a supplementary embarkation tax (*epibatikon*) collected for the benefit of the Anakes, in addition to the regular embarkation tax paid to the *dêmos*. Since this tax was apparently handed over to the Treasurers of the Other Gods (lines 13-14 as restored), and since this was the procedure which was probably used, as we have seen,[2] in handling rental funds used to support other cult activities in honor of other deities, it is reasonable to assume that this supplementary embarkation tax was similarly intended to be used to support the cult activities in honor of the Anakes.[3]

There may also have been other taxes devoted to specific cults, but we have no evidence for them. It is perhaps significant that except for the problematic *pôlêtai*-inscription mentioned above, the only evidence we have for special taxes for religious is from the fifth century, and we have no example of any revenue source other than rentals specifically dedicated to the funding of any *polis* cult in the fourth century.

H. TAXES FOR RELIGIOUS PURPOSES:

[1] The inscription has been re-edited by Langdon (1991, 105-17, no. P26), who also supplies the date; the taxes are at lines 479-80 and 487-88 in Langdon's edition.

[2] Above, pp. 122-24.

[3] The 2% tax (*pentêkostê*) mentioned later in *IG* 1³ 133.25 and .28 is, however, unrelated to the cult of the Anakes; this tax raised far too much money for any single cult, and was in fact a major source of the *polis'* general income.

BIBLIOGRAPHY

Ampolo (1981) = C. Ampolo, "Tra finanza e politica: carriera e affari del Signor Moirokles," *RFIC* 109 187-204.

Ampolo (1982) = _____, "Le cave di pietra dell'Attica: problemi giuridici ed economici," *Opus* 1 251-60.

Andreyev (1974) = V. N. Andreyev, "Some Aspects of Agrarian Conditions in Attica in the Fifth to Third Centuries B.C.," *Eirene* 12 5-46.

Behrend (1970) = D. Behrend, *Attische Pachturkunden: ein Beitrag zur Beschreibung der misthôsis nach den griechischen Inschriften*, Vestigia 12 (München).

Berthiaume (1982) = G. Berthiaume, *Les rôles du mageiros: Étude sur la boucherie, la cuisine et le sacrifice dans la Grèce ancienne*, Mnemosyne supplementum, 70 (Leiden).

Bicknell (1976) = P. J. Bicknell, "Clisthène et Kytherros," *REG* 89 599-603.

Boeckh (1886) = A. Boeckh, *Die Staatshaushaltung der Athener*, 3rd ed. by M. Fränkel (Berlin).

Bouffartigue and Patillon (1979) = J. Bouffartigue and M. Patillon, *Porphyre: de l'abstinence*, vol. 2 (Paris).

Burkert (1983) = W. Burkert, *Homo Necans: The Anthropology of Ancient Greek Sacrificial Ritual and Myth*, tr. P. Bing (Berkeley, Los Angeles and London).

Burkert (1985) = _____, *Greek Religion*, tr. J. Raffan (Cambridge MA).

Casabona (1966) = J.Casabona, *Recherches sur le vocabulaire des sacrifices en grec* (Aix-en-Provence).

Clinton (1982) = K. Clinton, "The Nature of the Late Fifth-Century Revision of the Athenian Law Code," in *Studies Vanderpool* (1982) 27-37.

Connor (1989) = W. R. Connor, "City Dionysia and Athenian Democracy," *C&M* 40 7-32.

Dahl and Hjort (1976) = G. Dahl and A. Hjort, *Having Herds: Pastoral Herd Growth and Household Economy*, Stockholm Studies in Social Anthropology, 2 (Stockholm).

Daux (1963) = G. Daux, "La grande démarchie: un nouveau calendrier sacrificiel d'Attique," *BCH* 87 603-34.

Daux (1964) = _____, "Notes de lecture," *BCH* 88 676-79.

Daux (1983) = _____, "Le calendrier de Thorikos au Musée J. Paul Getty," *AC* 52 150-74.

Davies (1971), = J. K. Davies, *Athenian Propertied Families 600-300 B.C.* (Oxford).

Davies (1981) = _____, *Wealth and the Power of Wealth in Classical Athens* (New York).

Davison (1958) = J. A. Davison, "Notes on the Panathenaea," *JHS* 78 23-41.

Deubner (1932) = L. Deubner, *Attische Feste* (Berlin).

Dow (1941) = S. Dow, "Greek Inscriptions: The Athenian Law Code of 411-01 B.C.," *Hesperia* 10 31-37.

Dow (1959) = _____, "The Law Codes of Athens," *Proceedings of the Massachusetts Historical Society* 71 3-35.

Dow (1961) = _____, "The Wall Inscribed with Nikomakhos' Law Code," *Hesperia* 30 58-73.

Dow (1965) = _____, "The Greater Demarkhia of Erkhia," *BCH* 89 180-213.

Dow (1968) = _____, "Six Athenian Sacrificial Calendars," *BCH* 92 170-86.

Dunst (1977) = G. Dunst, "Der Opferkalender des attischen Demos Thorikos," *ZPE* 25 243-64.

Durant (1979) = J.-L. Durant, "Bêtes grecs: propositions pour une topologie des corps à manger," in *La cuisine du sacrifice en pays grec*, edd. M. Detienne and J. P. Vernant (Paris) 133-65.

Durant (1986) = _____, *Sacrifice et labour en grèce ancienne* (Paris-Rome).

Edmonds (1957) = J. M. Edmonds, *The Fragments of Attic Comedy*, vol. 1 (Leiden).

Ferguson (1932) = W. S. Ferguson, *The Treasurers of Athena* (Cambridge MA).

Ferguson (1938) = _____, "The Salaminioi of Heptaphylai and Sounion," *Hesperia* 7 1-74.

Ferguson (1944) = _____, "The Attic Orgeones," *Harvard Theological Review* 37 61-140.

Finley (1973) = M. I. Finley, *Studies in Land and Credit in Ancient Athens, 500-200 B.C.: The Horos-Inscriptions* (New Brunswick).

Foxall and Forbes (1982) = L. Foxall and H. A. Forbes, "Σιτομετρία: The Role of Grain as a Staple Food in Classical Antiquity," *Chiron* 12 41-90.
Frandson (1986) = R. D. Frandson, *Anatomy and Physiology of Farm Animals*, 4th ed. (Philadelphia).
Gallo (1983) = L. Gallo, "Alimentazione e classi sociali: una nota su orzo e frumento in Grecia," *Opus* 2 449-72.
Garland (1987) = R. Garland, *The Piraeus From the Fifth to the First Century B.C.* (Ithaca).
Garland (1992) = _____, *Introducing New Gods: The Politics of Athenian Religion* (Ithaca).
Gomme (1933) = A. W. Gomme, *The Population of Athens in the Fifth and Fourth Centuries B.C.* (Oxford).
Handley (1965) = E. W. Handley, *The Dyskolos of Menander* (London).
Hansen (1973) = H. Hansen, "The Meaning of λειπογνώμων," *GRBS* 14 325-32.
Hansen (1980) = M. H. Hansen, "Seven Hundred *Archai* in Classical Athens," *GRBS* 21 227-38.
Hansen (1983) = _____, "Political Activity and the Organization of Attica in the Fourth Century, B.C.," *GRBS* 24 227-38.
Hansen (1986) = _____, *Demography and Democracy* (Herning, Denmark).
Hansen (1990) = H. Hansen, *Aspects of the Athenian Law Code of 410/09 - 400/399 B.C.* (New York and London).
Haussoullier (1884) = B. Haussoullier, *La vie municipale en Attique: essai sur l'organisation des dèmes au quatrième siècle* (Paris).
Hauvette-Busnault (1879) = A. Hauvette-Busnault, "Fragments d'inscriptions athéniennes," *BCH* 3 69-74.
Healey (1984) = R. F. Healey, S.J., "A Gennetic Sacrifice List in the Athenian State Calendar," in *Studies Presented to Sterling Dow on His Eightieth Birthday* (Durham NC) 135-41.
Healey (1990) = _____, *Eleusinian Sacrifices in the Athenian Law Code* (New York and London).
Hiller von Gaertringen (1897) = F. Hiller von Gaertringen, "Βοῶναι," *RE*, vol. 3^1, coll. 716-17.

Hodkinson (1986) = S. Hodkinson, "Animal Husbandry in the Greek Polis," in *Papers of the Ancient History (Greece and Rome) Section of the 9th International Economic History Congress* (Bern) 11-13.

Hodkinson (1988) = _____, "Animal Husbandry in the Greek Polis," in Whittaker (1988) 35-74.

Hodkinson (1992) = _____, "Imperial Democracy and Market-Oriented Pastoral Production in Classical Athens," *Anthropozoologica* 16 53-60.

Jameson (1965) = M. Jameson, "Notes on the Sacrificial Calendar from Erchia," *BCH* 89 154-72.

Jameson (1980) = _____. "Apollo Lykeios in Athens," Αρχαιογνωσία 1 213-35.

Jameson (1982) = _____, "The Leasing of Land in Rhamnous," in *Studies Vanderpool* (1982) 66-74.

Jameson (1988) = _____, "Sacrifice and Animal Husbandry in Classical Greece," in Whittaker (1988) 87-119.

Jones (1966) = A. H. M. Jones, *Athenian Democracy* (Oxford).

Lalonde *et al.* (1991) = G. V. Lalonde, M. K. Langdon and M. B. Walbank, *The Athenian Agora*, vol. 19, *Inscriptions: Horoi, Poletai Records, Leases on Publc Lands* (Princeton).

Langdon (1991) = M. K. Langdon, "Poletai Records," in Lalonde *et al.* (1991) 53-143.

Lewis (1960) = D. M. Lewis, "Apollo Delios," *BSA* 55 190-94.

Lewis (1973) = _____, "The Athenian Rationes Centesimarum," in *Problèmes de la terre en Grèce ancienne*, ed. M. I. Finley (Paris-La Haye) 187-212.

Lewis (1985) = _____, "A New Athenian Decree," *ZPE* 60 108.

Linders and Nordquist (1987) = *Gifts to the Gods: Proceedings of the Uppsala Symposium 1985*, ed. T. Linders and G. Nordquist, *Boreas*, 15 (Uppsala).

Meritt (1934) = B. D. Meritt, "The Inscriptions," *Hesperia* 3 1-128.

Mikalson (1975) = J. D. Mikalson, *The Sacred and Civil Calendar of the Athenian Year* (Princeton).

Mikalson (1977) = _____, "Religion in the Attic Demes," *AJP* 98 424-35.

Mikalson (1982) = _____, "The *Heorte* of Heortology," *GRBS* 23 213-21.
Murray and Price (1990) = *The Greek City from Homer to Alexander*, ed. O. Murray and S. Price (Oxford).
Oliver (1935) = J. H. Oliver, "Greek Inscriptions," *Hesperia* 4 1-70.
Osborne (1988) = R. Osborne, "Social and Economic Implications of the Leasing of Land and Property in Classical and Hellenistic Athens," *Chiron* 18 279-323.
Osborne (1990) = _____, "The *Demos* and its Divisions in Classical Athens," in Murray and Price (1990) 265-93.
Parke (1977) = H. W. Parke, *Festivals of the Athenians* (London).
Parker (1984) = R. Parker, "The Herakleidai at Thorikos," *ZPE* 57 59.
Parker (1987) = _____, "Festivals of the Attic Demes," in Linders and Nordquist (1987) 137-47.
Payne (1985) = S. Payne, "Zoo-Archaeology in Greece: A Reader's Guide," in *Contributions to Aegean Archaeology: Studies in Honor of William A. McDonald*, ed. N. C. Wilkie and W. D. E. Coulson (Minneapolis) 211-44.
Pickard-Cambridge (1968) = A. W. Pickard-Cambridge, *The Dramatic Festivals of Athens*, 2nd ed. by J. Gould and D. M. Lewis (Oxford).
Pollitt (1961) = J. J. Pollitt, "Fragment of a Sacred Calendar and Other Inscriptions from the Attic Deme of Teithras," *Hesperia* 30 293-97.
Pötscher (1964) = W. Pötscher, *Theophrastos:* ΠΕΡΙ ΕΥΣΕΒΕΙΑΣ, Philosophia antiqua, 11 (Leiden).
Pritchett (1953) = W. K. Pritchett, "The Attic Stelai, Part I," *Hesperia* 22 225-99.
Pritchett (1956) = _____, "The Attic Stelai, Part II," *Hesperia* 25 178-317.
Prott (1896) = I. de Prott, *Leges graecorum sacrae e titulis collectae*, pars prima *(fasti sacri)* (Lipsiae).
Rhodes (1972) = P. J. Rhodes, *The Athenian Boule* (Oxford).
Rhodes (1981) = _____, *A Commentary on the Aristotelian Athenaion Politeia* (Oxford).
Robertson (1985) = N. Robertson, "The Origin of The Panathenaea," *RhM* 128 231-95.

Robertson (1991) = _____, "The Laws of Athens, 410-399 BC: The Evidence for Review and Publication," *JHS*, 110 74-75.

Romans and Ziegler (1977) = J. R. Romans and P. Thomas Ziegler, *The Meat We Eat*, 11th ed. (Danville IL).

Rosivach (1985) = V. J. Rosivach, "Manning the Athenian Fleet, 433-426 B.C.," *AJAH* 10 41-66.

Rosivach (1991) = _____, "*IG* 2^2 334 and the Panathenaic Hekatomb," *PP* 46 430-42.

Rosivach (forthcoming) = _____, "The *rationes centesimarum* (*IG* 2^2 1594-1603+)," *Eirene*.

Schlaifer (1940) = R. Schlaifer, "Notes on Athenian Public Cults," *HSCP* 51 233-60.

Schöne (1909) = H. Schöne, "Zu den Aratscholien," *RhM* 64 476-78.

Shapiro (1989) = H. A. Shapiro, *Art and Cult Under the Tyrants in Athens* (Mainz am Rhein).

Simms (1975) = R. M. Simms, "The Eleusinia in the Sixth to Fourth Centuries B.C.," *GRBS* 16 269-78.

Simon (1983) = E. Simon, *Festivals of Attica: An Archaeological Commentary* (Madison).

Sloan and Duncan (1978) = R. E. Sloan and M. A. Duncan, "Zooarchaeology of Nichoria," in *Excavations at Nichoria in Southwest Greece*, ed. G. Rapp, Jr. and S. E. Aschenbrenner, (Minneapolis) 1. 60-77.

Sokolowski (1962) = F. Sokolowski, *Lois sacrées des cités grecques: Supplément* (Paris).

Sokolowksi (1969) = _____, *Lois sacrées des cités grecques* (Paris).

Sourvino-Inwood (1990) = C. Sourvino-Inwood, "What is *Polis* Religion," in Murray and Price (1990) 295-322.

Stengel (1912) = P. Stengel, ‛Εκατόμβη," *RE*, vol. 7^2, coll. 2786-87.

Stengel (1920) = _____, *Die griechischen Kultusaltertümer*, 3rd ed. (München).

Studies Vanderpool (1982) = *Studies in Attic Epigraphy, History and Topography Presented to Eugene Vanderpool*, *Hesperia* supplement, 19 (Princeton).

Threpsiades (1939) = J. C. Threpsiades, "Decree in Honor of Euthydemos of Eleusis," *Hesperia* 8 177-80.

Todd (1990) = S. Todd, "*Lady Chatterley's Lover* and the Attic Orators: The Social Composition of the Athenian Jury," *JHS* 110 146-73.
Traill (1975) = J. S. Traill, *The Political Organization of Attica*, Hesperia Supplement, 14 (Princeton).
Vanderpool (1965) = E. Vanderpool, "The Location of the Attic Deme Erchia," *BCH* 89 21-26.
Vanderpool (1975) = _____, "A South Attica Miscellany," in *Thorikos and the Laurion in Archaic and Classical Times*, ed. H. Mussche et al. (Ghent) 21-42.
van Straten (1987) = F. van Straten, "Greek Sacrificial Representations: Livestock Prices and Religious Mentality," in Linders and Nordquist (1987) 159-70.
Veyne (1976) = P. Veyne, *Le pain et le cirque* (Paris).
Walbank (1983) = M. B. Walbank, "Leases of Sacred Properties in Attica, Parts I-IV," *Hesperia* 52 100-35, 177-231.
Walbank (1991) = _____, "Leases on Public Lands," in Lalonde et al. (1991) 145-207.
Whitehead (1983) = D. Whitehead, "Competitive Outlay and Community Profit: Φιλοτιμία in Classical Athens," *C&M* 34 55-74.
Whitehead (1986) = _____, "The 'Greater Demarchy' of Erchia," *AncW* 14 57-64.
Whitehead (1986a) = _____, *The Demes of Attica, 508/7 - Ca. 250 B.C.* (Princeton).
Whittaker (1988) = *Pastoral Economies in Classical Antiquity*, ed. C. R. Whittaker, *PCPS* supplementary volume 14 (Cambridge).
Wiesner (1939) = J. Wiesner, "Oropos," *RE* vol. 18^1, col. 1171-74.
Wilson (1902) = J. C. Wilson, "On Aristotle, *Nic. Eth.* VII. xiv. 2 and xii.2,", *CR* 16 23-28.
Ziehen (1896) = L. Ziehen, "Die panathenäischen und eleusinischen ἱεροποιοί," *RhM* 51 211-25.
Ziehen (1906) = _____, *Leges graecorum sacrae e titulis collectae*, pars altera, fasc. 1 (*leges graeciae et insularum*) (Lipsiae).
Ziehen (1949) = _____. "Panathenaia," *RE* vol. 18^3, col. 457-93.

www.ingramcontent.com/pod-product-compliance
Ingram Content Group UK Ltd.
Pitfield, Milton Keynes, MK11 3LW, UK
UKHW041428180426
11947UKWH00007B/354